Therapy Beyond All Expectations

The self-help book that takes your therapy to a whole new level

JACK ITO, PH.D.

Loving Solutions Publishing
Kingsport, Tennessee

Therapy Beyond All Expectations
Taking Your Therapy To a Whole New Level
by Jack Ito

Published by:
Loving Solutions Publishing
1000 University Boulevard
Suite F30
Kingsport, TN 37660 USA
orders@lovingsolutionspublishing.com

Unattributed quotations are by Jack Ito

ISBN, print ed.   978-0-9890999-0-5

Library of Congress Control Number: 2014901350

DEDICATION

This book is dedicated to my friend and mentor, Rev. Dr. Paul L. Holland, who taught me the valuable early lessons for being a therapist:

- ➤ You work for God,
- ➤ The best person to be is yourself,
- ➤ Caring comes before curing,
- ➤ Don't hold back laughter, and
- ➤ A man of integrity will despised by those who don't need him, until they do.

CONTENTS

A NOTE TO THERAPISTS, PSYCHOLOGISTS, AND COUNSELORS OF ALL SORTS

Therapists will be encouraged to know that this book was written to supplement every style of therapy. Unless your clients continue in therapy long enough for beneficial results, no style of therapy will be effective. This is a book of hope, explanation, clarification, hand-holding, and activities to encourage clients to stick with you until lasting benefit can be obtained.

WARNING –DISCLAIMER

This book was written to provide general guidance for seeking help through psychotherapy. It was not written as a substitute for psychotherapy. The recommendations are general enough to apply to most kinds of psychological treatment. If the reader should encounter any situation where the advice in this book contradicts that of their therapist, the reader is advised to follow the recommendations of their therapist.

A resolution to mental health and behavioral problems does not happen quickly. Anyone who decides to improve their functioning must work on it continuously, both addressing problems and symptoms as well as promoting healthy functioning and learning life skills. This book addresses only some important aspects of life functioning. It can't be used as a comprehensive manual for healthy living. No book could conceivably offer all that is needed to guarantee a problem free life. Human life is far too complex, and the unexpected happens far too often.

Great care has been taken to make this manual as complete and accurate as possible regarding its content. However, there *may be mistakes*, both typographical and in content. Therefore this book should be used only as a general guide and not as the ultimate source of managing psychological problems. Furthermore, this book is current only up until the printing date.

In a book of this sort it is not possible to take into account individual differences that influence the success or failure of these methods. The author and publisher have no responsibility to any person or entity in regard to loss or damage caused, or thought to have been caused, directly or indirectly by the contents of this book.

If you are not in agreement with this disclaimer, you may return this book to the seller for a refund.

Really Getting Help

This book provides examples and self-help exercises which provide a powerful boost to whichever kind of psychotherapy you use. It bridges the gap between client and therapist, between self-help and therapy. It provides insights and guidance to make therapy more understandable and more helpful.

This book gives you a unique opportunity to benefit from a combination of self-help and psychotherapy. Used together the power of each is greatly multiplied. Overcoming a lifetime of dysfunctional thinking and behaving is very difficult to do alone. One of the reasons that therapy succeeds is because it helps people to sustain change long enough to replace old behavior patterns. Without such sustained work, people regress to their former, less effective selves. The self help exercises in this book differ from other self help books in that they are designed to be done while you are in therapy. Used by themselves, they would be no more powerful than those of any other self help book.

Using the self help exercises while attending therapy will have multiple benefits for you:

Firstly, you will have a better understanding of the therapy process. This will help you to be more patient with therapy as well as more hopeful about its outcome.

Secondly, you will get more out of your therapy sessions. By understanding the kinds of information that your therapist needs and some of the complexities of therapy, you will become a more active participant in the therapy process. You will get more done in fewer sessions. Rather than thinking of this as a way to shorten therapy, think of this as a way to get even more from therapy using the same number of sessions as you originally would have.

Thirdly, it will help you in your application of your therapy hour (typically 45 minutes) to the other 167 hours in your week. By completing the self help exercises, you will experience and realize substantial changes in your life. These will encourage you to continue in therapy until you have reached what therapists call "the maintenance phase." It is as this point that you will experience lasting and positive change in your life. Using this book you will find that the time you spend in counseling is some of the most valuable time you have ever spent in your life. You will become closer to the goal I help all of my clients with—living without regrets.

The Number One Problem for Both Clients and Therapists

Therapists across the country are seeing half of their clients drop out of treatment before any lasting improvement can be made. The average number of sessions that clients have before they drop out of treatment is one. Just one session before they call it quits with therapy. Most of those who drop out will never return despite a continuation of the pain and problems that brought them into counseling in the first place. What is happening or not happening in the first session that is causing people to abandon therapy? What are people thinking or feeling that's making them give up before they get started? What can be done to improve *your* therapy experience and to encourage you to continue?

For professionals, it's tempting to blame clients for giving up, while giving themselves credit for clients who improve. But, blaming clients for treatment failures and crediting therapists for treatment success is self-serving and does nothing to help clients. My job as a therapist is to help clients with every aspect of their lives that is ethically proper. I can't just provide treatment and expect them to get better. I need to help them find my office, be comfortable, and understand the forms I'm asking them to fill out. I need to give them a sense of hope and at least an outline of my approach. If they don't leave the first session with these things, then I haven't done my job.

The gap between the needs of people and the services of therapists must be bridged for the sake of both clients and providers. It needs to be a win-win situation. People with emotional and family problems need to understand better how therapy works before they can be expected to call for help. Misconceptions need to be removed so that people can make more educated choices. There are no reasons for the processes of therapy to be shrouded in secrecy. There is no voodoo going on.

Due to a misunderstanding about what psychotherapy is, clients often bring with them expectations that do not match the expectations of the therapist. Therapists' expectations come from their training and experience. First time clients have neither. The ideas that first time clients bring into therapy necessarily come from what they have heard about therapy from others—most often the media. Television and movies have alternately presented therapists as palm readers ("look at this ink blot and tell me what you see") or miracle workers who effect a cure with some witty piece of advice. The existence of call-in help lines and call-in radio shows gives the impression that there are quick fixes available. Radio show listeners have the expectation that a caller's problems have been solved simply because the answer made sense. Were they able to see how these same people are faring even a week after receiving their quick fix, they would see that although there are simple answers, there are no simple solutions. Receiving advice is not the same as applying it—which must happen before problems can really be solved. Solutions, and not merely answers, are the work of psychotherapy.

Therapists, for their part, have often done a poor job of educating their clients about what to expect in the different phases of therapy. Even second time or third time clients may not be familiar with the different phases of therapy if they dropped out early from their previous treatment. These different treatment phases are not seen in Hollywood portrayals. Therapeutic relationships have a beginning, a middle, and an end. Although it may feel like a friendship at times, it isn't and can't be. The goal of counseling is, after all, to make the therapist *unnecessary*.

Therapists necessarily must start by getting to know very many particulars about their clients. Therapists do what they can to help clients to feel comfortable and supported while they share details of their lives that they perhaps have not shared with others. It is during this initial information gathering process that most clients drop out of treatment.

Talking about problems always brings to the front the feelings associated with those problems. Tissues are always available in therapist's offices because feelings can be intense. But some people are so unaccustomed to expressing their feelings in front of others or even in private that they drop out of therapy within the first few weeks when emotions are at their peak. They may come to the conclusion that things have gotten worse because they feel worse. It does not fit their expectation of therapy as a place where you go to feel better. What they don't know is that we must first dig up the painful stuff before we can deal with it. Digging up the painful stuff is painful and that pain is a sign of progress. Therapists know that clients will necessarily feel worse before they feel better and are encouraged by this at the same time that clients may be feeling discouraged. If this difference is not talked about by the therapist, they may never see their client again.

Clients have serious doubts and false assumptions about therapy long before they call to make an appointment. These doubts and assumptions keep the vast majority of people who need help from making an appointment at all. These same doubts and assumptions make people wait until their situation becomes desperate before they call a therapist. This explains why many couples who go for marriage counseling are nearly ready to divorce. How much easier it would have been for them and their therapist if they had gone to counseling much sooner. Problems, like fires, are always most easily dealt with when they are small.

Unfortunately, therapists have no chance to clear up assumptions until the appointment has been made and kept. One of the contributing factors to these assumptions is the lack of understanding about how thoughts, feelings, and behaviors are all tied together. Because of the lack of such education in our culture, it is often easier to conceive how a pill can relieve our depression (or anxiety) than it is to conceive how talking can remove the internal conflicts that create those feelings. This is particularly true for clients with a background of low social support. They have never experienced healing through talking, so have no reason to believe that is going to happen in therapy.

There are good answers to client's doubts, but there are no simple answers. In the process of therapy clients gradually come to understand the answer to the question, "How will talking with a therapist about my problems help?" Although this is an important question and must be explained, there is a sense in which it is not helpful to explain. Like love, some things must be experienced to be understood. Even a thorough explanation by the therapist in the first session would do little to really satisfy the client about this question. More important than explanations, it must be seen that the therapist truly cares and some belief must be carried by the client that the therapist indeed does have a way to help. Therapy is a professional, helping *relationship*. There has to be some kind of personal connection from the first session.

I wrote this book to bridge the gap between fear and trust that will help people to seek and stick with counseling until they get what they want and need from it, to help people see how talking with a therapist can bring new understanding as well as changes in behavior, and to clear up misconceptions about the way therapy actually works. Therapy is more than talk—a lot more. Words are the tools that equip clients to think, do, and make sense of their feelings *between* sessions so that their situation can improve. Clients and therapists are allies in the change process. Without their clients' help, therapists would be quite powerless to effect change. Therapists guide, but the going is the client's. Therapists are not "brain mechanics"—they are simply the ones who know the way.

Therapists must necessarily adjust to every client, providing what they need, at the time they need it. Clients who enter therapy in any kind of crisis must be stabilized and receive rather direct advice. Once stabilized, the more gradual work of change can begin—if the client returns to therapy. Unfortunately, once the fire is out, many clients no longer see the need for therapy—until their next fire.

When the crisis is over, therapists need to continue to educate clients in the process of therapy. They do this by giving a brief explanation of their particular way of working with clients to help them make long term changes. Unfortunately, there are still too many therapists, kindhearted and eager to help, who don't explain soon enough. As a result, clients may drop out of treatment simply because they don't have a clear understanding of why it's important for them to remain in counseling. Both therapist and client need to be on the same page or they risk not even being in the same room

One thing therapists excel at is helping their clients restate or rethink their problems in ways that give them more control over both what happens to them and within them. Therapists therefore spend very little time helping clients to blame others and instead help them to see where they can make positive changes *despite* the behavior of other people, and *despite* whatever happened to them in the past. For clients who insist that others must change before their life can improve, this approach is difficult to swallow. They must choose between pointing a finger at others (sometimes long gone) and looking in the mirror at who is responsible for what happens from now on. People who are not ready to make this shift may drop out of treatment. They know that if they continue in treatment, their therapist must nudge them away from blame and toward responsibility. A therapist who didn't do this would be colluding with their client in blaming others, and blocking growth for the client. Caring won't allow that.

Successful outcomes in therapy are the result of the client and therapist working as a team, regardless of the style of therapy. A rule of thumb learned by therapists is "never work harder than your client." Yet, clients would not know how to do the work without the help of the therapist. It's when clients apply the wisdom, insights, and skills they learn in therapy *outside* of therapy, that they experience lasting change. Attending therapy without applying the benefits of therapy to your life is like reading a cookbook to satisfy your hunger. Until you actually cook the food, you will not really be satisfied.

I encourage you to see the exercises in this book like everything else in life—as an experiment. Don't try to figure out ahead of time what is going to be helpful for you or not, and instead, let the results guide you. With such an approach to life and self-help, you will no doubt go down some paths which end up being dead ends. But, you will go down enough paths that lead to a brighter, more beautiful place, as to make all the missteps worth it.

CHAPTER ONE

1. GETTING MOTIVATED TO GET PSYCHOTHERAPY

"What if the therapist thinks I'm crazy?" "How could just talking help me with this?" "What will my friends think if they find out I'm seeing a shrink?" "What if I can't think of anything to say?" "What if I say something really stupid?" These "what if" kinds of questions keep people in their comfort zones by keeping them from getting professional help. But professional help is what we need to get when we have a problem that is beyond our ability to deal with effectively. When our problems are related to the way we think, the way we feel, the way we behave, or the way we get along with others, that professional help is most often a psychotherapist (in this book, I will say "therapist" for short). Therapists help us to move forward again when we are just spinning our wheels. But, before we can even get that help, we must somehow get past the mental security gate that blocks us from seeking help. That is a gate electrified by our fears that hinders, rather than helps, us.

Fears both Prevent and Maintain Risk

Fears are helpful things and often they prevent us from taking unnecessary risks, but sometimes fear *keeps us* taking unnecessary risks. When inaction is risky, fear often increases risk.

We take a risk, for example, when we don't work on damaged relationships. How could fear prevent people from working on their relationships? People often fear talking about relationship problems with their partner because they believe they will be blamed and rejected. But, because they don't work

Here's What You Will Learn...

- **How to decide if counseling is appropriate for you.**
- **How to overcome the anxiety that keeps you from getting counseling.**
- **How to find the right counselor for you.**
- **How to make your first appointment.**

A psychotherapist (mental health counselor, social worker, or psychologist) can help with:

- **Our feelings**
- **Our thoughts**
- **Our behaviors**
- **Our interactions with others**

on their relationship problems, they risk losing their relationship as the problems grow. Instead of fearing working on relationship problems, a more realistic fear would be the fear of working on relationship problems *in the wrong way*. With that fear clearly identified, the benefit of having a therapist to help not only makes a lot of sense, it also reduces the fear.

Fear can also keep us from working on harmful habits, like avoiding others, excessive drinking, or excessive worry. We may fear that if we get help with such things, we will find out something is terribly wrong with us—that our secret will get out. Or, we might fear that we can't be helped because we are so messed up. Such fears actually result in our lives becoming more messed up. A more realistic fear would be fearing what will happen if we continue such behaviors. Then, getting help from a therapist makes sense.

We may also fear working on painful memories. Because we don't believe that anyone can take away our memories, working in therapy sounds like a very scary thing. We would repeatedly come face to face with those memories and might lose control or make the memories stronger. The reality is that therapists can help to take the pain and trauma out of memories, even if they are not removed, so that people can move on with their lives and be happy again. I frequently did this work with marines who had traumatic deployment experiences. Once treated, their fear of therapy disappeared since it helped so much. Greatly reduced fears and improved relationships made them into believers.

How seriously we take our fears (which includes our doubt about trying new things) should be in direct proportion to the amount of real *danger* involved. Doubt about whether a pond is frozen solid enough to walk on may save our life. Doubt about whether therapy may be helpful is more likely to hurt us than to help us. With counseling, the potential to make your life better is much greater than the potential to cause harm. Counseling helps with the preparation, action, and follow through which is necessary for becoming the way we really want to be. None of the changes happen overnight, or against our will and it is possible to withdraw from counseling at any time. These factors add up to high potential gain and low potential risk.

Have a Crisis or Borrow One

Therapy is for personal growth. If we want to grow something good, then we must till, plant, and tend the soil. We need to put in the effort. But before we can do that, we must get past the resistance of not feeling like it. At some point we must just do it. A crisis can give us the push we need. Crises are very motivating. When there is no crisis, we need to "borrow" the crisis from the future by anticipating what will happen if our problems continue. We need to be able to predict not only what will happen to us and our relationships, but also what we will miss out on. Regrets can only be prevented if we anticipate the long term results of our actions and *inaction* and use that anticipation to make the best choices today. To borrow a crisis, ask yourself what will eventually happen if you don't get therapy. Try to answer that question now.

Proactive questions are a good way to overcome the obstacle of doubt about counseling. Proactive (*pro*-for, *active*-action) questions help us to overcome inertia and get moving. Here are some good proactive questions for deciding about therapy. Ask and answer these questions:

How long have I had this problem?

Have my efforts to resolve the problem on my own been successful?

Which is likely to be more helpful—letting this problem go unresolved or getting professional help?

What would my life be like if I didn't have this problem?

Is it worth it to work on this problem?

If I do work on this problem, when would be the best time to do it (now, or in the future)?

To increase our willpower to do something now, we need to borrow the crisis from the future. What's going to happen?...How bad could it be?...What will I regret?

On the next two pages are an example self assessment form and a blank assessment form which you can use to answer these questions in a structured way. Structure helps us to organize both our thinking and our actions, resulting in less confusion and more accomplishment. This form and your answers will also be helpful should you decide to go to counseling. These same questions will also prepare you for your first session and take the worry out of what to say at your first session.

Seeing a Counselor Means You Probably Are Not Crazy

According to the National Institute of Mental Health, mental disorders are common, affect tens of millions of people each year in the U.S. and only a fraction of those people get help.[2] The people who do tend to use psychotherapy are those who have healthier coping skills. Recognizing and getting help for our problems is a sign of mental health. Those who either don't recognize their problems, or don't get help for them are needlessly making their lives worse. And that's not healthy.

The fact that you are reading this book demonstrates that you have both the insight and the motivation to effectively deal with your problems. And you have used your motivation to take an action step (reading this book). Even if you were to do nothing else, you are way ahead of most other people. Recognizing that you have a problem and doing something positive about it is a sign of your mental health. When you combine your motivation, the exercises from this book, and counseling, you will be using powerful tools for change.

Locating a Therapist

Once you have made the decision to begin counseling, the next step is to locate an appropriate therapist. Of course, everyone would like to have an experienced, well-trained, affordable and wise counselor. As in any field, however, some therapists are better than others, and there are a variety of

Seeing a licensed or certified professional will help you to be sure that the therapist is well trained.

Exercise: Do I Need Counseling?

A few questions are all you need to determine if you need counseling. This is an *example* self assessment. <u>On the next page</u> is a form you can use for *your* self assessment. If you decide to go to counseling, take a completed copy of it with you. Then you won't need to worry about what to say.

Example

What is the problem?	*I feel depressed most of the time*
When did this problem start?	*About 3 years ago when I moved to the Countryside.*
What do I usually do to deal with this problem?	*1. Eat a lot* *2. Sleep a lot* *3. Don't go out* *4. Call my mother*
What are the results of how I deal with this problem?	*1. I am gaining weight* *2. I have very little energy* *3. I am becoming socially isolated*
What will happen if I don't change?	*I won't have any friends and my life will be miserable. I will also be very overweight and my self-esteem will be even worse. I will be more depressed.*
How would life be if I didn't have this problem?	*I would have more energy, spend more time with friends and be happier.*
All of my ways of coping are helpful	Y (N) *They don't fix my depression*
Some of my ways of coping are helpful	(Y) N *Calling my mother is helpful.*
I need to learn better ways to cope	(Y) N *I need to learn what works because I am still depressed.*
I should get professional counseling	(Y) N *I want to feel better and enjoy my life.*
The best time for counseling is:	Now

Exercise 1, Part B: Do I Need Counseling?

A few questions are all you need to determine if you need counseling. This is a self assessment. <u>On the previous page</u> is a completed form you can use as an example. If you decide to go to counseling, take a completed copy of it with you. Then you won't need to worry about what to say.

Self-Assessment

What is the problem?	
When did this problem start?	
What do I usually do to deal with this problem?	1. 2. 3. 4.
What are the results of how I deal with this problem?	1. 2. 3.
What will happen if I don't change?	
How would life be if I didn't have this problem?	
All of my ways of coping are helpful	Y N
Some of my ways of coping are helpful	Y N
I need to learn better ways to cope	Y N
I should get professional counseling	Y N
The best time for counseling is:	Now Later (when?)

specialties. Careful selection on the front end can help you to find a therapist who is right for you, making you feel more assured that you can get the right help. Finding a therapist that is right for you will take a little work. As with anything, a step-by-step approach will help you to find what you need without becoming overwhelmed. It takes time, but it doesn't have to be hard.

There are a surprising number of professionals who are permitted to do counseling under the various state laws. Even professionals from seemingly unrelated fields (such as dentistry) are allowed to call themselves counselors in some states. Although it is impossible to tell how good therapists are by their titles, all things being equal, a person trained in psychotherapy is going to be better at doing psychotherapy than someone who is not. And, if you are seeking counseling consistent with your religious beliefs, you may consider pastoral counseling. It may even be desirable to have both pastoral counseling and psychotherapy.

People who are certified or licensed by the state in which they practice have met minimum training requirements and have also passed proficiency tests in psychology and ethics. They have also had their counseling supervised by other qualified professionals. Maintaining their license or certification compels them to remain competent and ethical. It also means they must take annual continuing education seminars in order to keep up with modern treatment methods. Seeing a licensed or certified professional will help you to be sure the therapist is well trained. In the unlikely event that a serious problem would arise, you would also have a licensing or certification board that you could take your complaints to.

There are various levels of certification. Doctorate level (PhD, PsyD, and DMFT) have more training than other psychotherapists and are the only ones who can call themselves psychologists. In general and as with all specialists, the higher the level of training and licensure, the higher the cost of counseling. If possible, don't let cost dictate your choice of a therapist. It is far better to match the therapist's skills and personality with your needs than with your wallet. Many

Levels of Counselors:

- **MA Psychotherapist**
- **MA MFT Marriage and Family Therapist (Masters Level)**
- **MSW Social Worker**

- **LCSW Licensed Clinical Social Worker**

- **DMFT Doctor of Marriage and Family Therapy**
- **PHD/PSYD Psychologist**
- **MD Psychiatrists**

Good Sources for Referrals:
- **Clergy**
- **Medical Doctors**
- **Lawyers**
- **School Counselors**

When you get a referral, ask why that particular counselor is being recommended to you. If you use a referral website or agency, determine what criteria are used for the selection of counselors.

people have been helped by students in training, while others have not benefited from seeing the most expensive therapists in the world. Because of individual differences, no therapist is "best" for all people.

The best way to locate a therapist is by recommendation. Good sources of recommendations are large churches in your area. It is not necessary that you attend the church or be religious at all. Clergy are usually happy to help and are accustomed to giving referrals. They are not paid for the referral. National referral websites and help lines can be good sources of referral information depending on how they screen their list of providers. Some, like Focus on the Family,[3] have multi-page questionnaires they use to assess providers before they will recommend them. Others may list the provider for free or for a small fee without doing any kind of check of the counselor's competence. When you get a referral, ask why that particular counselor is being recommended to you. If you use a referral website or agency, determine what criteria are used for the selection of counselors. If you want counseling for a child, you can call a few schools and ask the guidance counselor or principal for recommendations.

Other professionals you already work with can also be an excellent source of referrals. Since they want to retain your business, they are likely to give you their best recommendation. Your medical doctor, dentist, or lawyer, for example, may know both you and the counselors well enough that they can refer you to someone who is more likely to be a good match for you.

Using Health Insurance for Counseling

If you want to use your health insurance to pay for counseling, you will also need to choose a counselor who can take your insurance. Rather than call around to various providers it is usually best to directly contact your insurance company and ask who you may see in your area. They are also likely to have a list of their providers by geographic area on the Internet. You can then match up any recommendations that you have received against the list of providers who work for your insurance company. You may find that the most highly recommended therapist does not accept your insurance. The more urgent or serious your problem, the more important it is to get the best you can afford. Do your best to find a good match, but remember you can change later if things aren't working out. It's better to see a counselor you are uncertain about than to see no counselor at all.

Be aware that insurance does not cover marital or couple's counseling. There are some legitimate ways around this, however. If one of the people seen has a covered diagnosis that would be helped by couple's counseling, then services *are* likely to be covered. This is considered family therapy. For example, depression or anxiety, which is severely impacted by relationship problems, is likely to be improved by working together with the family or spouse. Psychotherapists are well aware of how this works although insurance companies are not likely to volunteer such information. If you are seeking marital counseling, when you call your insurance company, ask if you are covered for "family therapy," and not if you are covered for marriage counseling. The therapist will determine if family therapy is appropriate after the initial evaluation. Even if it is not, the initial evaluation is still covered by your insurance. This is because an initial evaluation is never considered to be family therapy (it is called an "intake evaluation").

Insurance does not cover marital counseling, but most cover "family therapy"—even if it's just you and your spouse.

If you have no insurance coverage or are unable to afford your copayments, do not despair. Many locations have agencies that operate on a sliding scale basis and will charge you according to your income level. These agencies don't advertise because they don't have the budget for it, although they do want your business. A call to any local psychologist's office should be all you need to find out the name of such an agency, because they undoubtedly refer other people there who cannot afford their services. Medicaid and Medicare both have provision for mental health services and function like other insurances. Be aware that with Medicare, you may still have to pay a large portion of the session fee (typically 50%).

On the following page is a step by step approach you can use

Exercise: Locating A Therapist

Locating a therapist is as easy as picking up the telephone book, but locating a good therapist is another matter. Your goal will be to get the best skilled therapist that you can afford.

1. Ask for names of therapists from professionals you already trust and whom you have a professional relationship with. This could be your medical doctor, pastor, college dean, etc. You don't need to give them any detailed information or even admit that you are searching for a therapist for yourself.

2. If possible, get the name of more than one therapist. The therapist you contact may not be taking new clients, may not accept your insurance, or may not treat your particular kind of problem.

3. When you call the therapist's office, ask for references. Understandably they cannot give you their client's names, but they can usually give references to professionals in the community such as psychiatrists they work with, pastors who have referred to them, school counselors, etc.

4. If they refuse to give references, make a note of that and keep checking. Everyone, including new therapists should be able to provide a reference to someone, even if it is with one of the agencies they trained with.

5. Call the references they gave you. Occasionally, references have bad things to say. On the other hand, good references can make you more confident about the therapist and help you to feel like you are in good hands.

6. Call your insurance company to find out about coverage for counseling and if they will pay for a particular therapist you have checked out. Do this after checking out the therapists though, as your decision should not just be based on insurance coverage. Your goal is to get the best treatment you can afford, not to save the most money that you can.

7. Use the form on the next page to call the therapists you have checked out and to make an appointment.

8. When you go to counseling, be sure to tell the therapist which references you talked to. Since these are important referral sources for them, they will want to send a thank you note to the referral source and they will also be on their toes to give you good service. They would probably do that anyway, but it doesn't hurt to let them know.

Exercise: Scheduling an Appointment

Instructions: Partially complete the forms with the information you already know (your insurance company, etc.). Call the therapist and complete the other parts while still on the phone. Do not schedule more than one appointment or more than one therapist.

Therapist or Agency Name:
Phone Number:
Recommended by:
My problem is _____.   Treated ☐ Not Treated ☐
My health insurance is _____.   Accepted ☐ Not Accepted ☐ Fee $_____
Appointment Date:
Appointment Time:
Directions to the Office:
What to bring (e.g., list of medications, etc.):

Therapist or Agency Name:
Phone Number:
Recommended by:
My problem is _____.   Treated ☐ Not Treated ☐
My health insurance is _____.   Accepted ☐ Not Accepted ☐ Fee $_____
Appointment Date:
Appointment Time:
Directions to the Office:
What to bring (e.g., list of medications, etc.):

Therapist or Agency Name:
Phone Number:
Recommended by:
My problem is _____.   Treated ☐ Not Treated ☐
My health insurance is _____.   Accepted ☐ Not Accepted ☐ Fee $_____
Appointment Date:
Appointment Time:
Directions to the Office:
What to bring (e.g., list of medications, etc.):

*NOTE: If for any reason you cannot make your scheduled appointment, call the therapist's office immediately. Many therapists are reluctant to reschedule someone who does not show up for their first appointment or who cancels at the last minute. Missed appointments are a significant expense to therapists who can typically only schedule one person per hour. Use the same courtesy you would with a good friend.

to locate a therapist who is likely to be good for you.

Once you have located a counselor, call to make an appointment. When you call, briefly state what you are wanting help with. For example, "I want to make an appointment for counseling for depression," or "I want to make an appointment for marital counseling," etc. The main reason for this is to be sure that the counselors provide the type of counseling that you want. If they don't, then ask for a recommendation to someone who does. Some problems are mainly treated by specialists. Counseling for these problems may only be done by a small percentage of therapists in your area. Drug and alcohol abuse, eating disorders, and child abuse, in particular, are areas often treated by specialists.

You can use the forms on page 11 to prepare for your call and to make an appointment. Once you have made the appointment, post it on your refrigerator or in another prominent place. Making the call to a therapist is a major step on your path to success. After you schedule the appointment, take the time to celebrate and reward yourself. Making the appointment is a major step and shows that you are capable of making your life better. Don't expect encouragement from others, although if you get it, consider it a bonus. Sometimes other people won't want you to get counseling. Family members are often afraid that counseling will bring about changes that will make their lives worse. Don't let their negativity spoil your pro-activity. Their fears won't subside until you are in counseling for a while and they see that nothing drastic has happened. When your problem is your family, you must decide between being miserable to appease them or to make your life better–even if they don't like it.

Case Example: Tony

Tony was a student at a small, private college in Ohio. He made fairly good grades and was praised by his family. But Tony was never able to feel happy about his successes. He just had a sense of relief at having passed another test. After-hours and on semester breaks he was never able to enjoy himself like he saw other students doing. This had been the story of Tony's life and he felt doomed to live a joyless life. Although he wasn't happy, it never occurred to him that therapy could help. He just figured that this was the way his life was and that he would just need to bear it as best he could.

After a psychology class, Tony's professor had asked him to come to his office for a few minutes. The professor remarked how Tony never seemed to be happy and recommended that Tony get counseling. This was a new idea for Tony because he never considered that his life could change. Although he was hesitant to schedule an appointment, Tony started to consider that he might have a psychological problem and that if he did, that was great news because it meant that there were ways to treat it. Tony started to consider his thoughts, feelings, and behaviors as "symptoms." Previously unrecognized by Tony, his lack of pleasure, low energy, social isolation, and feelings of doom were typical of a person with a type of depression called dysthymia.

—

Tony began to see a therapist recommended by his professor. Within three months he was able to replace some of the thinking habits which were taking the fun out of his life. After one year, he was feeling consistently happy and positive for the first time in his life.

In Tony's case, he didn't recognize he had a psychological problem because he had been depressed since early childhood. People who have always felt anxious or depressed often don't realize that life doesn't have to be that way. They don't realize that something is *wrong*, because things have never been *right* for them.

People who used to be happy, but now are not, realize that something has gone wrong and desire to get back to the happier way they were before. Their change in feeling is a clear signal to them that something happened—that life is not supposed to feel like this. The greater the difference between how they felt before and how they feel now, the more distressed they feel, and the greater their desire to change.

Finding out you have a psychological problem can be both a relief and a reason for hope. Disorders, after all, are treatable.

Both people who were never happy and people who have become unhappy, may not know how to change. Both are in need of professional help and can begin to have a realistic hope from the time they decide to make a therapy appointment.

Summary

Most people feel nervous about getting counseling for the first time, although almost everyone could benefit from counseling at some point in their life. Knowing more about what will be asked of you in your therapy session will help you to be more prepared and comfortable with the process. Just like every profession, not all therapists are alike and there are steps you can take to make sure you find the therapist that is best for you. If you have had a problem for most of your life, it may not seem to you like you need counseling, because what is unhealthy to other people seems normal to you. On the other hand, if you were much happier with your life at some time in the past than now, you can recognize the importance, and your potential, to return to that happier way of living.

CHAPTER TWO

2. YOUR FIRST FEW SESSIONS

Client's who come to my practice encounter a form which is called "Checklist of Concerns." It asks clients to check off all symptoms and concerns which apply to them. It has items such as "anger, confusion, sadness, financial problems, marital conflict, etc." From a therapist's perspective, it is important to know everything that is going on with a client in order to get a clear picture of the client's strengths and weaknesses as well as any issues that may get in the way of treatment. Clients, however, are usually focused on the one or two problems that are causing the most distress at the moment. They often forget about the little problems which led up to those big problems. Our major problems usually start as minor problems, much like giant oak trees start as small acorns. Our large credit card bills start as small credit card bills, depressions can start with just one bad day, and every addiction started with just one use. Even the small problems you are less concerned about today could become the big problems of tomorrow. That's why it's important to be forthcoming with *all* of your difficulties—big and small.

Small problems are the seeds of tomorrow's big problems unless we take care of them now.

Your Feelings Are Important

On the "Checklist of Concerns" it's not unusual to have someone check off "marital conflict," or "parent-child conflict," but then not check off anger, sadness, guilt, or any number of unpleasant feelings. This simply cannot be. People are not robots, after all. When we are having problems with others, we have a variety of feelings that go along with our problems. A

You are the sum of your experiences:

- **Your losses**
- **Your attachments**
- **Your biggest problems**
- **Your problem resolutions**
- **Your past goals**
- **Your success in reaching them**
- **And every relationship you have ever had**

Your past performance is the best indicator of your future performance. Talking about your past provides information for every type of therapy.

therapist wants to know your feelings because they provide important information. Knowing what kind of feelings, when they started, how strong they are, and how long they last help the therapist to understand you. The therapist, in turn, will better help you to understand yourself. Knowing that you are angry says something different about your situation than if you are sad. Maybe you are both angry and sad. That is different still. Although you are not a therapist, could you guess at the differences in the following situations?: 1) a man's wife leaves him and he feels sad; 2) a man's wife leaves him and he feels angry; and 3) a man's wife leaves him and he feels nothing. Just knowing these two pieces of information (his wife leaving plus his feelings about that) can tell you how well he is coping, what kinds of thoughts he is having, and what might be the best way to help him.

Sad people have experienced a loss of something or someone important to them. If the man whose wife left is primarily sad, it is a clue to the therapist that the man needs help grieving and accepting his loss so that he can move on. This is particularly true if he has been sad for a very long time without any improvement.

Angry people cope by blaming someone else for their problems. It helps them to avoid taking personal responsibility. If a man was angry at his wife for having left him, he would be seeing her as the cause of his problems. He will probably have some valid points to tell the therapist. Where he is most likely to need help is in seeing what he can do to help his own situation and to focus on that rather than his wife.

If a man feels nothing, in a situation where he should, it tells the therapist that the he is using denial to cope. At some level, he fears being overwhelmed by his emotions and so blocks them off. Because denial will also prevent him from experiencing positive emotions, the therapist would help this him to feel safe and gradually experience the loss of his wife.

The presence or absence of a feeling is as important a part of what happened as whatever your eyes saw, or your ears heard. Be as accurate and as open as possible. Although you may not be used to such openness, your therapist is only there to help. He or she will not belittle you in any way for having many difficulties

The Intake Interview

Before figuring out the best way to proceed, a therapist needs to collect lots of information. Of course, you will have to provide general information such as your name, age, and address, but the total amount of information needed to correctly identify how to help you is immense. It may take your therapist a few sessions to gather all the information needed to understand how best to help. Therapy can then be tailored to your specific needs. A therapist who does a careful intake can save you months of treatment because she can catch valuable information which could have delayed your recovery, if it had been missed. Don't mistakenly assume that since the therapist is asking questions about many seemingly unrelated things, that the reason you came to therapy is being ignored. The therapist is gathering many bits of information that will help both of you to understand the origin of your problem as well as the best approach for making things better. On the following page you can see the typical kinds of information gathered in an intake interview.

Most people who drop out of therapy, do so during this intake process, which may take from one to three sessions. You also may find it hard to be patient with the intake process. For one thing, you will need to not only tell the therapist detailed information about what is bothering you now, but the therapist will also want to know details about other problems that you are having and have had before. A family history is a typical part of the assessment process. The therapist will want to know about your life as a child (even if you are now elderly), relationships with family members, successes and failures and any number of other things. Who you are today is a result of the interactions of heredity, environment, experiences, and all the choices that you have made in the past. Did you ever look at a photo of a stranger and try to figure out what that person must be like? In order to know what that person is *really* like, what would you need to know? If you only had one to three

Some possible biological causes of the most common psychological problems:

depression – genetic predisposition; menopause; hypothyroidism; any illness including the flu, overworking; medication; and sleep deprivation

anxiety –genetic predisposition; menopause; hyperthyroidism; heart disease; respiratory disorders; medications; and head injury.

Example: Information Typically Gathered in an Intake Interview

Problem client is seeking help with:

details, how the problem came about, course, methods tried to cope with the problem

Client's current situation:

family structure and relationships, work, activities, interests, hobbies, desired changes to current situation

Client's family history:

characteristics and nature of relationships with parents, siblings, and other important childhood family relationships.

Client's school/work History:

successes, failures, choices, problems, satisfactions, regrets

Client's social history:

friendships and rivalries in early, middle, and late childhood; romantic and intimate relationships; successes and failures in friendship, dating, and marital relationships

Client's key life events:

traumatic experiences to self or significant others; structural changes to family; medical, alcohol, or drug abuse problems; emotional, physical, and/or sexual abuse

Client's physical health history:

current health status and time since wellness checkups; medications and dosages; allergies; history of medical problems for client and family.

Client's mental health history:

Previous psychological and psychiatric treatments, their reasons and outcomes.

Client's mental status:

Estimated by the therapist from your appearance, speech, behavior, mood, and interactions. Possible direct testing of memory, attention, and orientation.

Client's stated counseling goals:

Regarding presenting problem as well as other concerns.

hours to know this person well enough to give counsel about life changes and your answers might make the difference between getting better or struggling for years, what would you ask? This is what your therapist is doing in the intake. Your therapist is not "nosey"; your therapist is determined to give you the best help possible.

The Psychological and the Physical Are Closely Related

Your therapist will also want to know about any physical conditions that you have and any medications that you take (whether prescriptions or over the counter). What affects the body affects the mind and vice versa. Sometimes a client's problems are the result of some underlying physical problem. The therapist may ask you to get a physical examination and possibly blood tests to rule out an underlying condition. Although this may seem unnecessary to you, it is much better than spending months in counseling before finding out that a physical condition is causing your problems. Depression, for example, can be caused by many different physical conditions.[4] If you take several medications, it is often helpful to bring in a written list of your medications and dosages. If you want to, you can bring the prescription containers so the counselor can copy the required information from the containers.

Thoroughness Is a Mark of a Skilled Professional

What makes getting through the assessment phase of therapy difficult is that while the counselor is gathering information, it doesn't seem like your problem is being addressed. After all, you came to the therapist in distress about some matter that you no longer want to live with and two or three sessions later it seems the counselor still has not gotten to work on it. But, this type of thoroughness is the mark of a skilled professional.

The counselor that does a thorough evaluation is likely to gain a good understanding of your problem and the potential obstacles to your progress. By taking the extra time to be

Physical problems can be symptoms of psychological problems and vice versa. It is really important to try to figure out which came first.

Remembering is mentally re-experiencing. This just strengthens our original feelings, whether they were bad or good. Talking about experiences objectifies them. Talking can be like a small light that can erase even a large shadow.

thorough, the therapist may actually be reducing the total number of sessions that you will need and he will be better prepared to help you deal with the obstacles which have, until now, been stopping you from doing better.

By presenting all this information to the therapist, you will be saying things that you have probably never said aloud before. This is therapeutic in itself. Talking about something is different from thinking about something, especially if it's your own life. Your inner thoughts about events most often reflect the way that you thought at the time something happened to you. For example, if your parents divorced while you were young, you will tend to think about the conflicts and split-up of your family from the perspective of a child. If you describe aloud the situation as an adult, you will more objectively talk about what happened—"When I was 10, my parents divorced; after that I just didn't care about things as much and my school grades went downhill." In explaining the situation, you will see more of the connections between what happened to you, the choices that you made, and the choices that you continue to make. You will see things in a more *objective* way rather than just continually re-experiencing the emotions. Re-experiencing heightens emotional intensity, whereas re-telling decreases emotional intensity. Remembering is re-experiencing. The things that we don't like to remember are the things we need to talk about. Repeatedly talking about a traumatic event does not take away the memory, but it does make the feelings connected with them less intense and easier to manage.[6]

The Therapeutic Alliance

The revealing that you do in the intake process will help to strengthen your relationship with your therapist. By the way your therapist responds to you, you will gain a trust and comfort level with your therapist that you didn't have when you first came in. This relationship with your therapist is called a "therapeutic alliance" and means that you and your therapist are on the same side—both working to help you. This alliance is also often experienced with other kinds of helping professionals such as medical doctors, pastors, and even hairdressers. Wounding and healing both occur within the context of *relationships*. Healing happens in alliances, and wounding happens with antagonism. Face to face contact with a therapist is more powerful than any self-help book, telephone conversation, or internet chat, because it is the most conducive to a real, human relationship.

The therapist will share little or nothing private about herself with you. This is mainly for your benefit. Things that you learn about the therapist could unduly influence your thoughts and behaviors toward your therapist and hinder your progress. Still, your therapist will probably tell you enough to let you know that he or she is a human being and you will probably be able to figure that out just by looking around the office. Don't consider your therapist's lack of self-revelation to be a reflection of whether the therapist likes you. You will be able to detect that just in the way he or she responds to you.

In addition to not saying much about himself or herself, the therapist will keep therapy times and payments standard in order to protect you and help you. Some clients feel "cut off" at the end of a session, although you need to keep in mind that what the therapist is doing is modeling good boundaries and protecting you from becoming too dependent. The more needy you are, the more this will hurt—at first. But as therapy progresses and you see that the therapeutic alliance remains strong, you may even start to let your therapist know that time is nearly up. Therapists also need to practice what they teach. If therapists keep clients longer than their scheduled time, they will feel rushed, may have to stay late to finish their paperwork and may gradually come to resent their clients, grow disinterested, and burn out. Your therapist doesn't want that for you and surely you don't want that for your therapist.

As in no other profession, your therapist's personality will influence what happens in therapy. When you go to get your car repaired, you don't get to know much about the mechanic. He may be introverted, outgoing, good at reading, hate sports, or any number of characteristics that won't affect in the least how your car is repaired. Replacing a muffler takes exactly the

The boundaries that help therapists keep you feeling safe (even when you don't like them):

- Appointments start and end on time
- Billing for services
- Charging late fees
- Maintaining confidentiality
- Complying with the law regarding abuse and danger reporting
- Not taking calls outside of office hours
- Charging for telephone time
- Limiting self revelation
- Not taking sides in couples or group therapy
- Being non-judgmental

same steps regardless of the personality of the mechanic. The personality of the therapist, however, will influence both the style of therapy and the therapeutic alliance. Therapy is a helping relationship that promotes emotional healing and self understanding.

The fact that therapist's styles vary with their personality turns out to be a good thing. For example, a patient and easygoing therapist is more likely to have a style which draws information from you in a way that you feel comfortable giving. An energetic and assertive therapist is more likely to have a directive style that helps you to feel like you are in capable hands. It is not possible to say which style (or if another style) will be best for you. Either could be just as helpful as long as you know the therapist cares.

Beware of Premature Judgment

Unless the therapist does something unethical or obviously incompetent in your initial session, you should hang in there regardless of your initial reaction. Some of the most brilliant therapists have personalities that are boring, outlandish, or even confrontational. They have one characteristic in common however—they are motivated to help you. The "feel good" therapist often is helpful, but not always. The "boring therapist" may have a systematic approach that is very effective. The "outlandish therapist" may help you to see things from perspectives that you never thought of, and the "confrontational therapist" may bring out strong feelings that will help you to get unstuck and get moving.

Barring unethical or incompetent behavior, stick with your therapist for a month before deciding that the therapeutic alliance is just not going to happen. If, after that time, you don't feel comfortable with your therapist, then switch to another. Actually, this is a reasonable recommendation for any kind of professional that you are seeing. Some of your doctors could never be friends with you in another context, but really know their stuff and care about your health. These are worth

Don't be quick to judge your therapist by personality differences:

- **Some of the best (and worst) therapists are very different than anyone you might meet "in real life."**
- **The one thing that all good therapists have in common is their motivation to help you.**
- **Unless there is obvious unethical behavior, stay with your therapist at least a month before passing judgment.**
- **If you are using progress as your criteria, wait at least three months.**
- **There is always a part of us that doesn't want to change which will find reasons to doubt our therapy or therapist.**

keeping and following from practice to practice should they move. It is much better to have a competent doctor than a friendly but incompetent one. With a therapist, by the end of a month, you will have a pretty good idea of which case it is. Do not, however, judge your therapist according to how much *progress* you have made in only one month. You will need at least three months for that, as you will read about later on.

In the unlikely event that you did need to change to a different therapist, you wouldn't be exactly starting over. Even though you would go through the same processes, it wouldn't be your first time through and that would make it much easier. The second time you give your information will be even more therapeutic than the first.

If you changed therapists and found you were having the same negative reaction to your second therapist, you would want to consider continuing anyway. Some people, through no fault of their own, have a naturally hard time developing trust. By sticking with therapy you can greatly improve your ability to trust. If trust is not the issue, there could be another reason some part of you is resisting counseling. A good rule of thumb is to stick with your first counselor at least a month before passing judgment and with your second therapist at least three months. Quickly changing from therapist to therapist would leave you not knowing what was going on.

Any counselor who has been in practice for a little while has had clients who switched from or switched to a different counselor. It is not something that counselors take personally. You can feel perfectly free in the future to see any counselor that you have seen before without fear that the counselor will hold some kind of grudge (unless, perhaps, you left without paying your bill).

In summary, the first session consists of filling out paperwork and talking about your problems. The next one or two sessions may be spent providing other information about your life so that the therapist can design a treatment plan tailored to your needs. You may or may not like your therapist at first, but you will be able to detect whether the therapist truly

Any counselor who has been in practice for a little while has had clients who switched from or switched to a different counselor. It is not something that counselors take personally.

wants to help you by the end of the first month. The therapist is not your friend, but is an ally who really cares and who will work in a professional way to help you do what you are unable to do on your own.

The Treatment Plan

Once the therapist has gathered enough information, a custom made treatment plan will be written for you. Besides being helpful, treatment plans are also required documentation by insurance companies. If you are using insurance, you will be asked to sign the treatment plan to acknowledge that you have seen it and agree with it. If you do not agree with the treatment plan, you should say so before you sign. It is important that you and your therapist be on the same page in terms of which problems you are focusing on and how you will proceed. If you are not using health insurance, your therapist may not have a formal, written treatment plan, but will never the less have a plan of approach. If your therapist does not mention it, be sure to ask your therapist about short and long term goals that she thinks will be helpful to you. Just knowing your goals can help you to achieve them. Knowing our goals clearly sets our unconscious minds to work on them.

The essential elements of a written treatment plan include the symptoms that are present when you begin therapy, the diagnosis, other treatments that may be recommended (such as psychiatric evaluation, medical evaluation, group therapy, etc.), treatment goals, session frequency and estimated length of treatment (you can see an example of a treatment plan on the next page).

Although many clients consider the diagnosis to be the most critical part of the treatment plan, actually the treatment goals are much more important. Diagnoses are required by insurance companies because they need some justification for the money they are spending on your treatment. If they discover a lot of their members are seeking treatment for a particular type of disorder, they will often offer lower cost

Treatment Plans Include:

- **Symptoms**
- **Diagnoses**
- **Recommendations**
- **Goals**
- **Estimated completion dates**

Treatment goals are measurable items that indicate normal or improved functioning such as:

- **Sleeping within 30 minutes of going to bed on five of seven nights**
- **Normal appetite and weight within 10 pounds of ideal body weight**
- **Agree and follow through with partner on methods of Disciplining children**
- **Resolve the problem that led to current crisis**
- **Increase self-esteem as measured by self-esteem inventory**

24

Example Treatment Plan

DATE:	9/15/2013	INITIAL GAF:	50
CLIENT NAME:	DOE, JANE	CASE NO.:	00283A

PRESENTING PROBLEM:

anxiety, worry, feeling stressed, difficulty concentrating, racing thoughts, frightening fantasies, fears of criticism/disapproval; depression, confusion, low energy

DSM IV PRELIMINARY DIAGNOSES:

Axis I: Generalized Anxiety Disorder

Axis II: None

Axis III: Acid Reflux

Axis IV: Job Stress, Financial Problems

INITIAL EVALUATION OBJECTIVES   Specifics/Target Dates

☒	1.	Psychological Evaluation	ANXIETY AND DEPRESSION INVENTORIES by 1/23/14
☒	2.	Psychiatric Referral	MEDICATION EVALUATION FOR ANXIETY
☒	3.	Medical Referral	COLLABORATION
☐	4.	Drug and Alcohol Referral	
☒	5.	Other	FINANCIAL COUNSELING

TREATMENT GOALS (progress evaluated at each session and changes noted in *Progress Notes*)

☐	1.	Understand purpose of treatment	9.	☐	Increase assertiveness
☒	2.	Solve situational distress	10.	☐	Improve communication
☒	3.	Decrease anxiety	11.	☐	Explore educational/vocational needs
☒	4.	Decrease depression	12.	☒	Do better in school/work
☐	5.	Decrease uncontrolled behavior	13.	☒	Improve daily living skills
☒	6.	Increase self-esteem	14.	☒	Learn to cope with illness
☐	7.	Improve family relationships	15.	☐	Work toward leaving therapy
☐	8.	Eliminate harmful habits	16.	☐	Other:

Goal	Measurable Objectives	Target Dates
1	Identify major life conflicts from the past and present	1/15/2014
2	Develop relaxation and diversion activities to decrease anxiety	1/15/2014
3	Increase daily social and vocational involvement	1/15/2014
4	Identify beliefs and messages that produce worry and anxiety	1/15/2014
5	Use self-help exercises to correct beliefs and reduce anxiety	1/15/2014

25

Don't get overly attached to your diagnosis. It describes how you are to a limited extent, at this point in time. It doesn't explain how you came to be this way or what your life is going to be like in the future.

policies to employers that exclude that particular diagnosis. A good recent example of this is Attention Deficit/Hyperactivity Disorder (ADHD). Many children and adults were being diagnosed with ADHD. As a result, ADHD is often excluded by insurance policies as a covered diagnosis. This keeps insurance policy costs low (relatively) for people who purchase insurance, while helping the insurance company to maintain a profit. When a diagnosis is not covered by an insurance company, the common practice by counselors is to use another diagnosis that could also apply. So, the result of the ADHD exclusion was a greater number of children being diagnosed with Oppositional Defiant Disorder or Conduct Disorder. Not surprisingly, ODD and CD were then excluded by many insurance policies. Since therapists still want to work with children who need to be treated for ADHD, ODD, or CD, these children are often diagnosed with less accurate, but applicable, diagnoses that the insurance companies will pay for. All this is to say that there is some flexibility in diagnosing and sometimes the diagnosis has more to do with insurance policies than the exact symptoms. Fortunately, similar diagnoses entail similar treatment, so the end result is the same.

For these reasons, and because therapy is not an exact science, two clients may receive different diagnoses although they have the exact same symptoms. It happens all the time. Most likely each of the therapists can make a strong case to defend their diagnosis, so they are not actually lying. Although the diagnoses differ, the treatment goals for the two clients may be almost the same. More importantly than diagnoses, treatment goals must be a good match for your problems and for what you want to accomplish.

Don't get overly attached to your diagnosis. Like a photo, it shows how things look, at this point in time. It doesn't explain how you came to be this way or what your life is going to be like in the future.

As you would expect, if two clients are being treated for similar problems, then the treatment goals are likely to be similar as well. If one client is anxious, has no friends, low energy, and is unhappy, he may be diagnosed with an anxiety disorder. Another client may have the same symptoms but receive a diagnosis of depression. Both people will probably have "increase socialization" as one of their treatment goals. This is because social support is important for coping with both anxiety and depression.

Often the treatment plan will include words that you don't understand. That is not because the therapist is trying to trick you. As in any profession, therapists get used to the jargon of their trade. The therapist will be happy to explain anything about the treatment plan that you don't understand.

You may also find something in the treatment plan that needs to be corrected. Therapists are human after all. For example, a target date for completion of the goals may be dated wrong (a frequent mistake at the end of the year). Therapists are always thankful when clients correct them as it keeps their records in order. In the managed care marketplace, a therapist's livelihood depends more on the quality of their documentation than on the quality of their care. Many wonderful therapists have been penalized for problems in their documentation.

When you are first shown your treatment plan, you may feel a little overwhelmed. It's likely to be the first time that you have seen someone spell out your problems on paper and put a name to it. The treatment plan can make you feel like you are all messed up and like there couldn't be anyone as troubled as you. What you need to keep in mind, is that because insurance companies continue to follow the medical model for mental health, treatment plans focus on your problems rather than your strengths. You have a great number of strengths that far exceed your problems. If they were included on the treatment plan, you would feel much better about it. Think of the treatment plan as a snapshot of you early in the morning on your worst day–hair disheveled, tired and bloodshot eyes. Of course you are not like that all of the time (hopefully). The treatment plan is the "before" picture in the before and after comparison. The very positive thing about treatment plans is: 1) they reassure you that the therapist is taking your problems seriously and has not overlooked something; 2) they reassure

Think of the treatment plan as a snapshot of you early in the morning on your worst day.

27

you that although you may have many symptoms, there are ways to get better; 3) they give you guidance and a step by step plan for improvement; and 4) they reassure you that the therapist is focusing on your priorities. Once signed, the therapist will keep your treatment plan in your file and you can also have a copy. If you would like to try your hand at making your own treatment plan, you can follow the instructions on the next page, and fill in the blank treatment plan on the page following. If you prefer a "no-label" treatment plan, I've included a form and help for doing that. This style is a good alternative when you are not using insurance (insurance companies like labels).

One of the great benefits of counseling is being able to rest assured that you can say what is on your mind without worrying the information is going to show up somewhere else.

What Your Therapist Has in Your File

You will probably notice that therapists keep a file for each of their clients. There is nothing mysterious about it. Files generally contain dates of service, billing records, consent forms, the treatment plan, test results (if any), and progress notes. Progress notes are written by the therapist after your session. They are brief and don't provide details about your life. They mainly contain current symptoms, techniques used by the therapist, and any significant changes such as the addition of a medication. The vast majority of the time, no one will read your file to try to figure out anything about you. In a clinic setting, there is likely to be a medical records person that will check the files to make sure that all forms, signatures, and record keeping is in place. An insurance company may audit a therapist (much as the IRS can audit your taxes) by choosing a small sample of files that the therapist must submit for review. Like the medical records person, the insurance company is looking for complete and accurate records and has no personal interest in your situation.

What the Insurance Company Gets

When a therapist bills an insurance company, the information provided includes your name and address, date of

Exercise: Making Your Own Treatment Plan (Instructions)

On the following page is a blank treatment plan. To feel more engaged in the process of therapy, try to develop your own treatment plan. Use the example treatment plan presented earlier in this chapter for reference.

1. Start by entering your name and today's date.

2. For "Presenting Problem," list all of the symptoms that you have related to what you want help with.

3. For "Preliminary Diagnosis," go ahead and take a guess at your diagnosis if you like.   You may have some guesses based on information you got from the internet, from your past experiences, or from your family history. If you have no clue about this, just skip the diagnosis.

4. For "Initial Evaluation Objectives," consider other services that may be helpful to you in addition to counseling. Medical treatment or a medication evaluation? Financial or legal consultation? Drug or alcohol counseling? Someone severely depressed as a result of a recent family crisis may need counseling, medication, and legal advice, for example.

5. For "Treatment Goals," check the boxes that apply to what would be good for you to achieve.

6. For "Measurable Objectives," list some things that other people could observe about you to see that you are doing better, or have overcome your presenting problem. If you are suffering from depression, for example, how will other people be able to tell when you are no longer depressed (e.g., move around more energetically, participate more in social events, keep your home organized, etc.)? Whatever people can observe is "measurable." Try to get away from simply wanting to feel better. Work on doing better, and then you will feel better as a result.

There are very many different styles of therapy. Some therapists will welcome you to bring your treatment plan for discussion while others will just see it as a distraction from other work that needs to be done. If you tell a therapist that you made your own treatment plan, you may give them one of the few surprises of their careers (it's good for them).

Exercise: Making Your Own Treatment Plan (Form)

DATE: INITIAL GAF:

CLIENT NAME: CASE NO.:

PRESENTING PROBLEM:

DSM IV PRELIMINARY DIAGNOSES:

Axis I:

Axis II:

Axis III:

Axis IV:

INITIAL EVALUATION OBJECTIVES   **Specifics/Target Dates**

☐   1.   Psychological Evaluation

☐   2 .   Psychiatric Referral

☐   3.   Medical Referral

☐   4.   Drug and Alcohol Referral

☐   5.   Other

TREATMENT GOALS (progress evaluated at each session and changes noted in *Progress Notes*)

☐	1.	Understand purpose of treatment	9.	☐	Increase assertiveness
☐	2.	Solve situational distress	10.	☐	Improve communication
☐	3.	Decrease anxiety	11.	☐	Explore educational/vocational needs
☐	4.	Decrease depression	12.	☐	Do better in school/work
☐	5.	Decrease uncontrolled behavior	13.	☐	Improve daily living skills
☐	6.	Increase self-esteem	14.	☐	Learn to cope with illness
☐	7.	Improve family relationships	15.	☐	Work toward leaving therapy
☐	8.	Eliminate harmful habits	16.	☐	Other:

Goal	Measurable Objectives	Target Dates
1		
2		
3		
4		
5		

birth, marital status, employment or student status, whether you have other insurance, diagnoses, dates of service, procedure used (e.g., individual, family, group, etc.), and therapist identity information. One of the great benefits of counseling is being able to rest assured that you can say what is on your mind without worrying the information is going to show up somewhere else. The reputation of the entire profession is at stake, not to mention the job of the individual therapist, if your confidentiality should be compromised. Files are kept under lock and key within a locked facility. Therapists do not talk about you with others, and after a period of time files are purged and eventually destroyed. They are stored for at least several years in case you need information transferred to another provider/facility, and for insurance review.

Case Example: Jordan

Jordan was a 42 year old telephone receptionist for a major telecommunications company. She was referred to me for counseling by her supervisor. Her supervisor had noticed that Jordan was increasingly short-tempered and that other staff would need to "tip toe" around her in order not to set her off. When Jordan showed up for counseling, she admitted that her job was stressful, but added that anyone would be stressed out if they had to do what she did all day long. Jordan was not happy to be in counseling and did not see how talking to a therapist would help her since she still had to go back to the same working conditions.

Jordan was reluctant to fill out the form which asked about her symptoms and after pouring over it for 10 minutes only checked off "stress." When she was called into my office, Jordan only gave brief answers to my questions. She was surprised when I asked, "You don't really want to be here, do you, Jordan?" Jordan admitted that she did not, although she added that it was not my fault. I thanked her for saying so and added that I appreciated her honesty in admitting that she didn't want to be there. I told Jordan that she could leave at any time and that she didn't need to cooperate with anything she was asked to do. But,

Your File:

- **Contains what is required by law.**
- **Does not contain personal opinions about you.**
- **Does not contain a record of what you said during the session.**
- **Is mainly for the benefit of insurance companies' record keeping requirements.**
- **Does have a history of your diagnoses, test results, treatment dates, and types of service received.**
- **Is normally kept for 10 years in case you need information transferred to another therapist or for legal purposes.**
- **You do have the right to see your file or to obtain a summary of it's contents, but it is generally not helpful.**

The therapy was drawing out many bad memories, but it was also making her feel less crazy and giving her a sense of hope.

I also asked her, "Would you please just answer one thing before you decide whether to leave?" Jordan agreed. I asked, "Jordan, if you return to work, and things continue as they are, what do you foresee happening?" Jordan thought about that for a moment and slowly said that she guessed that she would either really lose her temper someday and be fired or she would quit. I asked her how she will feel and what her life will be like when that time comes. Jordan said her life will be "like hell" and that it already was. She became tearful and said she didn't know why she was crying. I told Jordan that it must be a very painful way to live and that I would like to help her learn how to feel better.

"Well, I guess that's better than just keeping on the way that I am," Jordan said. I told Jordan that in order to help her, she would have to help me. "What do you want me to do?" Jordan cautiously asked. I said that I wanted her to tell me what her life was really like so that I could truly understand her situation better. By the end of the first session, Jordan couldn't believe how much she had shared with someone she only met for the first time. She had talked about her bad divorce, her struggles to make ends meet as a single mom, and how she felt like a trapped animal. I had listened attentively to her, which made her feel truly understood. It was something that she had not experienced for a long time—maybe ever.

Over the next two sessions, Jordan filled me in on the details of her life. I helped her think about old things in a new way. She saw clearly how her life was repeating some of the same patterns that her parents followed and how her feeling helpless had happened in her childhood and her marriage as well as her job. She was starting to recognize how her choices had gotten her to where she is and that if only she could make better choices, her life might become better. The therapy was drawing out many bad memories, but it was also making her feel less crazy and giving her a sense of hope. I had her fill out the symptom checklist again. She found that she had many symptoms besides stress. When I put together the information into a treatment plan, it really helped her to see how her symptoms related to each other and how they could be overcome by working in therapy. Not for the last time was she glad that she had "decided" to get *counseling.*

———

If you are in counseling and haven't yet seen your treatment plan, you might like to try making your own. It can help you to start thinking about how you want to be once counseling is ended. It can help you to focus on the rainbow and not just the rain.

Summary

Therapy has been mystified by the media, but in actuality, it is no more mysterious than a trip to your medical doctor. Therapists use your emotions, behaviors, and thoughts, as symptoms of your psychological health. Your therapist will follow a certain structure according to the style of therapy he or she uses, but all therapists essentially do the same thing. You don't need to be concerned about what you need to say in therapy and do not have to tell your therapist more than you are comfortable telling. The more accurately you report your thoughts, feelings, and behaviors, the better your therapist will be able to design a treatment plan for you. Although the diagnosis is important for insurance coverage, it is the treatment goals which matter most. Being knowledgeable about your treatment plan will help you and your therapist to collaborate and will help you make progress faster.

Exercise: How to Make a "No-Label" Treatment Plan

Instead of conceptualizing your problems in terms of diagnostic categories, you can conceptualize your problems in terms of deficits and excesses. So, for example, if I think I should be more active, then I would have an activity deficit. This would be true even if everyone around me were couch potatoes who were more inactive than me. This kind of treatment plan works well for people who have good judgment about what their needs are. It is half-way between counseling (which focuses on overcoming problems) and coaching (which focuses on creating success).

Follow These Steps:

1. Start by asking yourself, "What would benefit me to decrease or stop doing?"
2. List out these excesses (you do them too much). For example, smoking, arguing, using credit cards, thinking about mistakes, feeling anxious, having panic attacks, etc.
3. Continue by asking yourself, "What would benefit me to increase or start doing?"
4. List out these deficits (you don't do them enough). For example, exercising, giving compliments to others, making a budget, calming yourself when you start to feel anxious, etc.
6. Choose up to five in any combination of excesses and deficits.
5. Transform these into goals by making them measurable and by giving them a deadline. For example, "reduce smoking to no more than two cigarettes per day within three months," "build up to exercising for 30 minutes, three times per week within three months." It's important to make goals you can *easily* achieve rather than goals you would ideally like to achieve. This will help you to have faster success and encourage you to continue. Your result might look something like the following table:

Goal	Target Date (at least 3 months in the future)
Smoke no more than 2 cigarettes per day.	10/15/2014
Exercise for 30 minutes, 3 times per week	10/15/2014
Use a relaxation technique every time I start to feel panicky	10/15/2014
Make a budget and follow it for one month	10/15/2014
Compliment my wife and children 5 times per week	10/15/2014

7. Go over your treatment goals with your therapist to make sure they are realistic.
8. As you achieve your goals, replace them with new goals.

This kind of structure will help both you and your therapist to work collaboratively and to get more done in a shorter period of time. If you are not comfortable sharing this with your therapist, it will be helpful to do for yourself, to track your progress. This style of treatment plan can be written to work with every kind of therapy. It makes little difference if your goals relate to changes in behavior, thinking, or feeling. Changes in one is evidence for changes in the other. Regardless of the kind of therapy you are receiving, it should result in more of what is helpful, and less of what is unhelpful, in your life.

3. NEEDS, DESIRES, AND PROBLEMS

If you are like most people, 99% of your thinking is either focused on what you already know you have to do, what you are doing, or what you have done. Thinking about the future requires more effort and imagination because it hasn't happened yet. And when people have problems, they become very focused on their problems—so much so that they may not even consider how they would really like their life to be. They just know that they don't want to have their problems anymore. They go to therapy to get rid of their problems.

What Do You Want?

If I were to ask you what you want, what would you say? When people enter therapy for the first time, they usually say what they don't want—"I don't want to feel so depressed," "I don't want to fight anymore." This is a place to start, but it still doesn't tell the therapist what is wanted. The therapist will then ask, "How do you want to feel instead of depressed?" or "What do you want to do instead of fight?" This question often takes people by surprise because they are so focused on what they don't want, they may not even know what they do want. The answer to the first question might be, "I want to feel happy." (The exercise on the next page will help you to identify what you really want—your desires).

The second question to come out of the therapist's mouth may well be, "What do you *need* to be happy?" The answer to this question is usually even harder to come up with than the answer to "What do you want?" but may get at some of the

> *It's easier to dwell on the past than it is to think about the future. The past has already happened. Thinking about the future requires more effort and imagination. It also offers more hope.*

Exercise: Identifying Desires

On a separate piece of paper, give yourself permission to list all of the things that you want for your life. These should be present and future things only. This paper will only be for you. It will also be useful for the exercise on identifying your needs. Try to list 100 things.

Examples:

1. have better communication with my partner,
2. a new car,
3. see Niagara Falls,
4. allow people to get close to me,
5. allow my partner to disagree with me,
6. build a birdhouse,
7. learn to play the piano
8. go scuba diving
9. teach children to sing
10. plan a bicycle trip across Europe
11. plant a garden
12. ride all the world's roller coasters
13. have a million dollars in my retirement account

If you are stuck for ideas, think about what you want to have, see, allow, build, discuss, do, fix, get, learn, plan, teach, and write. Do not be concerned about whether these are possible to have, good to have, legal, etc. Be honest with yourself.

issues causing the problem. If I were your therapist, and I asked you what you need to be happy, fulfilled, and satisfied with your life, what would your answer be? How can we begin to think about the best answer to that question?

Everything that people desire relates to an inner need. The better we fulfill our inner needs, the more content we become. So, there is a relationship between what we desire and what we need, but desires and needs are not the same thing. If you're hungry, you may desire pizza, or a steak, or a sandwich. You don't need any of these things. What you really need is food. However, if you weren't hungry then you wouldn't desire a pizza, a steak, or a sandwich. (The exercise on the next page will help you to identify your needs).

Problems are problems because they thwart one or more of our needs. Emotional problems may thwart our need to feel secure, relational problems may thwart our need for love or companionship, physical pain will thwart our need for comfort, etc. For somebody who is functioning really well, their needs will make them desire things, which in turn will satisfy those needs. The less healthy, or functional someone is, the more they will desire something which only partially fulfills their needs. So, a person may have an attraction for someone who treats them badly because they do help them to feel loved just a little. And if they lose the relationship, they may seek out another which is just as bad. When people have an underlying need, partially meeting it is better than getting nothing at all. The major task of therapy is to find healthier and more satisfying ways to take care of those underlying needs.

People are Need Driven

If you want to become better at understanding what makes people tick, listen to what they say, and look at what they do and try to relate that to underlying needs. It explains almost all of human behavior. If you think about the successful people you know, you will realize that they're successful because they are very good at fulfilling their underlying needs. People who are very successful think more about their *future* needs, plan for them, and work on them. People who are only partially

Where do your desires come from?

- **Your needs, and**
- **Your beliefs.**
- **Every desire is connected to what we believe will meet an inner need that we feel.**
- **What differs among people are not the needs, but the beliefs about how to satisfy them.**
- **The best beliefs about your future are the ones that will really help you to meet your inner needs.**

Exercise: Identifying Needs

1. By folding or drawing lines, divide a paper into three vertical columns (as shown in the example below).

2. In the first column make a list of everything you desire. You may already have such a list from the previous exercise. Be sure to list all of your desires—big, small, appropriate, inappropriate, etc. Be as specific as possible (e.g., cup of coffee, trip to Hawaii, win the lottery, work as a bikini contest judge, etc.).

3. In the second column, write the reason(s) that you desire that thing. For example, a desire for coffee could be because you are tired. Or because it tastes good, or both.

4. In the third column write what the underlying need is. An underlying need for the coffee may be pleasure (related to the good taste) or sleep (because you need sleep, you desire coffee to diminish that need).

5. Determine what need (from column three) comes up most often on your list. Meeting this need in appropriate, achievable, and healthy ways is key to your life satisfaction.

6. Talk about your important needs with your therapist. Some items on your paper may be embarrassing, so there's no need to share the whole paper.

Short Example (your list should actually have about 100 items) *

What I Desire	Why I Desire It	The Underlying Need(s)
Coffee	Tastes good	Pleasure
	To wake up	Sleep
Win the lottery	Travel	Excitement
	Meet fun people	Excitement/socialization
	Pay the bills	Security/feel in control
Trip to Hawaii	Fun	Excitement/adventure
Allow people to get close to me	Share my life	Intimacy/companionship
	Someone to do things with	Excitement/adventure
Bikini Contest Judge	Fun	Excitement/adventure

*Even in this very short example, you can detect this person's need for excitement. Since it emerges frequently, it is probably being met only occasionally. This makes the person vulnerable for choosing exciting options even when they are not in the person's best interest (such as flirting with someone other than their spouse or overspending). Until this need is met consistently, in healthy ways, it will be very hard to give up the unhealthy behaviors.

successful try to meet their needs as they happen. Without any long term planning, they end up repeating the same behaviors over and over. And that's fine if their life is going well. But for people with emotional pain, it becomes a treadmill. For therapists to help out such people, a shift needs to happen to more long-term thinking. Just as we put food in the cupboard because we know we will be hungry again, so also we need to "stock up" on friends, activities, and beliefs that will continue to meet our needs.

Most people do some combination of long-term thinking and short-term, habitual gratification. For example, they may put money away for their retirement on a regular basis and also spend money on daily necessities. But, at the same time they may neglect physical and emotional needs by overeating, failing to exercise, and by becoming increasingly distant from their spouse. Because of these mixed behaviors, they may have money for their retirement but not be able to enjoy it because of poor health, or a failed relationship. "Health" is another word for physical or emotional balance in the many facets of our life.

Are you familiar with the "little bit more" syndrome? This is the belief that if only we have a little bit more of this or that, then we will be happy. And did you know that there are millions of people in the world who believe that if they had the things that you have (whatever you have), that they would be happy? Much of the world lives in poverty on one meal a day and a few dollars per month. Many live in bondage or else need to work 16 hour days even from the time they are young children. They desire things that you and I take for granted. Yet, many of us are neither satisfied nor happy. We often long for what someone richer or freer than us has, even though we may be no less happy than the people we envy. And, even if we don't want to be rich, most of us still want just a little bit more. Do we really have any control over how happy we can be? How satisfied we can be with what we have? And can we make choices from the options that we have that will help us to be happier and more satisfied? Fortunately, we can.

Are you familiar with the "little bit more" syndrome? This is the belief that if only we had a little bit more of this or that, then we would be happy. And did you know that there are millions of people in the world who believe that if they had the things that you have right now, they would be happy?

Regardless of when your problems started, or who is to blame for them, something will need to change practically for your life to become better.

Better Choices Are the Key to Fulfillment

For rich people and for poor people alike, the solution to unhappiness is understanding what our needs are and to choose ways that are likely to fulfill our needs in the long-term. These ways can be as practical as getting proper nutrition, spending time with the family, getting out of debt, saving for retirement, making friends, etc. These "practical" choices turn out to be the most powerful way of creating change and the most important for both long term and day to day happiness. Regardless of when your problems started, or who is to blame for your problems, something will need to change *practically* for your life to become better. Finding out what that is and doing it is the best use of your time. When you can't do that, the best use of your time is dealing with the psychological issues that get in the way of making practical changes. Your therapist will help you to work at the level you need to move ahead in your life.

Another way to understand needs is as requirements for physical and mental health—much like vitamins. If any of our needs continue to go unfulfilled, then we suffer—just as a plant would without water or sunshine. You can't give a plant extra water to compensate for a lack of sunshine. It needs both. A person suffering from an anxiety disorder may take care of her need to feel secure by staying home, by avoiding people, or by becoming very passive. But, that would only contribute to other needs going unmet, like the need for intimacy and to feel important to someone else. Balance needs to be restored.

The greater the deprivation of any of our needs, the greater the suffering and the more hunger or desires we will have for anything that even partially meets that need. Some examples of physical needs are the need for air, water, food, sleep, activity, and shelter. If you deprive a person of one of these, even for a short period of time, it can have disastrous consequences. In our world, there are many people suffering both physical and psychological problems because of deprivations of these basic needs. If you deprive someone of something they don't need, there won't be any long term consequences. That's why it's a lot easier to break up with someone who no longer loves you at all. They supply very little of your emotional needs. After a short time, they won't be missed. If you take drugs or alcohol away from an addict, there may be short term stress to both the body and mind, but the long term consequences will be beneficial. That is the proof that drugs and alcohol are not meeting needs.

We Get Used to Toxic Living

In reality, it is often confusing whether we should continue to act, think, or relate with others in a certain way. What we do may partially meet our needs, and partially meet our desires, but partially hurt us, too. If you were dying of thirst, would you drink polluted water? I'm sure you would hold out as long as you could, but eventually you would probably drink the water. And, if the water just made you a little sick, you might not even try to find other sources of water. You might get used to it. In the place of drinking polluted water, you can substitute many things that people do and think. If I shut down (suppress) my emotions, that may help me to have the feeling of safety that I need. But, it also poisons my relationships to some extent. After awhile though, I can get used to relating to my partner as a roommate, or not talking to my coworkers. People are remarkably adept at getting used to living in a substandard way. So used to it, that it becomes the normal way, the expected way, and the way our families have done things for generations.

People go to therapists for problems related to psychological needs that are being poorly satisfied. This is true whether their problems are emotional or relational. You can see how the needs for security, love, acceptance, importance, and purpose have emotional, thinking, behavioral, and relational components. When we are young, these needs are primarily met by our interactions with our caregivers. As we grow older, they are increasingly met by our own self-care and by the people we have relationships with.

Your therapist will be interested both in your past relationships, as well as your current relationships, to help

Change is Hard Mainly Because:

- **The way we do things works at least a little.**
- **We don't have experience doing things a different way (even if we've observed them or heard about them).**
- **We risk losing what little we get now by trying to do things differently.**
- **People are more afraid to lose what they have (even if it is little), than they are to lose what they could potentially have if they changed.**
- **Our subconscious works to minimize risk by creating comfort for our habits, and fear of change.**
- **Change requires leaving our comfort zone, which means we won't "feel like changing," until after we have changed.**

41

All valid therapies are based on helping a person to identify both physical and psychological needs and to meet them in healthy ways.

identify your emotional needs and how well they are being met. Sometimes our previous experiences, especially deprivations, can drive us to seek out the fulfillment of those needs to a much greater extent than other people. People who are constantly seeking reassurance, for example, often come from backgrounds in which their safety, importance, or care was not assured. At other times, we may have learned to live on a very low level of one of these needs, with resulting depressions and anxieties. Optimally meeting your needs in an important focus of any psychotherapy. (The exercise on the next page will help you to gain a long term perspective of your needs. As I said before, none of your needs started yesterday).

All valid therapies are based on helping a person to identify both physical and psychological needs and to meet them in healthy ways. Toxic relationships can be detoxified, as can toxic thinking and behavior. You can learn the many ways that you hurt yourself with patterns of thinking and interacting that you may have had since childhood. It is not your fault that they are there or that you have continued to follow them. But, as you learn in therapy, it is your responsibility and to your advantage, to change them now. And that is just what your therapist will help you do.

Although Our Desires Are Different, We All Have the Same Needs

Every single technique used by therapists is aimed at one purpose—helping you to get what you need in a healthy way so that you can do and feel better. All people have the same needs. What differs is how they go about trying to get those needs met. A person may eat junk food or healthy food. A person can feel important by providing to a family, contributing to the community, or by committing crimes. A person can have a healthy sexual relationship with another person or spend hours every day looking at pornography. You can take every problem common to man (except for accidents, natural disasters, and genetic conditions) and see how each is an attempt to get physical or emotional needs met in unhealthy ways. Every person in prison has attempted to meet their needs in ways that were not only unhealthy, but also illegal. But their needs are

Exercise: How My Needs Developed

Sometimes we try to meet our adults needs in the same way we did as a child, even though it doesn't serve us very well. Becoming aware of this can help to free us to make other choices. Relax and don't try to get the "right" answer to the following questions. Just go with the answers that come to you.

Childhood

When I was a child I most needed...

I got that, at least a little by...

Teen Years

When I was a teen I most needed...

I got that, at least a little by...

Adulthood

As an adult what I most need is...

I get that, at least a little by...

Self-Analysis:

1. How well have your needs been met throughout your lifetime?
2. Are you still trying to get something you needed as a child or teen?
3. Is this way of getting this need met based on your earlier experiences?
4. If you had a better family or social environment as a child or teen, how else might you have learned to get these needs met?
5. Is it possible for you to benefit from using these other ways now?

Every Emotion and Feeling is Designed to Help Us Meet a Need:

- Hunger,
- Thirst,
- Sleepiness,
- Sadness,
- Anger,
- Frustration,
- Love,
- Sexual desire, and
- All the rest

the same as ours. We are all humans and we all desire in our life those things which we *believe* will meet some underlying unmet need, even if it only meets it a little. Understanding this principle will help you to better understand your family, friends, children, and coworkers. It explains why people do foolish things—not to be foolish, but to meet one of their underlying needs—a need that we can understand and relate to. Your therapist will never think you are foolish, because he or she will relate to the very human need that underlies what you do. Therapists are people of compassion.

Counseling will help you to identify your unmet needs. And you have them—otherwise you would not be in counseling. Your needs are going unmet because they are either not currently available to you or you are using the wrong ways to get them met. It is also possible that what you desire is actually in conflict with getting your needs met. We can get really confused about what we need, what we want, and how we feel. Therapy will help you to sort that out. (On the next page is a needs self-assessment to help you identify unmet, or poorly met, needs).

Temporarily Stopping a Bad Habit Helps to Identify the Need

The short term deprivation of your usual bad habits, whether in thinking or in behavior, will be a big step toward your life satisfaction. Depriving yourself of unhealthy behavior brings your needs closer to the surface. You will feel them more intensely. Just as depriving yourself of food would make you feel hungry, depriving yourself of your usual attempts to escape, avoid, or drug your feelings will get to the root of your problem. Your unmet need will appear as some kind of pain or fear.

Stopping bad habits takes us out of our current comfort zone so that we can choose to meet our needs in healthier ways. All growth in our life from infancy until now has involved our leaving our comfort zones. When we were a child, we didn't have much choice about it. As adults, our parents can't make us change. We need to have the self discipline to make the

Exercise: Psychological Needs Assessment
Complete the following statements

I feel secure when:

I feel loved when:

I feel important when:

My life's purpose is to:

In order to be happy, I need:

Answer the following questions

I can freely give love to others without holding back: Yes/No

I can freely love others without expecting anything in return: Yes/No

I am angry with others who haven't, or aren't, meeting my needs: Yes/No

Memories of my past get in the way of my happiness: Yes/No

Considerations:

Frequency: How often are your needs for love, security, and importance being met? Are you on a starvation diet?

Quality: Are you accepting low quality substitutes that don't quite satisfy your need? For example, are you eating when you are really needing to be loved? Are you buying things to make you feel happy or secure? Are you having conflict with people just to get their attention?

Increasing both the frequency and the quality of the way you get your needs met will contribute to your happiness and life satisfaction. It will also make you a more loving and loveable person. The more ways you have to feel loved, secure, and important, the less needy you will be, the less important past hurts will be, and the better able you will be to emotionally connect with others. Working in therapy can help you to make this happen and save you years of emotional subsistence living.

Therapists are great at knowing how to get needs met in healthy ways. After all, this is what they are working on with every single client they see.

changes ourselves. For really hard changes, it helps a lot to have support from someone else who wants to help us make positive changes. That is one of the prime uses of therapy. And, although you may feel like dropping out of therapy when you first leave your comfort zone, it is imperative that you don't. Dropping out during this painful transition would just make you fall back into old patterns and your progress would be lost.

Therapists strongly suggest that you work on getting your needs met before seeking the desires of your heart. Every day you can see needy people going from one unhealthy relationship to another hoping that the next one will make them permanently happy. And they have the same kind of problem relationships again and again. Rather than learn from past mistakes, they return to whatever satisfied their desires before—even though it was for just a little while. They find someone who is just like how their previous partner used to be, which is of course a recipe for making the same kind of relationship again.

Eating a chocolate cake really can't cure depression. Keeping busy does not cure anxiety. Having sex outside of marriage doesn't cure loneliness. To truly get away from the same old mud hole that they are used to wallowing in, people must find healthy ways to meet their needs. Then, the cake will taste better, work will be more productive, and sex will be more meaningful. People don't *need* to have affairs. What they need is to have a good relationship with their spouse.

This principle works for raising children as well. Give your children what they really need to be healthy—physically and emotionally, and teach them practical ways to deal with problems. Then, they will be less drawn to unhealthy ways to get their needs met. If you shower your children with games and toys but deprive them of love and acceptance, they will seek it elsewhere and get it where they can. This is not because they are sick—it is because they have unfulfilled needs. Of course, they also need reasonable limits and expectations—this helps to fill their security needs and to keep them safe.

Resistance to Change

Therapists are great at knowing how to get needs met in healthy ways. After all, this is what they are working on with every single client they see. Yet, there are two major obstacles to you getting your needs met in healthier ways—resistance and adjustment. You need to be aware of them because they will both motivate you to leave therapy too soon. *Resistance* can be experienced in many ways, but what you will usually feel is just a lack of desire to do what your therapist is suggesting. If you normally find comfort in a box of ice cream, television, or online gaming, it may be very difficult for you to get involved socially. You will be able to come up with a number of reasons not to, although you agree in theory that it is a good idea. You may not believe you have the time, social skills, money, opportunity, etc. to meet people. But when your therapist tries to help you to overcome those obstacles, you just don't find any of the ideas appealing or think up reasons why they wouldn't work. This unconsciously motivated lack of desire to do a more healthy behavior is what therapists call resistance. It feels like trying to push a car uphill. Resistance keeps us in our present comfort zone—which is safe and predictable, because it is what we are used to. Resistance is also one of the main two obstacles to overcoming problems by ourselves (the other is lack of skills). Overcoming resistance may take months of therapy. Once the resistance is broken, change can happen quite rapidly.

Resistance is the main reason that therapists can't just hand you a list of 10 things that you need to do to overcome your problem the first day you come into therapy. Just knowing the steps to take will not get you to your goal because the steps don't do anything to counter your resistance. You can usually find the answers to your problems in a book or online, but you will not be able to implement them for more than a short period of time. Your commitment to therapy and the help of your therapist will enable you to overcome the resistance and to make real, lasting progress.

When you run into resistance (a lack of desire to follow

Resistance:

- **That unconscious part of us that fights against changes that we try to make.**
- **Everyone has resistance.**
- **It is something to plan for and deal with.**
- **It is not something to be blamed for.**
- **It is as natural as your heart beating.**

When you have your needs met, you won't be desperate for anything and will be freer to enjoy your life and make good choices. You will more easily be able to pass up unhealthy choices that you would have chosen in the past.

through on your therapist's recommendations), you may be tempted to say that your therapist just "doesn't get it," is "out of touch," and is altogether unrealistic. You will be tempted to drop out of therapy. This is all part of resistance, because there is a part of you that knows that what the therapist wants you to do would be healthier than what you are now doing. When that is the case, HANG IN THERE! Your therapist expects you to resist, knows that it is normal, and won't blame you for it. Your therapist will work with you until you break through that resistance. Then it will be full speed ahead for both of you. Both your therapist and you will be excited when that happens. It may be a new experience for you if you have never overcome your resistance before.

Adjustment

The second obstacle to getting your needs met is *adjustment*. You must maintain the new way of getting your needs met for at least three months before you can be sure that you won't fall back into the old, unhealthy, temporarily satisfying behaviors. The new comfort zone has to become comfortable. When we stop doing something that we have done for a long time, our desire to return to that behavior, especially when under stress, can be enormous. Continuing to refuse to return to our old behaviors, with the support of a therapist, makes it much more likely that we can continue our progress.

With resistance broken and adjustment well underway, the most exciting and fun part of therapy can now begin. This is because once your basic needs are met, you can start pursuing your *desires for the future* with more confidence and without desperation. The best time to find a job is when you already have one, the best time to shop for food is after you have eaten, the best time to find a partner is when you are happy being by yourself. When you have your needs met, you won't be desperate for anything and will be freer to enjoy your life and make good choices. You will more easily be able to pass up unhealthy choices that you would have chosen in the past. You will be less likely to get into bad relationships or argue just because you are hungry for attention or intimacy.

Need-Based Relationships

Getting your needs met is especially important for the health of your relationships. Need-based relationships (being with someone because he or she gives you what you need) most often fail. Needy people attract each other like the positive and negative poles of two magnets. The relationship is close until one person no longer feels their partner is meeting their needs. Anger and disappointment result. The strong attraction stops. The relationship becomes more distant and both people become dissatisfied, needy, and angry. The needy partners demand that their needs be met. Resentment and insecurity create a wedge between them. Their relationship can struggle on for a long time even if each is only getting scraps of what they need—until a better source is found. Need based relationships are stable only as long as both people stay needy and each continue to provide at a least a little for the needs of their partner.

The advantages of meeting your needs in healthy ways:

- You become mentally free to pursue your desires.
- You have self respect and confidence.
- You have more respect from others.
- You become a better candidate for relationships— both personal and professional.
- You feel secure enough to take reasonable risks which are necessary for having success.

Case Example—Sandy

Sandy was a very charming young woman who had a series of short term relationships with men. Although her desire was to marry and have a family, her relationships never seemed to work out. She would find a man who she thought was "wonderful," her "soul mate," or "Mr. Right," only to be proven wrong a few months later after increasingly tense conflict.

The point where her relationships started to go bad was when her boyfriends would desire to do activities with their friends which did not include her. She would insist that either she accompany her boyfriend or that he choose her over his friends. Although her boyfriends at first would do just that, they would gradually have more and more conflict and eventually her boyfriends would go out without her.

Because it felt so bad to be second choice to his friends, she believed that if he really loved her, he would not let her feel so bad, but would instead stay with her. She wanted desperately to be taken care of (what she had thought was "true love") and

The point where her relationships started to go bad was when her boyfriend would desire to do activities with his friends which did not include her. She would insist that either she accompany her boyfriend or that he choose her over his friends.

when her boyfriends refused to do this, she could only conclude that they didn't really love her.

As Sandy's therapist, I helped her to see that her main concern in her relationships centered around being taken care of. In order for men to take care of her, they had to neglect their own needs for friendships. It became her needs verses their needs. Neither of them wanted to sacrifice what they needed for the sake of the other. When they did make such sacrifices, it would cause resentment. As long as they had competing needs, the relationships could not last.

Sandy was not immediately ready to accept such an idea and in fact felt that I was siding with her old boyfriends against her. I did not try to stop her from quitting therapy, but did help her to see her choices clearly so that she could at least make an informed decision. If I was right, then she would need my help if she were to be able to have the kind of stable relationship and family that she wanted. If she was right, then she still had the problem of choosing men she thought were wonderful, but who were not. She would have to find men who had no friends and who would not make any.

Sandy struggled for two weeks with whether to quit therapy and canceled one appointment during that time. She rescheduled, however, because she did not want to be stuck in the same kind of pattern which could lead her to hate men altogether and cheat her out of a family. She also thought that if she could only have men with no friends, then something must be wrong with either them or her.

My approach with Sandy was straightforward. She needed to have friends of her own and activities of her own so that she would be able to let her boyfriends have the same. Freedom, and not control, was the real path to greater intimacy. Sandy had never felt the need for friends other than a boyfriend, but was willing to try having some "experimental" friends. I knew that it would be important for her to have more than one friend so as not to be too demanding with her friend and run into the same problem that she had with her boyfriends.

With my help, Sandy's friendships developed, and she became more patient about having a boyfriend. She no longer got instantly attached to men who gave her attention, and could look more at how their lifestyles either matched or did not match her own. She did not want a "needy" man, but rather a man who wanted her as she was. She wanted a man with friends, just as she had friends.

——

It is very important that you work with your therapist to get your needs met in healthy ways before entering into any long term relationship. If you are already in a need based relationship, your therapist can help both of you to get your needs met in healthy ways. That will strengthen and preserve your relationship. When two people overcome their neediness, they can love each other more deeply than ever before because their underlying insecurity will no longer get in the way.

Summary

Your desires spring from internal needs that you are trying to meet. Although you may desire a particular food, for example, the need you are trying to satisfy may be hunger, comfort, or the relief of boredom. Although it makes sense to eat to satisfy hunger, there are more healthy ways to deal with feeling bad or being bored. Attempting to satisfy a psychological need accounts for many of our self-destructive thoughts and behaviors.

Each person has different desires, but we are all trying to satisfy the same needs. Unhappy people are having difficulty satisfying their needs and may desire things that only bring temporary relief, at best. Although psychological problems can happen for other reasons, it makes sense to take a look at what your desires are, and how well what you desire actually meets your needs.

People often confuse needs and desires, and as a result hold on to unhealthy relationships and ways of doing things that they really don't need. Therapists always strive to help clients

She needed to have friends of her own and activities of her own so that she would be able to let her boyfriends have the same.

get their needs met in healthy ways, while also helping them to give up unhealthy desires. If you do that, you will feel more at peace and happier. Your therapy may focus on understanding how you developed unhealthy desires, letting go of ways of thinking that you don't really need, or gaining new ways of coping that meet your needs better. Whichever of these methods is emphasized in your counseling, you can be assured that you are addressing something important.

CHAPTER FOUR

4. THERAPY HURTS BEFORE IT HEALS

"I thought therapy was supposed to make me feel better, not worse!" Therapy does help people to feel better, but healing and overcoming psychological problems takes time. Due to misconceptions about how easy therapy is, the percentage of people who drop out of therapy too soon is high. The estimate is 50%. This misconception about the ease of change in therapy also applies to other human endeavors. As a result, people drop out from all kinds of activities every day. New Year's resolutions are well intended, but rarely result in successful completion. In fact, most people are no longer resolved to keep their resolutions just shortly after making them.[5] Why is it that we *know* what is good for us, but find it so hard to *do* what is good for us? And why do we stop doing what's good for us after we've started? The answers are not as simple as laziness. If people were really lazy, they would do what makes life easier and not continue to do what makes it hard. The answer lies somewhere between knowing what to do and doing it.

Misconceptions About Therapy

Misconceptions about therapy often come from false expectations fed by mainstream media. The media has tended to portray therapy as quick, easy, and fun. Like all worthwhile things in life, making changes to thinking and behavior takes hard work. While it is true having good mental health and resolving problems makes life easier, there are no short cuts to doing that.

Therapy is not quick. If you only want to *find out* how to

Misconceptions About Therapy

- **Therapy is a quick way to get help.**
- **Therapy is supposed to be enjoyable.**
- **Progress is determined mainly by the skill of the therapist.**
- **Therapy is about getting the right answers to problems.**

Realities About Therapy

- **Therapy takes time.**
- **Talking about painful things is painful.**
- **Progress is determined mainly by the participation of the client, regardless of the style of therapy.**
- **Therapy is a process for creating change. The answers are already known.**

cope with a psychological disorder, that is pretty quick. Any therapist can provide a list of things for you to do at your first session that would, 99% of the time, cure whatever problem you have.

Self-help books, CD's, and DVD's by the thousands have been published with the same completely accurate information. These resources are for the most part filled with helpful advice and explanations by people who really know what they are talking about. Yet, 95% of people who read such books, watch such videos, or attend self-help seminars have no *lasting* benefit from them. Does this mean that these materials are not helpful? The fact is, they are very helpful for people who are able to put them to good use, but not very helpful for people who just read them or watch them. This is because *knowing* what to do does not automatically lead to us doing it. I am willing to bet that you could write out a list of things that, if you did them, would make you healthier, more attractive, and improve your relationships. Not only that, but I bet you could write out a list of things that would help your significant other to be healthier, more attractive, and have better relationships. Therapists, CD's, and books do not work any magic by giving you answers. But, if you learn how to benefit from these things, you can shoot ahead.

On the next page is an exercise that will help you to be part of the five percent of people who do benefit from self-help books. Just as even a cheap paint brush can create wonderful works in the hands of an artist, so too can any self-help book enrich your life when you know how to benefit from it.

Answers Are Not Solutions

More people than ever are actively searching for answers to all of their life problems. The wonderful accessibility of information on the internet makes it possible to quickly find not only one, but many answers to each question you have.

Why then, is the need for mental health care services on the increase, as well as health problems and broken relationships? With all the answers available at virtually no cost, life should be

It is a rare event in human endeavor that any problem can be solved simply by coming up with the right answer.

Exercise: How to Benefit from a Self Help Book

The Key: The key to benefitting from a self help book is *application*. Merely reading, or merely understanding, does not bring any lasting benefit.

Selection of Books:

Any self help book can be useful, no matter how well or poorly written. My suggestion is, though, that you start with a book that is easy to read and understand. Easy books are the foundation for more difficult books, just as learning algebra is a foundation for learning calculus.

Materials Needed:

Your book
A piece of paper
A pencil or pen

Forget colored highlighters and don't bother to underline the text or circle key words. Those are methods for preparing for a test on the book, but that is not your purpose. You are instead searching for one to three applications from the book that you will transfer to your piece of paper. After making your applications, you can go back to the book to harvest some more applications. Trying to get everything at once is counterproductive.

Method:

1. Read until you come to a good idea or example.
2. Write the idea on a separate piece of paper in your own words (this ensures that you understand it).
3. Write how you can apply that idea.
4. Write what results you can expect from applying that idea.
5. Write how long you will need to apply that idea before getting good results.
6. Transfer your application to your daily to do list.

Example: (This is taken from my own book. Don't get overly focused on the content here. Look at the method. This method takes you from reading to application, which is what you need to do to benefit. One good idea is worth the price of a book many times over).

IDEA	MY APPLICATION	MY EXPECTAION	HOW LONG
Every criticism has some truth. Focusing on that part can build cooperation.	*When my partner criticizes me, look for the part I agree with without arguing.*	*My partner will be surprised at first and won't change quickly. But, we will fight less and less and the criticism will decrease.*	*I will need to persist at least a couple of weeks before I see any changes. If I keep it up, we can have a better relationship.*

getting better for more people than ever before, shouldn't it? If there is anything to learn from this, it's that *answers* to problems are very different from *solutions* to problems. And, seeing how something is done is very different from being able to do it yourself.

Making changes is far more difficult than getting answers. Most people would agree that the Ten Commandments of the Bible are excellent and if followed would lead to better lives. Honesty, loving one's neighbor, and loving God is hardly advice that's going to get you into trouble. But, thousands of years of history has shown that putting it into action is quite another thing. The key to losing weight also seems very simple—eat fewer calories. If you eat fewer calories than you use in your day, you will lose weight—no ifs, ands, or butts. Does that 100% accurate answer help people to lose weight? No. How about a psychological example (this is a book about psychology, after all). The keys to overcoming depression—thinking positive thoughts, exercising, and letting go of the past, also are not hard to discover. Although this is the answer, the typical length of therapy for people who are overcoming depression is anywhere from three months to a year.

In school, children learn that the solutions to problems are the answers. For math problems, solutions and answers have the same meaning. Most adults also think that finding out the answers will solve their problems. But, when we are talking about people, solutions and answers are two different things.. *Answers* are like a map—they tell you where to go, but they don't take you to where you want to go. For that, you have to drive, fly, walk, swim, etc. You could buy a thousand maps that all tell you great ways to get somewhere, and still be right where you are. Likewise, a thousand self-help books won't *do* anything for you. Like the map, they show you where to go, or what to do, but it is you who must do the doing. This also why, when you tell your kids, parents, significant other, or friends what to do, their lives do not automatically get better. Some people think if they repeat the answer enough times that others will start to change. But, that doesn't work anymore than looking at a map 1000 times will get you to your destination.

Answers tell you what to do. The solution doesn't come until you follow through.

Answers are free and available in abundance. Everyday millions of people search for and find answers on the internet. The number of those being helped *simply* by the answer?...Zero.

Likewise reading a self-help book over and over again is not going to do anything for you. Nor is reading many self-help books that say the same thing. That would be like reading many different maps to see where to go. Perhaps you are thinking that reading many self-help books would help you *understand* better, but would that really achieve anything?

Have you ever had the experience of reading an instruction manual and thinking that you knew exactly how to do something, but then when you went to do it, it was confusing and difficult? Many people study very thick books to pass difficult tests in college. They get a good understanding of the material. But, virtually none of it helps them to make any changes in their life or even on their jobs. The fact is that no matter how well we understand something, learning only happens when we *do* something. No matter how well we have studied, the first time is going to be hard—because we haven't done it before. The second time will be a little easier, and the third easier still. This is because practice brings improvement in a way that repeated study cannot. Specifically, *successful* practice brings improvement. Practicing doing something the wrong way will not bring any improvement. That's because we don't learn from mistakes. People who make mistakes continue to make mistakes. People who have success, continue to have more and more success. We learn from success—not from failure.

Practice brings improvement in a way that repeated study cannot.

The solution to problems is *sustained* action. Answers do not lead to actions and so answers don't bring about change. Only action can bring about change. Only *sustained* action can bring about *lasting* change. Eating fewer calories will help you lose weight. But just knowing that won't help you lose weight. You will need to take some kind of action that results in your eating fewer calories. Likewise, in terms of mental health, staying in therapy and doing the work of change long enough for stable gains, and then continuing to do them on your own after you finish therapy, are the keys to success.

Not only is therapy not about just getting the right answers, therapy is also not fun. This is mainly because it requires people to see and to feel the unpleasantness in their past and

Some people have tried so hard and waited so long to enter therapy that they feel hopeless from the very start. They often don't show up for their first appointment rather than face their fear that there is something incurably wrong with them.

present, as well as the misery that awaits if they continue on a destructive course. Therapy will bring to mind your darkest fears and how your actions and ways of thinking mess up your life. It will bring back memories of things forgotten or buried and you will experience some of the pain you have been mostly able to avoid in your daily life. That box of tissues in the therapist's office is not for tears of joy.

No Gain without Pain

Therapy is also not fun because it requires action from you. Once your insecurities and responsibilities are laid bare, only positive action and changes to thinking can help you to improve. Truths, once exposed to the light, cannot be hidden again. The early stages of therapy will expose some of these truths. They may make you want to drop out of therapy and to pretend that the therapist is wrong. But, some part of you will know that the therapist is right and you won't be able to have peace about it again until you do something about it. People who cope with their problems by pretending they don't have any (denial) need to have tremendous courage to enter and continue with counseling.

Helping you to overcome these difficulties will be the realization that identifying your problems and setting goals will make positive change possible. And that's why people go to therapy in the first place. Your life can change for the better and will change for the better when you work on the heart of the issue. That's painful, but that's also hopeful. Throughout the course of therapy, you are likely to struggle with the opposing feelings of discouragement and hopefulness. If you can hang in there through the periods of discouragement, your life will improve. Nobody has to be stuck being unhappy.

Many people have tried on their own to make changes in their lives and have failed. Some people have tried so hard and waited so long to enter therapy that they feel hopeless from the very start of therapy. Although they see that change is possible, they still don't believe it is possible *for them.* They are handicapped with doubts from the first time they call for an appointment. They are highly likely not to show up for their

58

first session and to drop out of treatment soon if they do come. It's not that they don't want to get better. It's just that they don't want to face the disappointment and discouragement of failing again.

Others realize that change is possible even for them, and have high hopes when they start therapy, but find that the process of changing is much harder and takes much longer than they expected. Like the person who signs up for a membership at the gym, the first couple of weeks bring soreness, tiredness, and no indication of progress. Although they know that all people who are in good physical or mental shape started out struggling through the pain, they wonder if it is worth it when they feel the reality of it. Faced with the choice of soreness from working out or being out of shape, they often settle for being out of shape. The more people give up on something, the less they are bothered about it. This goes for being in shape, happiness, relationships, finding a good job, or what have you. "It's not so bad to be overweight—most of my friends are overweight," "Is anyone truly happy? The best we can have are some happy moments," "I wouldn't really want to have a job where I had to dress up every day and work a lot of overtime," etc. Aesop hit the nail on the head with his fable of the sour grapes. We devalue whatever we believe is out of our reach. Not only does that make us want it less, it keeps us from trying.

The Challenges of Therapy

There are other challenges to our motivation to work on making positive changes. For example, other people may discourage you from continuing in therapy. Not understanding the process of therapy, they may believe that you are worse off than when you started, or they may not like the person you are becoming. Often the people around you will want you to stay just the way you are because it helps their lives to be predictable. Sometimes, they will be afraid that you will reject them if you get healthier and would rather you just stay the way you are. The sicker the people in your life are, the more afraid they will be of you getting healthy. Unless the way you are already bothers your friends or family, they are unlikely to

The Benefits of Therapy

- **Feeling unburdened by sharing your cares,**
- **Feeling hopeful by having an effective way to make your future better,**
- **Gaining more respect from family and friends as you become healthier and/or more effective,**
- **A rise in productivity as you improve and have more energy and enthusiasm, and**
- **The end of creating new regrets.**

The Challenges of Therapy

- **Talking openly and honestly about things you don't like to reveal,**
- **Time commitment,**
- **The financial cost,**
- **Discouraging family or friends, and**
- **The temporary stress of change.**

Can you imagine someone saying to you, "I went to the gym two times last month, and I'm still out of shape—I guess gyms just can't help me"? Therapy requires sustained action in order to bring about improvement.

encourage you to stick with therapy.

Therapy also requires a time commitment. You will need to meet frequently enough to keep up a healthy pace. Most often, this is once a week or more. Any less than that and you may not make any progress at all. Just like working out once a week at the gym won't help you to get into shape, neither will going too seldom to therapy. For therapy to work requires a commitment. Appointments need to be kept. Self-help assignments need to be done. If you don't have the time or don't want to make the time commitment, then don't start therapy! In such a situation, therapy is likely to do more harm than good.

Psychotherapy can be compared to physical therapy. In physical therapy you go to your session and use muscles that you don't normally use. That places stress on your body. This small amount of stress helps your body to become stronger. Your next physical therapy session needs to happen before you have lost all the gains from the previous session or you will make no improvement. You will feel fatigued and a little sore after your PT, but you will become stronger and more flexible with regular sessions. Likewise, in psychotherapy, you will talk about and process things that you don't normally talk about and in ways that you don't normally talk. Some of the things may be really hard to talk about and will also fatigue you. Do this regularly enough and you will overcome your problems. Do this just once in a while and you will keep reinjuring yourself the same as if you only went to the gym once in a while. You would see no progress from your therapy and would conclude that therapy does not work. Can you imagine someone saying to you, "I went to the gym two times last month, and I'm still out of shape—I guess gyms just can't help me"? Therapy requires sustained action in order to bring about improvement.

On the next page is an exercise to help you cope with any mixed feelings you may have about whether to continue in therapy.

Exercise: Deciding Whether to Continue Therapy

Everyone has mixed feelings about therapy—especially at the beginning. The biggest danger is quitting therapy without considering the cost of quitting. Almost always the cost of quitting is more than the cost of continuing.

Directions: Write out your answers to the following questions which deal with negative feelings about your therapy.

1. Is what I am doing in therapy actually harmful to me, or just unpleasant?

2. How much time does it actually take me to do therapy homework?

3. Why did I start therapy in the first place? Has that reason stopped being important?

4. Do I have any method that is more effective than going to therapy?

5. Would quitting therapy really help me to achieve the results I want?

6. Are there things that I can do to make my therapy more successful?

7. Is it the healthy or unhealthy part of me that is motivating me to quit therapy?

8. Which am I more likely to regret later—quitting therapy or not quitting therapy?

9. Have I really learned to let things go that are keeping me down or holding me back?

10. Are my negative feelings the result of positive changes (e.g., talking about important issues, finally dealing with old, unresolved issues, grieving an unresolved loss, etc.)?

Improving the Odds

As you can see, the odds of your making progress in therapy are much better if you make the decision to attend therapy on a weekly basis rather than according to how you feel or according to how busy you are. The odds are also in your favor if you realistically expect it to be both difficult and worthwhile. You really can be a person who benefits from therapy and who achieves more than you had at first hoped or expected. You, like many others, can reach your goals and achieve greater life satisfaction. Therapy, like dieting, does work *if* you make and keep your commitment to change. Sustained action will always lead to results.

Your therapist is an expert at helping people to make changes and will help you to change. Making change on your own would be very difficult. The people that can do that generally have done it already. Your therapist cannot make changes for you or make therapy painless. Your therapist will, however, help you in several important ways. Your therapist will provide emotional support, keep you accountable, keep you at the appropriate pace, give expert guidance on the best way to accomplish your goals, and help you to shift your thinking and priorities to what matters most for your happiness.

The most important change necessary for success is to make all of your important decisions based on long term consequences. Even if your thoughts about the short term are true, they may not be helpful in the accomplishment of success. Thoughts like, "Just one won't hurt," "I can always change tomorrow," "Everyone does it," "Someone will get upset if I use healthy boundaries," and "I'm too busy," may all be true at the time that you think them. But, it is also true that none of these thoughts will get you closer to your goals.

Learning to Self-Evaluate

Every action you take needs to be evaluated as though it were a habit. A new self-assessment question that you can learn from your therapist might be, "If I did this regularly,

---

How to Make a Good Decision

- Ask yourself, "If I did this regularly, would the result lead to a better life or a worse one?" Follow the path to better results and you will find the end of the rainbow.

How to Evaluate Past Decisions

- Ask yourself if something you have been doing continues to be the best thing for your future. Even though it might have made sense once, it may be time to give it up.

would it lead to a bad result?" If the answer to that question is yes, then don't take the action. Every bad habit you have now, started with just one bad action. The single biggest obstacle to change is using short term consequences to decide what to do. While you might think this makes a lot of sense, right now as you read this book, it is not likely to stay with you. It's not a habit. However, when you are in therapy, your therapist will keep bringing you back to this question in session after session—"What effect will this have on your long term goals?" The therapist is in a sense helping you to develop healthier, positive habits. Therapy is a chance for you to create habits that serve you and those around you so that your life can be richer and fuller.

In addition to considering long term consequences on a regular basis, you will come to understand what it means to be truly healthy. It is likely to be somewhat different than what you thought. Depending on how distorted your thinking was before you entered therapy, your understanding of what is healthy may be skewed. Most people believe that they are doing the healthiest and best thing for themselves even when it continues to cause them problems and even when their problems are obvious to others. You are probably better at identifying problems that other people have than in identifying your own problems.

To take just one example of ineffective self-evaluation, people with codependency problems often use other people's reactions to them as an indication of what is the best thing to do. If someone is upset, they assume they did the wrong thing. If people are pleased with them, they assume they did the right thing. This way of thinking has some good short term consequences, but also some very bad long term consequences. Codependent people initially receive good reactions from others, however their relationships generally get worse and worse because problems are never resolved. Any attempt to resolve problems makes others upset and shuts the codependent person down. After awhile, they feel trapped and enslaved by the very people they have been attempting to please. They also are unable to see that it is their own

Therapy is a chance for you to create habits that serve you and those around you so that your life can be richer and fuller.

63

Rescuing people often does more harm than good because it prevents them from making the changes they need to make.

Emotional Dependency Says

- **Whenever you show your love to me or take care of me, I am happy. Whenever you don't, I am not.**

codependent behavior that keeps them in the trap.

As a more tangible example of this, a wife may buy beer for her alcoholic husband because it keeps him calm and less abusive toward her and the children. The alcoholism, however, makes it impossible for her husband to have a good relationship with her or the children. She is then caught between two seemingly bad choices—feed the alcoholism or face the wrath of her husband. If she can learn, in therapy, to keep herself and her children safe while not feeding the alcoholism, she will remove herself from the trap. It does not depend on her husband getting healthy—it just depends on her getting healthy. This is incredibly difficult for the codependent person to learn on her own, outside of therapy.

Just as people can be unwittingly codependent, they can also be dependent on someone else's codependency. A mom protecting her adult son from the consequences of his depression may be an obstacle to his seeking help. A certain level of bad results needs to happen to motivate people to change. Rescuing people often does more harm than good because it prevents them from making the changes they need to make. Having healthy relationships means becoming aware of and escaping both of these codependency and dependency traps. Staying in therapy is your best chance for working on these and other psychological issues. Your therapist can help you, for example, to identify unhelpful dependencies. The most common dependency is requiring that someone else (partner, parents, etc.) or some environmental circumstance (job, finances, etc.) be a particular way before you can be happy, successful, or at peace. If I need you to love me in order to be happy, then I give up control of my own happiness to you. I put my feelings under your control and become desperate and resentful whenever you pull away from me. Whenever you love me, I'm happy; whenever you don't, I'm not. While it is wonderful to be loved by others, making our own emotional states depend on others makes us feel less in control of our lives and contributes to unstable emotional states. Our feelings and our relationships can be like roller coaster rides—up one minute and down the next. Generally, whenever you place your happiness on any one worldly thing, you have an unhealthy dependency, whether it is your job, your relationship, your finances, your children, or something else.

Learn to Take Responsibility

Being healthy and being responsible (as opposed to blaming others or circumstances) go hand in hand. Your therapist will help you take responsibility. That doesn't mean blaming you—it means equipping you to be able to make the changes. The more you take responsibility for everything that happens to you, the more in control you will feel, and the happier you will become. Not taking responsibility keeps us stuck in a cycle of sadness and anger.

Blaming others for our problems makes us feel angry, and does not improve our lives. We then get stuck waiting for others to change, or trying to make them change. Whereas others may create problems for you, it is up to you to deal with those problems and to deal with those people. You do that not by changing others, but by changing the way that you think and by changing the way that you respond to others. It is always nice when others change in ways that benefit us, but waiting for them to do that keeps us trapped in anger, sadness, and despair. Our life time is far too valuable to waste waiting for others to change, especially because many people never will.

Case Example: David

When David first came to see me, he was not used to taking responsibility for his problems. He had a history of failed relationships that he had believed were caused by his partners being unfaithful, controlling, and demanding. He found that while the relationships were initially fun, that after a while, the women would start to act like they were his mother. At first, he figured he was just unlucky with his choice of partners, but the more it happened, the more he thought that he might have something to do with it. He went to therapy on the advice of an older friend that he respected.

Responsibility Does Not Equal Blame

- **When I take responsibility, it doesn't mean I'm at fault. It means I will do something to make the situation better.**
- **Firefighters are not to blame for fires, but they are responsible for putting them out.**
- **Taking responsibility for everything in your life means taking charge of making it better in every area.**
- **Stop looking to blame and start looking for ways to take responsibility for change.**

Not Everyone Wants You to Change

- **People who need you to be unhealthy in some way so that they can feel better are not good people to have in your life.**
- **Never be afraid of becoming healthy because other people won't like it.**
- **They will either adjust or leave you alone. Either option is preferable to your needing to be unhealthy for them.**

I asked him what changes he had made in himself so that his problem would not keep recurring. Although he felt better, he hadn't made any changes.

David found that at first therapy seemed to be pretty good. He could unload what was on his mind and he found me (his therapist) to be understanding. I was able to guess a lot about David's feelings of anger, sadness, and frustration and empathized with his problems. This helped David to get out of the slump that he had been in and he was thinking about quitting therapy. I suspected this and told David that he was probably thinking about quitting therapy. I asked him what changes he had made in himself so that his problem would not keep recurring. That question stumped David. Although he felt better, he hadn't made any changes. He might very well get right back into another bad relationship. I challenged David to continue and to learn how to have a long-lasting relationship with women. Unfortunately, against my recommendations, David dropped out of therapy and didn't return until two years later, after a particularly hard break-up.

I welcomed David back to therapy and was not upset with him in the least. David stuck with therapy this time and learned to look at what he was doing that drove his partners away. He had a choice—to keep on driving partners away or to make some changes in himself. Slowly, working together, David started to change the way he looked at things and learned how he created his own feelings of anger, sadness, and frustration. He learned that his feelings of insecurity made him attempt to control his partners. When he couldn't, he became angry and frustrated. And it pushed his partners away. He also learned that his beliefs came out of his family background and had contributed to a lot of turmoil for his parents as well. He didn't want to repeat what his parents had gone through in his own relationships. David got involved in another relationship while in therapy and although he continued to make many of his old mistakes, his relationship was longer and more satisfying than any he had before. This encouraged him to continue his therapy and to continue to change his habits. When he left therapy, he was still in the same relationship and determined to make it work

———

Just like David, you may have desires for your life which

have been frustrated, or have gone unfulfilled. And, just like David, you may be doubtful about how therapy can help you with that. The exercise on the next page will help you to look more hopefully at the potential of therapy to help you. You may be able to achieve much more than you had imagined.

Summary

Staying in therapy and using the specialized help of a therapist is not quick, easy, or fun. It will mean facing parts of yourself that you would rather not see. It will mean giving up ways of thinking and behaving that have become very comfortable for you but which are not helpful for you in the long run. Instead, you will be working on long term, positive results, that will help your life to be richer and fuller. Your increased self-confidence may be disturbing to others who have become dependent on your unhealthiness. They will then either adjust to the new you or leave you alone. Either way, you will feel in control of your life and your destiny—possibly for the first time. The emotional roller coaster ride will be over.

Your ultimate success in therapy will mean that the emotional roller coaster ride will be over.

Exercise: What Can Therapy Do for Me?

Answer the following questions to both encourage yourself, and to open your eyes wider to the possibilities for a richer, fuller life with the help of therapy.

Instructions: Answer the following questions aloud, or in writing (don't just think them).

1. What are some examples of things that were difficult in your life and which took time, but which you are glad that you did (e.g., learning to ride a bike, graduating high school, learning to do your job, etc.)?

2. What is the number one obstacle which is keeping you from having what you really want in life?

3. How could you use therapy to overcome this obstacle?

4. How will your life be different when you don't have that obstacle anymore (name some specific examples)?

CHAPTER FIVE

5. ACCOMPLISHING MORE WITH LESS EFFORT

Entering therapy was a big step, but you did it. To do that, you had to get past the resistance to going in. You could do it because your desire to go to therapy was greater than your desire not to. The closer your desire to go and your desire not to go were, the more you had to struggle with taking action—making and keeping your appointment. If you entered therapy in a crisis, then your desire to go to therapy was a lot bigger than your desire not to, and so it wasn't much of a struggle. Although we can make almost all decisions without much resistance, whenever we want to take action on those decisions, there is some resistance that comes along with it. How you manage that resistance will largely determine your success both in and out of therapy.

One Step at a Time

If you are in therapy, by now you and your therapist have set goals and you can picture what your life will be like when you accomplish those goals. As you make progress, you will become more and more eager to reap the rewards of therapy. If all goes well, at some point the resistance to ending therapy will be as great as the resistance you initially had to starting. It's hard to stop a good thing, once we've made a habit out of it. To make sure your therapy goals come true, it will be important to focus your energy on just one important step at a time. That way, you will move steadily toward your goals without feeling bogged down or overwhelmed. Taking small steps will actually help you to go further, with less effort.

Resistance

- **Internal and external forces that oppose us.**
- **Resistance prevents us from taking harmful risks.**
- **It can also stop us from making positive changes.**
- **The purpose of internal resistance is to keep us safe by keeping us from making changes.**
- **Unfortunately, when our habits are not healthy, resistance also gets in the way of us creating better ones.**
- **Resistance is not based on logic. It is based on habit.**
- **Because of that, both negative and positive changes are resisted.**

When people get enthusiastic about new goals, they tend to overestimate their ability to quickly accomplish them. Infomercials on television seem to give the impression that we only need to buy that new ultra gym set (in three easy payments) to quickly and easily get into muscle rippling shape. As anyone who has bought one of those ultra gym sets knows, change is possible, but it doesn't happen easily or quickly. In fact, it often takes so long to get into muscle rippling shape that people give up before reaching their goal. Expecting it to be quick and easy helps to make the purchase, but it is the wrong expectation for sticking with it. The problem isn't that the product doesn't work—the problem is the difficulty *persisting* with the work long enough to benefit. The natural tendency is to start out with too much weight on the ultra gym. Then, the eager-but-out-of-shape home athlete becomes tired, sore, and gives up. The same kind of eagerness to make progress in therapy can also prompt you to deal with too much "emotional weight" at one time.

Two Important Motivators

Regardless of what you set out to achieve, whether it is getting in physical shape, mental shape, or relational shape, there are two important motivators which will help you to follow through and reach your goals. It is the *idea of success* that initially motivates a person and it is *actual success* which keeps a person motivated. The actions of starting and continuing are motivated by two different factors. No one would enter therapy if they believed that they could not possibly be successful. And, no one would continue if they didn't experience any success. The more successes you can have, the more motivated you will be to continue.

Success Is Related to the Way We Set Goals

The principle of maximizing success will keep you positive and motivated. The way you set goals both on your own and with your therapist will result in more or fewer successes. Notice I didn't say working hard will get you more successes. I said the way you *set* goals will result in more or fewer successes.

It is the idea of success that initially motivates a person and it is actual success which keeps a person motivated.

Let me illustrate that with two examples. I am using the goal of weight loss because it's an easily understood problem. The same principles apply to any goals—physical, or psychological.

Goal Setting Example 1: Susan's Weight Loss Goal

Susan joined a weight loss program with the goal of losing 50 pounds to arrive at her ideal weight. She has visualized herself standing in a swimsuit at the beach feeling good about herself. She has even cut a picture of a bikini model out of a magazine and pasted a picture of her own head over the model's and stuck it on the refrigerator. These images are a good motivator to help her get started. At the start of her weight loss program, she has done well motivating herself. She anticipates difficulty, but that's ok with her—she knows it will require sweat and deprivation.

After being in the program for three months, Susan has lost 20 pounds. It's a big weight loss, but it's not even half-way to her goal of losing 50 pounds. That picture is still on the refrigerator, but it's not as motivating as it was before. Although at first she liked going to her weight loss meetings, now it seems a chore. What's more, the more weight she loses, the harder it is to lose more weight. Susan is beginning to realize that it may be a year or more before she can lose the 50 pounds. And she's not looking forward to another year of meetings. It won't be long before she starts missing meetings and she may quit altogether.

Susan's problems began when she set her goal at losing 50 pounds. By setting one large goal, she couldn't experience success until she lost 50 pounds. Stopping anywhere short of that would seem like a failure to achieve her goal. If she can force herself to stick with her program, then she might make it to her 50 pound weight loss goal. Provided she can do that (which is unlikely), she will have achieved exactly one goal. If it took her a year, then her rate of success would be one goal per year.

If we set our goals too high, our small achievements pale in comparison and we lose motivation.

71

- **We can't use logic to reason our resistance away, but we can reduce resistance by reducing the size of the changes we make.**
- **Nine little steps will get you just as far as three big ones, but with less resistance.**

To Achieve More Goals:

- **Make small short term goals.**
- **Be sure your short term goals are relevant to your long term goals.**
- **Reward yourself for your successes on short term goals.**
- **Success with something (positive experience) reduces our internal resistance to continuing.**
- **Always try to experience some kind of success as quickly as possible.**

Few people have the discipline to work so long and so hard for one goal. This is why most people drop out of new programs in the first month. Only a few make it to three months. This is not just with weight loss, but with every kind of health benefit program you can imagine, including counseling.

Now, we will consider another way to set goals:

Goal Setting Example 2: Jan's Weight Loss Goals

Jan was in the same shape as Susan, but instead of making a goal of losing 50 pounds, she set a goal of losing only 2 pounds. Two pounds sounded too easy to her and she knew that she wanted to lose more, but the instructor encouraged her to have a goal of losing two pounds. She agreed and lost two pounds within a week. Her instructor told her that she did a great job and she was praised in front of the entire weight loss group. Getting that kind of praise gave Jan a really good feeling that she wasn't used to. She had only been in the program for a week and had successfully achieved one goal.

She set a new goal of losing two more pounds, which she did without much difficulty. This pattern of: 1) setting a goal, 2) accomplishing the goal, and 3) praise, continued over a three month period. By that time Jan had lost 20 pounds and achieved 10 goals (successfully losing 2 pounds 10 times)! Her successes demonstrated her capacity to lose weight, and she learned to praise herself for small successes.

She now knows she can lose weight because she has already had so many successes. She likes going to her meetings, and she knows it is only a matter of time before she will both look and feel great. Already she can see that she looks better and feels lighter.

The difference between Susan and Jan is not the amount of weight lost over a three month period (both lost 20 pounds), but the number of goals achieved (0 vs. 10). Jan achieved 10 goals, but lost no more weight than Susan. She did, however, remain enthusiastic and felt a sense of pride and success. Jan is highly likely to continue her weight loss program. When Jan reaches 50 pounds of weight loss, she will have had 25 successes (25 x 2 lbs.= 50 lbs.). Whether it takes a year or more won't make much difference. The *idea of success* provided her initial motivation. The *achievement of success* continued to motivate her. More smaller goals lead to greater long term success than one or even a few big goals.

A similar example can be seen with modern martial arts versus traditional martial arts. Modern martial arts reward small levels of success with different color belts (white, yellow, orange, etc.). Traditional martial arts do not award any belts until the accomplishment of black belt, which takes many years to achieve. Few today have the kind of discipline required to complete such a traditional program—even though it takes the same amount of time and effort.

What are the implications for therapy? Although you may have some big long term goals that make you initially enthusiastic (because you can picture the result), that goal won't carry you through the full course of therapy. The larger your goals, the longer and harder you will have to work to achieve them. The longer and harder you have to work to achieve your goals, the more likely you are to quit. To continue to stay motivated, you will need to have short term goals. Some people call them "baby steps."

To continue to stay motivated, you will need to have short term goals. Some people call them "baby steps."

Just as we must climb the rungs of a ladder one at a time, the only way to reach your big goals is one short term goal at a time. Each short term goal needs to be relatively easy to accomplish and lead toward your long term goal. Would you rather own a ladder that has rungs two feet apart or one foot apart? Although most people could climb a ladder with rungs two feet apart, it would be much harder to use and no faster.

If a person has been depressed and isolated, a goal of having fun with friends would be a nice long term goal. Short term goals would need to lead toward that, such as: understanding the cause of the initial isolation, learning social skills, identifying interests, making acquaintances, identifying potential friends, becoming active with potential friends, and further developing relationships with potential friends who are responsive. The accomplishment of each of these steps may take a month. Following them, however, leads to the long term goal of making friends.

Your therapist will help you to choose short term goals that really will take you where you want to go. You can help by keeping the challenges for yourself small along the way and seeing each accomplishment as a success. As long as your short term goals lead to your long term goal, then focusing on your short term goals is *guaranteed* to bring you many small successes as well as the achievement of your long term goal.

> *The only thing you ever need to work on in therapy is the next step. Working that way, you avoid becoming overwhelmed, you experience multiple successes, and you maintain your motivation.*

The only thing you ever need to work on in therapy is the next step. Working that way, you avoid becoming overwhelmed, you experience multiple successes, and you maintain your motivation. For a person who smokes two packs of cigarettes a day, is it a better goal to quit smoking, or to reduce smoking to one and a half packs a day? The person who sets step by step reduction goals is more likely to reach the long term goal of quitting. With the step-by-step method, people climb Mt. Everest. With the one-step method, no one climbs Mt. Everest. You can prove this to yourself by climbing several flights of stairs. First try climbing the stairs two or three steps at a time all the way to the top. Then try climbing the stairs one step at a time. Which method would you be able to maintain over a long period of time? Taking two steps at a time provides an initial burst of speed, followed by fatigue and quitting. The step-at-a-time approach will take you a lot further with a lot less effort.

Taking a Second Look at the First Step

The hardest step to take in reaching a goal is always the first one. Although it may take you a year or more in therapy to accomplish your long term goal, it may have taken you several years to make an appointment for therapy. The exception to this is people who come to therapy as the result of a crisis. However you came, when you entered therapy, you already accomplished the most difficult step! You are well on your way to a better life. Congratulate yourself. Praise yourself. Treat yourself. You accomplished the most difficult step of all that you need to take. The final step of reaching your goal will be the easiest to take. Mountain climbers never take a break when they are only one step from the summit of a mountain. No matter how long or hard they have hiked, the last steps are the easiest.

Each Day Also Has a Kind of First Step

Although the hardest step is behind you, you need to sleep, eat, work, and many other things throughout each day. Starting on your self-help work or other daily tasks presents its own little challenges. Many people say that they have a hard time getting started on their daily tasks or self help work. They become immobilized or spend a lot of time on low priority tasks. Although they want to get the priority tasks done, they can't bring themselves to actually do them. This is a kind of internal resistance that you can predict. And because you can predict it, you can also prepare for it. Everything that we can predict, we can prepare for.

Motivating Yourself in Your Day to Day Self-Help Work

You can use the principle of setting small goals to both get started on these daily tasks and to maintain momentum on your goals until you are finished. Let's use cleaning your house for an example of getting started. It's another easy example that most people can relate to. You can easily extend this example to apply to office work.

Everything that we can predict, we can prepare for:

- **We buy groceries because we know we will be hungry.**
- **We set the alarm clock because we know we need to get up.**
- **We learn to talk about problems because we know conflicts happen.**
- **We make a schedule because our time is limited.**
- **We save money because the bills will arrive.**
- **We make long and short term goals because life passes quickly.**

Example: Getting Started Cleaning Your House

The problem is you want to clean your house but can't seem to get off the couch. Start by asking yourself, "What is the smallest part of cleaning that I am willing to get off the couch and do *right now*?" Your answer might be, "I guess that I could vacuum the living room, at least." Let this be your goal—not cleaning the house, but just vacuuming the living room (a short term goal). Now, the test—do you actually get off the couch to vacuum? If you still can't get moving, then your short term goal (vacuuming just the living room) is still too big. *Any goal that doesn't motivate you is too big.* If you can't get started, the next step is to repeat the process by asking yourself, "What is the smallest part of vacuuming the *living room* that I am willing to get up and do right now?" You might now say to yourself, "I can surely vacuum the area just in front of the TV." Let's assume that you still can't get moving, even for this little goal. Going through the process of asking yourself again, you decide that you can at least get the vacuum out of the closet and plug it in.

Behold, you actually get off the couch, get the vacuum and plug it in. Success! Congratulate yourself because you did exactly what you set out to do. No doubt you will even think that it wasn't that hard. Now, before you sit back down, ask yourself if you could go ahead and vacuum that area in front of the TV. Just having had a success, you are much more likely to vacuum the area in front of the TV. As soon as you do, it is another success!

Before, you would have had to clean the whole house to experience a success, but now you have had two successes in only a few minutes with minimal effort. Anything you do from here on out is all gravy—a bonus on top of what you have achieved. Using this goal reducing system, you will get *more* done and feel better about yourself.

Using a small goal to get started primes the pump and helps you to get more done, more quickly. That's because once you are moving, it is easy to keep moving. Many is the time that I have not wanted to work on my book (which you are reading right now), but I was able to start simply by deciding to work on it for 15 minutes. Once I got started, the 15 minutes would grow to two hours. I like to write—once I get started.

Procrastination is the Result of Resistance.

- **Making small or even tiny goals reduces the resistance to the point where we can get started.**
- **Once we have started, the initial resistance is gone and we can often continue until we are stopped by other factors such as fatigue or time demands.**

"Have To" Thoughts Don't Motivate Anyone

Part of the reason first steps are so difficult is because people tell themselves that they "have to" do them. "I have to clean the house," "I have to do my self-help work," and so forth. These "have to" thoughts create feelings of guilt and obligation. Guilt and obligation are not motivating. They are de-motivating emotions. Trying to get yourself started with these feelings is like trying to start a fire with wet wood. When you set a tiny goal to get started, you avoid the thought that you have to do the whole job. You won't feel like you *have to* do more because you can choose to stop at any time after getting started. And, because getting started is easy, you can get started right away. People don't use *have to* self-statements with easily accomplished tasks. And, because doing small tasks is easy, many people spend their time doing little routine chores rather than working on their larger goals. Rather than trying to force yourself to work on the larger goals, make them as easy as the little routine chores by breaking them up into tiny goals (or "baby steps," if you prefer). Large goals can become as easy as our routine chores when we break them into tiny, manageable steps.

On the next page is an example of a process you can use to make an achievable, long term, tangible goal for yourself. On the page after that is an example of how to do the same thing with a psychological goal.

A Success Secret

Small goals are one of the secrets of success. If you want to be more successful, set smaller goals that you can accomplish quickly. Then, as soon as you finish them, set more small goals. You will be busier, but have more success with less effort. Working this way also makes people feel a lot happier. Accomplishment and progress are great for self-esteem and personal development.

The surest way to fail at your goals is to make them too big. Little goals give you more successes. More successes lead to the accomplishment of larger goals. There is no way to accomplish

Do More with Less Effort

- Small goals are one of the secrets of success. If you want to be more successful, set smaller goals that you can accomplish quickly. Then, as soon as you finish them, set more small goals.
- You will be able to do in a day more than most people do in a week.
- You will be able to do in a month more than most people do in a year (in terms of working on goals).
- By choosing the right small goals, your long term success is assured.
- Whether your goals are physical, financial, or psychological, the principles are the same.

Exercise: Making More Easily Achievable Real World Goals
Three Steps to Success
1. List your long term goals and prioritize them.
2. Break each long term goal into several intermediate size goals.
3. Break each intermediate size goal into daily, short term goals.

The mistake that most people make is to make their short term goals too big. They need to be accomplishable in one day, and ideally within 15 minutes. Making goals bigger or longer makes them more difficult to start, which delays accomplishing your long term goals.

BAD Example: Write a book (DON'T DO THIS!)

Long term goal: Write a 15 chapter book
Intermediate goal: Write half a book
Short term goals: Write one chapter per day

The long term goal is fine. The intermediate goal is also ok. But, the short term goals will take longer than 15 minutes. They will be hard to start, and on most days they will not be achievable. Although it sounds very productive, writing a book in 15 days is an unrealistic goal for most people.

The number of achievements with this plan are only 17:
- 1 long term goal (the finished book)
- 1 Intermediate goal (writing half a book)
- 15 short term goals (writing each chapter)

17 achievements in the process of writing a book are too few.

GOOD Example: Write a book

Long term goal: Write a 15 chapter book
Intermediate goals: Write chapter 15, 14, 13,...
Short term goals: Write a *minimum* of 15 minutes per day

Although this is a rather simple plan, it allows for:
- 1 long term goal (the finished book)
- 15 intermediate term goals (each chapter), and
- 30 short term goals per month (writing for 15 minutes).

With this plan, you will have hundreds of achievements and be able to keep up. It may take 6 months or a year to write your book, but this will be much faster than most first time authors take.

Note: If you miss a day, just get back on track with the daily goal. Don't try to make up for the work you missed. Piling up work will stop you dead in your tracks.

Exercise: Making More Easily Achievable Psychological Goals

Three Steps to Success
1. List your long term goals in terms of how you will be different.
2. Break each long term goal into several intermediate size goals.
3. Break each intermediate size goal into daily, short term goals.

BAD Example: Overcoming Depression (DON'T DO THIS)

Long term goal: Be happy
Intermediate goals: Be ok
Short term goals: Go to therapy

While this is a common plan (usually not written out), it is not achievable. Just going to therapy doesn't make people happy and being ok doesn't lead to happiness either. And it's hard to picture what the end result will look like, which makes it hard to achieve.

GOOD Example: Overcoming Depression

Long term goals: Think positively, have an active social life, and let go of all "excess baggage"
Intermediate goals: Forgive specific people from my past, make new friends, have a hobby I enjoy, attend therapy once a week, get a medication evaluation if my therapist recommends it
Short term goals: practice social skills and thinking skills learned in therapy 15 minutes a day (or review insights about self-acceptance and mentally giving others permission to be human and fallible); take medication daily (if prescribed)

This plan succeeds because it gives you specific things to do on a daily basis and provides a mental picture of where you are going. Your therapist will be happy to help you with know how to work daily in a way that complements your therapy.

Note: Going to therapy is only one part of working on yourself. No matter how helpful it is, only what you do on a daily basis will change your life and achieve your long term goals. You wouldn't go to the gym just once a week to get into good physical shape would you? But, you would do what your coach recommended on a daily basis. Think about your therapy the same way. Therapy plus daily self-help work is a formula for feeling and doing better.

long term goals without doing short term goals. Can you walk across the room without first walking half-way across the room? Can you walk half-way across the room without first taking a single step? Make simple goals and give yourself credit for achieving them. Maximize the number of small successes to maximize your momentum and get more done. This is as true in therapy as it is with your daily chores.

Example: Reducing Anxiety

Suppose that your long term goal for therapy is reducing your anxiety to the point that the anxiety doesn't interfere with any of your daily routines. That's a nice long-term goal, but if your anxiety is very high right now, then you will need smaller goals to give you successes along the way that will keep you motivated. There are many possibilities and your therapist will help you to make appropriate short term goals, but here are a few examples: 1) talk about your anxieties with your therapist; 2) get a medication evaluation; 3) get together with a friend and do something you enjoy; 3) start a walking routine or other exercise. You could use any of these that are appropriate for your situation. They would be your short term goals. Then you could have even shorter short term goals to work on each day. Each time you accomplish one, congratulate yourself on reaching your goal. Celebrate. Treat yourself. If you keep doing short term goals like these and others, you will arrive at your long-term goal of having a fairly normal daily routine.

If you only have the one long-term goal, you will likely chastise yourself when you lose momentum and won't feel like continuing. You can even become anxious about not working on your goals. Chastising yourself is not motivating. Worriers also tend not to be motivated by their worry. Guilt may help a person to stop a behavior, but it doesn't provide motivation to continue a behavior—like working on goals. Self-blame and guilt lead to avoidance, which leads to more guilt and self-blame. When the guilt and self-blame become bad enough, you will quit. Trying to achieve a long-term goal without short term goals is a terrible thing to do to yourself. Instead, focus

Avoid the (Self)Blame Game

- Self-blame and guilt lead to avoidance, which leads to more guilt and self-blame.
- Whenever you are tempted to blame yourself for something, find some small thing you can do to work on the situation and go do it.
- You will feel better and do better as a result.

80

on achieving short term goals. Then, your long term goals will seem to happen all on their own (e.g., "I didn't set out to climb the mountain. I just kept taking small steps, and one day I was at the top!").

How Public Schools Get People to Achieve a 13 Year Goal

There are many examples of successful long-term systems that use small steps. One which you have already had experience with is school. School is not only broken up by grades, but by even shorter terms or grading periods. And each grading period is broken up by tests, and the tests are broken up by assignments. Can you imagine if there were no grades or grading periods? A child would go off to school at age 5 and just continue until age 18. There would be no way to measure progress. Imagine, no feeling of growth and accomplishment for 13 years! It would be like working in a factory with no chance for promotion except that you would be promised a gold watch after 20 years of service. Delaying gratification too long leads to stagnation and quitting. Grades and report cards help children to feel like they are progressing. Every school day is broken up into a number of periods. Each period is one class, lunch, study hall, or activity. Because of this, the day goes by much quicker. Compare this to a job where you get one lunch break and the rest of the day is the same. The day drags and productivity decreases.

Is Marriage One Continuous Goal?

One of the reasons for failure in marriages is no doubt due to the lack of short-term goals. The idea, "We are married, so now we can just sit back and enjoy," is a product of the happily ever after fairy tales. Success requires goals—lots and lots of them. It is not the ratio of successes that is important, but the absolute number. Achieving 5 goals out of 10 is better than achieving 1 goal out of 2. A salesman who makes 5 sales out of 100 calls will earn more money than a salesman who has only 1 sale out of two calls. The number of sales determine the profit—not the ratio of sales and not the number of failures. So it is with all accomplishments in life. Thomas Edison only

Life is Like Basketball
- **Do you count baskets made or misses made?**
- **The number of failures in our life do not matter. It's the number of successes that count.**

Edison only created one working light bulb out of 1000. It didn't matter that 99.9% of his attempts were failures. He is only remembered for his successes.

created one working light bulb out of 1000. It didn't matter that 99.9% of his attempts were failures. Only that one success mattered. His small goals consisted of trying a different kind of filament in the bulb. Whether it worked or not did not matter since trying each one brought him one step closer to his long term goal.

Resting Is Not Part of the Plan

Once you have achieved a small goal, the next task is to set another small goal. Whether that is paying two more bills, vacuuming the hallway, calling a friend, studying one section of your statistics book or working 5 minutes on your therapy homework, it doesn't matter. Setting goals, achieving them, and setting new goals will help you to maintain momentum, keep you motivated, give you a feeling of success, and ultimately take you further than you ever thought you could go. No mountain can be climbed in a single step and anyone who tries will fail. But the person who focuses on taking the next step, and then the next one, will climb higher than she ever imagined.

Setting goals, achieving them, and setting new goals will help you to maintain momentum, keep you motivated, give you a feeling of success, and ultimately take you further than you ever thought you could go.

Case Example: Carley

Carley had reached a middle management position in a financial firm, but was growing increasingly dissatisfied with her job.

When she initially got the job, she enjoyed the prestige and the position of authority. As the years went by, however, her job had become routine, the prestige had worn off, and the hassles of supervising employees had long lost its appeal. Still, she made a good living and was concerned that a job change would be more difficult now that she was older. She also wasn't sure about the support of her husband if she were to change jobs, and was afraid of risking the ability to fully fund her children's college education.

82

Her dissatisfaction with her job was not motivating enough to overcome her fears of failure if she were to try to change jobs. She felt trapped—doomed to work in a job which brought her little satisfaction.

Carley entered therapy because of her feelings of depression. I helped her to see how her fears and inactivity were behind her depression, rather than her job. I knew that if she could find a way to take some actions, without risking her job, it might bring more excitement and enthusiasm into her life. Together, we made a list of all the steps that would be required if she were to get a new job. For example, her first step would be to revise her résumé; the second would be to put together a list of the types of work she enjoyed, and so forth.

I encouraged Carley not to focus on getting another job, but just to focus on the first step. Carley agreed, but week after week she only had excuses for why she did not work on her resume.

To overcome her resistance, I suggested that the step of making a resume be broken down into smaller steps. The first would be to print out her old resume, the second would be to update her personal information, and so forth. Carley's new self-help assignment was to do step one—printing out her old resume, with no obligation to continue to step two.

Carley easily accomplished her assignment and in fact had her complete resume done the next week. She told me that once she got started, the rest was easy. Step-by-step Carley worked toward getting a new job, with no obligation to continue if things seemed risky.

By the time Carley got to the final steps, she was very excited about a job offer for a position that not only interested her, but which offered more money and benefits than she was currently earning. She ended therapy at that point and accepted the new job offer.

Getting a new job had at first seemed like a very risky and difficult move for Carley, but it was just the final step in a long

The only thing harder to do than change is to not change.

series of small steps. When she concentrated on just taking little steps toward getting a new job, the final step of getting a new job was easy.

———

Summary

In order to be successful in therapy or anywhere, you need to use strategies which actually lead to success. Most of these strategies are not known by the general public, but are used every day by those who are highly successful. Your therapist is an expert in helping people to achieve goals. You can start today to learn the joy of doing more by focusing on doing less.

6. MAKING BETTER CHOICES

The number one reason that people give for not working on themselves is time. Because of that, time (or the lack of it) appears to be an obstacle to good physical and mental health. However, the simple fact is that both healthy and unhealthy people have the same amount of time in their day—exactly 24 hours! Successful people, unsuccessful people, happy people, sad people, people with good relationships and people with bad ones, all have the same 24 hours. No one on the face of the earth has more than 24 hours in their day and no one has any less than 24 hours. The difference between these groups of people is not time. It is the choices they make and the skills they use. Make the same choices, use the same skills as successful people, and you will be successful too. The essence of time management isn't finding time to do more; it's doing better with the time you have. In many cases, you don't have to work any harder than you already do. You just need to make better choices regarding what you do. Choosing to do things that matter most, first, will enable you to make progress in any area or on any endeavor you choose.

The Amount of Time Successful People Have:

- **24 Hours per day**

The Amount of Time Unsuccessful People Have:

- **24 Hours per day**

The Difference Between Successful and Unsuccessful People:

- **The choices they make (not the time they have)**

Your Three Best Choices

As boring and unoriginal as it sounds, the three best choices that people can make for their health (physical *and* mental) is to eat nutritious food, sleep enough, and exercise. You can pay a lot of money to get people to give you more fancy advice, but if you don't take care of these three, they will impact everything that you do.

The general principle is, the more free time that people have, the less that they get done. Successful people know this so they fill their to-do lists and schedules.

People who don't eat right often say, "I don't have time to cook decent meals—it's easier just to order out or take out." If you ask them what they order or what they pick up at a drive thru, they will say something like "pizza" or "burgers and fries." If you point out to them that it would take the same amount of time to order a chicken Caesar salad and juice or milk, suddenly the time excuse doesn't work anymore. The most common reply to this is, "Yeah, I know I should." Although at first time appeared to be the reason for their unhealthy food consumption, the real reason had to do with choice.

Sleeping is much the same issue. "I wish I could sleep more—I'm lucky to get 6 hours as it is." If you ask such people in detail about their schedules, you will find that they could sleep more if they turned off the TV or computer an hour earlier. "Yeah, I know I should..." Exercise? Same story. Lifestyle *choices* have a greater impact on mental and physical health, and relationships, than does time.

Whenever people claim that they do not have time to do their self help work for counseling, one thing I know for sure— lack of time is *not* what is stopping them.

Productivity Is Not a Time Issue

If a person sits around and watches TV all day, how much time do they have in their day? How about the busy executive that works more than 12 hours per day, 7 days a week? You already know the answer—they both have 24 hours in their day. Which one do you believe gets more done? Although they both have exactly the same amount of time every day, the busy executive gets more done than the person who sits around. The general principal is, the more free time that people have, the less that they get done. Successful people know this so they fill their to-do lists and schedules. The more successful *and* busy they are, the more they tend to eat right, sleep enough, and exercise. I'm sure the president of the U.S., as busy as he is, gets all the sleep he needs, eats three square meals a day and keeps in shape. Is it because he has plenty of free time? Or is it because he wants to be at his very best to deal with all the

86

important decisions he makes each and every day? Certainly getting more done is not a factor of having enough time or having more time or having free time. It is a matter of choice.

A Steady Pace Wins the Race

Getting more done does not happen by setting time aside. It is also not related to working faster. Working faster than your normal pace will stress you out and eventually lead to burnout. People who try to work faster do shorten (a little) the time it takes to do something, but also take away from the energy they have to do other things. The net result is that they get less done and are more tired. Working faster than a comfortable pace will result in *decreased* productivity. People who drive 75 mph on the highway rather than 65 mph do arrive at their destination a few minutes earlier, but it takes considerably more fuel for them to get there. It also places more wear and tear on their car and their car will require more frequent maintenance. The lifespan of their car will also be shorter.

If your tendency is to maintain a lifestyle that is bad for you psychologically, socially, or physically, then doing what you *want* to do will result in a continuation of your problems. People often believe that if they could only do what they want, they would be happy. The fact is, doing what they want is what gets them into trouble in the first place. They *want* to eat something tasty, so they buy pizza and burgers. They *want* to watch more TV, so they stay up later. They *want* to relax without stressing themselves so they put off exercise to some other day. If you want to know what a person really wants, watch what he or she does. If you could follow someone around for a day, you would get a very good idea of what he or she really wants. The person who wants to be financially sound will be doing something to earn, save, or invest money. The person who wants a better relationship with her husband will be setting better boundaries, earning respect, communicating better, or cooperating more (depending on the health and behavior of her partner). If someone says he or she wants these things, but does nothing to work on them, you can see that although they *think* they want it, they want something else even

To figure out what people want, you only need to observe what they do and what they try to do. Anything else they say they want is just self deception.

- Someone who really wants to be your friend will take an interest in you and be nice to you.
- Someone who really wants to make more money will get job skills, invest, or work more hours.
- Someone who really wants to quit smoking will start some kind of smoking reduction program.
- Someone who really wants to overcome a mental health problem will get help and/or do self-help work.

more. Even if that is just to relax.

Successful people spend some of their time every day working on a future goal. The more they want that future goal, the more single-mindedly they work on it, and the less they spend time on other things. The "me" generation wants things easy, cheap, or free, but there is not much of quality available at that price. Every person you admire has had to work at becoming that way, and that is what you need to do, too.

On the following two pages are exercises you can do to make a master to-do list, and a daily to-do list. These will help you to make better choices, get more done, have more success, feel better about yourself, and live without regrets.

Predicting the Future Can Help Us Make Better Choices

A simple, but powerful exercise is to guess what your life will be like in 5 to 10 years if you make no changes in your lifestyle. Where will you live? Who will be your friends? How happy will you be? What regrets will you have? And how will your relationship be with your significant other? If there is anything that you want to change about that picture, the changes need to start to happen *today*. For the people who go to therapy, the picture they typically have of how their life will be in 5 to 10 years can be really depressing. If that's true for you, remember that that picture does not have to stay that way. You have the power to make the choices that will make the difference.

I know that all of these things sound simplistic. When people enter therapy, they often want grand solutions. Many people have entered therapy reporting low energy, low motivation, and depressed mood. When the therapist learns that they are only sleeping half of the hours that they need and suggests that they sleep more, they have a reaction like the therapist just doesn't get it. The client often wants to search their childhood for the root of their depression or to get on antidepressant medication. To be told that they need more sleep, although right on target, is one of the last things that they

A simple, but powerful exercise is to guess what your life will be like in 5 to 10 years if you make no changes in your lifestyle. What choices could you make today to improve on your expected future?

Exercise: Making a Master To-Do List

Instructions: Plan to work on these steps for 15 minutes per day, every day, until you have completed step four. Planning in 15 minute steps will help you to keep going and have more successes. You can always work more than you planned, freely, without obligation.

Step 1 (Have to and should do)

List ALL of the things that you "have to" do (**B** activities) and "should do" (**C** activities) on separate pages. "Have to" do items are things, that if not done, will cause bigger problems (e.g., pay the electric bill, do the laundry, etc.). "Should do" items are things that would be helpful to get done, but won't create bigger problems if they are not done (e.g., wash the car, organize the desk, etc.). Plan to use at least one hour (15 minutes per day) for this step. Add to it throughout the day and week as you think of new things.

Step 2 (Long term goals)

On a separate sheet of paper, list ALL your long term goals (**A** activities). These are things you want to achieve or have. They are things you would regret not doing or having as you reach the end of your life. Examples could be "travel the world, double my income, have a great relationship with my spouse, retire to Jamaica, learn French, etc." Add to this list throughout the week as you think of new things.

Step 3 (Action Steps)

List the first step (just one) toward every "A" activity you have (from step 2). Be sure that the step would take only 15 minutes For example, if your goal is to write a book, your next step might be to brainstorm 5 book topics. If your goal is to find a great job, the next step might be to make a list of your interests. If your goal is to travel the world, the next step might be to make a list of 5 interesting places (Remember, all goals are accomplished one step at a time).

Step 4 (Prioritizing)

You now have three lists: A, B, and C activities. Now, put the number "1" next to the most important item on each list. Put a 2 next to the next important item on each list, and so on. Continue like this until all items are numbered.

USAGE

Since our mind can only help us to achieve what we imagine for ourselves, just having made this master to-do list will set your subconscious in motion on your goals. Even if you do nothing else, you will achieve more in the next year than you otherwise would. However, you can greatly accelerate how fast you achieve your goals by using this master to do list to make a daily to do list (see the next exercise).

Exercise: Making a Daily To-Do List

For this exercise, you will use your master to do list from the last exercise. The master to do list and daily to do list work together like gas in an engine to accelerate you on your way. You will be able to do more in the same amount of time and with more enjoyment than before. They will help you to create a life you really want—a life with positive energy and without regrets.

Use the following two steps each day:

1. <u>At the beginning of your day</u> (or the night before), list at least one "A" action step and all your "B" activities. If you wish, you can schedule them, but it is not necessary. Have the master C list available, but do not put those items on your daily schedule or to do list.

2. <u>During the day</u>, do not do any C items until the B items are done and at least one A action step (which takes 15 minutes). Check off the items as you do them. Put the next action step for the accomplished "A" items on your master action steps list.

Tweaking your lists:

When you first start using this system, you will need to make a few adjustment until things are going smoothly and you are rolling along. Use the following steps to make adjustments:

1. <u>Undone "B" items</u>: If you get to the end of the day and have not done some of the "B" items, it is likely that they were really "C" items that were mislabeled as "B" items. Relabel them on your master to do list.

2. <u>Undone "A" activities</u>: If you have worked on your "A" activities, but have not completed a step for the day, you have made it too big. Steps need to be completely achievable on the day you work on them. For example, if your "A" item was "write resume", and you only managed to list your job history, your "A" item should have been "write job history part of resume." The next day you can make the relevant "A" item to write the academic history section of your resume. Try to guess what amount will take 15 minutes. Small steps will help you to get started and maintain momentum.

3. <u>Failing to work on "A" activities</u>: If two weeks have gone by and you have not worked on some of your "A" activities, cross them off your master to do list. They were things you thought you wanted, but can now see that you don't really want them very much. Don't feel bad about it, it's good to know so you can focus on what you really want.

THE FINAL RESULT OF THIS PROCESS

- You will spend more time with what is more important,
- You will get more done with less effort
- You will be more enthusiastic about your future, and
- You will create a life you love and value.

want to hear.

Many medical doctors don't even inquire about sleep, food, or exercise, knowing that their patients don't want to hear these questions. Also, no one in the health care industry will profit from you being well, although they will profit from treating you. As a result, the advertising you are exposed to will tell you rather directly that the way to be healthy is to receive treatment and medication. There are a few public service messages and programs to promote healthy lifestyles, but they are poorly funded compared to pharmaceutical advertising.

I've helped many clients to make remarkable improvement just by improving their sleep. On the next page are ten steps you can follow to get a better night's sleep, improve your mood and energy level, and think more clearly.

Happiness Is in the Making

How many television or magazine advertisements have you seen urging you to sleep more, exercise, or eat right? Instead, they will urge you to buy beds, exercise equipment, particular foods, and medications. If the beds, exercise equipment, particular foods, or medications actually delivered what they promised, we would be a country full of fabulous looking, happy, healthy people rather than a country full of obese, depressed, and worried people on prescription medications. People try to substitute having a thing (a supposed cure or fix, for example) for the *process* of doing a thing. They want to get a good life without having to make one. But the happiness is in the *making*—not in the getting. Happy people are always working on something, whether they need to or not.

Health, whether a healthy body, mind, or spirit is not the result of something you buy or some place you go. It is a result of the process of how you live your life each day. For thousands of years, people slept enough without $2000 beds, stayed thin and energetic without exercise equipment, and ate healthy and natural food without going to a health food store. The advent of technology is not improving the quality of our lives and it will not improve yours. Do you believe that driving

"An apple a day keeps the doctor away." Who is motivated to tell you that?

- **The doctors?**
- **The drug companies?**
- **The apple growers' association?**
- **Your grandmother?**

We need to have a good understanding of how our mind and body work so that we can make the best choices about our health.

Exercise: Ten Steps to Better Sleeping

Introduction to the Steps: People who have had difficulty sleeping for years can often find it easier to get a night's rest from following these ten steps. Sleeping is a natural ability, but sometimes we train ourselves to sleep poorly. You will need to follow them for a few weeks before getting good results. But then you can keep them for a lifetime.

Step 1: Don't drink beverages with caffeine within 12 hours of bedtime. It takes that long for our bodies to get it out of our system.

Step 2: Go to bed the same time every night, and wake up the same time every morning. If you are constantly varying your sleeping and waking time, you are defeating the purpose of your internal clock.

Step 3: Don't take naps in the daytime. Many people have been able to get off of sleep medications simply by following this step.

Step 4: Don't drink alcohol before bedtime. Alcohol interferes with REM sleep. What this means is that although you could sleep through the night after drinking, you may not feel rested the next day. What good is sleep if you are just as tired the next day?

Step 5: Sleep in a dark room. Light is nature's alarm clock. Trying to sleep with the alarm clock sounding creates lighter, rather than deeper, sleep. The darker your room, the better. Wear a sleeping mask if you need to.

Step 6: If you can't fall asleep within half an hour, get up. Frustration about not sleeping will keep you awake. Get up and do something relaxing and dull (no tv, games, or internet) until you are sleepy then go back to bed. Repeat as often as necessary, until you fall asleep.

Step 7: Never try to sleep, as trying to sleep will keep you awake. Instead, try to relax by focusing on your breathing. Long slow breaths, over and over. Meditatively and quietly.

Step 8: If you need to get up to use the restroom, go back to bed after you finish. Don't check your text messages or get a snack. If possible, keep the lights dim as you go back and forth.

Step 9: Don't do anything in bed except sleep. Condition your body to automatically sleep when you get in bed by not eating, reading, having sex, talking on the phone, or any other thing in bed except sleeping.

Step 10: Exercise. Daily exercise increases your body's need for sleep, which will increase your ability to sleep quickly and deeply.

Comments: Your ability to sleep is intimately connected with your moods and your ability to think clearly. Sleeping well is one of the two most powerful things you can do for your mental health (the other is exercise).

a car makes you a happier person than an ancestor who rode a horse? Does using the internet or watching television truly make you happier than people used to be sitting around a campfire and telling stories? Technology increases corporate productivity and the rate of information exchange, but it does not increase satisfaction with life. More than ever, people feel they are working harder and are satisfied less. Meeting healthy needs, in healthy ways, makes people happier *and* more productive. And it will do the same for you.

Two Popular Myths About Productivity

This brief chapter holds the keys to your success and satisfaction with life. But, you cannot adopt better ways without letting go of worse ways. Following are two myths that many people hold, that are holding them back. As you read each myth, ask yourself if it is holding you back.

Myth 1: You need to work faster to get more done.

To get more done in your day, including your self-help assignments, make a "to-do list" at the beginning of each day (you can find an exercise on how to make a to-do list on the next page). Schedule the items from your to do list, starting with the most important ones that will bring the most long term gain. Fill your entire schedule, with no breaks at all, except for meals (don't worry—you will still have breaks). Remember, free time and getting things done don't go together. The busier you are, the more you can focus on getting the essential things done which will get you ahead. The less busy you are, the more you can goof off, which will result in you becoming more and more unhealthy. It won't make your life easier. It will make your life more and more difficult as you get further away from what you really want. Any successful person you can think of didn't get that way by sitting around.

When you need a break during the day, only take it during the least important activities scheduled or redefine a break as a change in activity (see the exercise on the next page). Using this method, you should *never* get everything done on your list or schedule. But, you will get the most important things done

Working faster is only beneficial for those things which you can complete without getting fatigued. Working fast while fatigued leads to depression and reduced immune response.

A man walks much more slowly than a horse can run. But, a man (or woman) can walk more miles in a day than a horse can run. For big jobs and long term goals, working steadily at a normal pace is more enjoyable *and* more productive.

Exercise: Take More Breaks and Get More Done

In the text, I said that breaks are never a problem—that you can take all the breaks you want and still get your work done.

One of the best ways to think of "breaks" is as changes from your current activity. A break does not mean *rest* necessarily, as resting is only one kind of activity.

All of these could be breaks:

- going for a short walk

- taking a nap

- reading part of a book

- writing part of a book

- using your exercise equipment

- making a phone call

- working on a report

- chopping some wood

The key to a good break is to shift the mental and/or physical muscles to a different task. When you take breaks, switch to working on another high-priority task, if only for 15 minutes. This way, you can take as many breaks as you want and still be very productive.

List some of the high-priority break activities that are available to you:

Keep this list in your work area or use other items from your to-do list the next time you want to take a break.

and you will have as many breaks as you need. Not only will you get more done, you will feel better about yourself and your life. Remember to work only at a comfortable pace. Working at a faster than comfortable pace, you would get fatigued, start avoiding your work, and before long get less and less done. By keeping busy, but not hurrying, you will get more done than ever before. Your therapist can play a crucial role in helping you figure out what your priorities should be in order to reach your personal goals.

Truth: You need to schedule more and work at a normal pace in order to get more done.

Myth 2: If you do what you want, you will be happy (or giving others what they want will make them happy).

To do more healthy things, replace unhealthy choices with healthy choices. For example, order the chicken Caesar salad. Buy fruit instead of chips when you are grocery shopping. Drink bottled water instead of soda pop. Get away from the idea that you have to enjoy everything that you do. Water doesn't taste as good as soda pop, but that is ok. At first, making such changes will be hard and you will crave your usual diet. But the more you make the substitutions, the easier it will become. The first few days are the toughest. Then it gets easier and easier. Do an experiment and find that out for yourself. Are you able to go without these products for a few days? Are you addicted to a product or behavior that will lead to that future picture of yourself that you don't want to see?

Try turning off the TV or computer one hour earlier than usual and going to bed. At first, it may be hard to sleep, but the more you do it, the easier it will become. You will have more energy the next day, and you will get colds and other illnesses less often. You will also think more clearly, be more positive, and enjoy your life more. Park your car in the furthest parking spot from the entrance everywhere you go. You will get more exercise but won't notice any actual increased time to do so. Make healthy eating, sleeping, and exercise your top priority.

Who Needs "Easy" When You Can Have "Good"?

- **Choose the most unhealthy thought or behavior you have and start substituting a better one for it, every time you have the urge. At first it will be difficult, but it will get much easier and so will your life. When you have that under control, choose another one and do the same thing. It worked for George Washington, Benjamin Franklin, and Abraham Lincoln. It will work for you, too.**

These are vital for keeping you healthy in every way. Your life, to you, should be just as important as the president's life to him.

As you go throughout your day, ask yourself, "Is there a healthier thing that I could be doing right now?" Make this a regular question and keep making substitutions of healthier things for less healthy things. You can make making healthy choices a habit. For every bad choice you remove and every healthy choice you add, you will feel physically and emotionally better and have more positive energy. What are some healthy choices you could start with? Have you ever put your television in your closet for a week? Have you ever gone a week without eating any junk food? Have you ever made it a priority to get eight to ten hours of sleep a night for a week? Have you ever tried to only say nice things to everyone for a week? I dare you to try it.

Truth: If you work toward what you want in the future, you will become increasingly successful and happier.

Simply knowing what is true and what is false does not automatically make our lives better. To live without regrets and become increasingly happy, we must substitute good habits for bad ones. We can't hold onto bad behaviors and somehow just add good ones on top. That would be like putting cream on a dish of mud. Likewise, to change bad beliefs, we must willingly give up our unhelpful beliefs and substitute new, good beliefs. Many unhealthy people know what they "should" do. To be different from them, you will need to actually make the changes. It will be hard for a little while, but that's ok. Not everything has to be easy.

Dealing with Temptation

One of the reasons that people give for making the choices they do is *temptation*. Simply speaking, temptation is the desire to do something which is harmful to yourself or another. Whether you see the temptation as coming from an external source such as Satan, advertising, or seductive talk from others, it is still the same thing. Temptations are unavoidable and

The Power to Change is Within You:

- **To live without regrets and become increasingly happy, we must substitute good habits for bad ones. Wise leaders have been teaching that for thousands of years, including Socrates, Christ, Gandhi, and Mother Theresa, to name a few.**

everyone has them. Old and young, rich and poor, successful people and failures all experience temptation on a daily basis.

What is the difference between someone who gives in to their temptations and someone who doesn't? In a word, *discipline*. Discipline separates the winners from the losers— the haves from the have nots.

Discipline is the habit of making good choices in the face of temptation. It takes no discipline to do what we have to do when there is no choice. The more choices that we have, the more we will need discipline in order to have success. Fortunately, discipline is like a muscle which grows stronger the more we use it. And, just like developing our muscles, we need to begin with easy workouts.

Many people come to the conclusion that they don't have enough discipline (also known as willpower) after they fail at a venture which was beyond their ability to sustain. When I was first becoming a runner, I started out by running half a mile as fast as I could. For the first week, I was able to push myself to do it, but then I quickly started finding excuses not to run. I would have given up completely if I hadn't bought Jim Fixx's book, *The Complete Book of Running*. I learned in that book that because I was a beginning runner, I needed to start out running slowly, not much faster than a walk, and gradually build the muscles I needed for running faster. By gradually increasing distance and pace, I was able to work up to running over 100 miles per week. No doubt you already have discipline for doing your job or taking care of your children. With other things, you will need to walk before you can run.

Besides gradually making changes, the other thing which will help you to avoid temptation and build discipline is prayer. When you are feeling tempted, pray for the strength to resist the temptation. For people who find strength in their relationship with God, this method works wonders.

I challenge you to work toward seeing your temptations as opportunities to improve yourself by increasingly making better choices.

Discipline:

- **Making good choices even when you are tempted to do something else.**
- **Gets stronger the more you exercise it.**

Stubbornness:
- **Refusing to make a change, even when it is beneficial.**
- **Unlike discipline, is unhealthy.**

Case Example: Jim

He was always too busy trying to meet other people's demands and if he did take a little time for himself, his level of guilt would not allow him to enjoy himself.

Jim was a very busy man. As a sole supporter of a family of five, he often worked 12 hour days. Jim came to therapy due to feelings of depression, low energy, job stress, and family conflict. He always felt guilty and especially felt like he was not spending enough time with his family.

Jim entered counseling on the condition that I could see him during his lunch hour. He thought that something must be terribly wrong with him and was afraid of other people finding out.

Besides being sleep deprived, Jim did not take time to do things which interested him. He was always too busy trying to meet other people's demands and if he did take a little time for himself, his level of guilt would not allow him to enjoy himself.

I had Jim start keeping a "to do" list of all the things he believed that he should do as well as things he would like to do, "if he had the time." Sales calls were on the list as well as getting 8 hours of sleep. Looking at the list of all the things that he had to do made Jim feel overwhelmed. Jim was asked to assign priorities to each thing on the to-do list based on its impact on his future. In other words, "What difference will it make tomorrow, next year, and in 10 years?"

Jim started to see that while everything that others wanted seemed to be important for tomorrow, what he wanted for himself seemed to be more important for the future. I helped Jim to see the way he was making choices regarding what to do. By doing the things that seemed immediately urgent, he was in fact sacrificing long term physical and mental health, as well as his relationship with his family. Jim also learned that he was sacrificing important friendships. He did not currently have friends and choosing to do other things was preventing him from making friends.

Every week when Jim returned to counseling, I would ask him, "What healthy choices did you make this week?" At first,

Jim made the same choices as always, But the longer he remained in therapy, the more he started to make healthy choices. He was just as busy, but was getting a little more time off from work to spend with his kids, began to date his wife, and would get a little more sleep. The more Jim did this, the better he felt. He was learning to measure his productivity in terms of long term benefits and peace of mind rather than hours spent at the office.

Jim remained a high energy individual, but learned to use his energy for better purposes. His depression lifted, and much to his surprise, he became more successful than ever at work although he was actually working less. When Jim left therapy, he still had the tendency to bury himself in his work whenever he was feeling stressed. But, he was doing enough important things that he could sense his life was moving forward.

———

There is only one thing standing between you and happiness—making healthy choices. Although you may see other obstacles, it's how you choose to deal with those obstacles which will make the difference. Your choices are the only things that make you have different experiences from other people. Every healthy choice moves you toward a healthier group of people, while every unhealthy choice moves you toward an unhealthier group of people. In order to make progress, your healthy choices must far outnumber your unhealthy choices. Do learn in therapy what the healthy choices are for you. Do discover what you are forfeiting in your life whenever you make the unhealthy choices (every unhealthy choice involves losing something good).

Summary

This book was written to supplement your counseling. Counseling is the process of change, which means letting go of false and harmful beliefs and habits, and taking on new and healthier ones. Letting go of beliefs and habits that we have held for most of our lives is very difficult. Although we can see the truth or value in a new way, it will require sustained effort

He was learning to measure his productivity in terms of long term benefits to his life rather than hours spent at the office.

There is only one thing standing between you and happiness—making healthy choices.

(perhaps several months) to make the changes that will bring life satisfaction. The value of getting help from a therapist dedicated to helping you make those changes cannot be overstated. On our own, old habits will quickly replace new thinking and prevent positive change. On our own it is too easy to slide back again and again. For the sake of your own health and happiness, do not end your counseling until you have maintained a healthy lifestyle for at least three months. You will never regret it.

CHAPTER SEVEN

7. PAIN IS NOT THE ENEMY

"Sticks and stones may break my bones, but names will never hurt me," is very far from the truth. Many of us live daily with the pain verbally inflicted on us by others. I recovered from my pain, but it took time and help. From age five to ten, I experienced physical abuse at the hands of my father. But it wasn't his steel toed boots or his fists that left the deepest marks on me. It was what he said over and over again to my mother and me. I am thankful for my counselors who taught me how to let go, move forward, and bring meaning out of my experience.

Time Does Not Heal All Wounds

It is simply not necessary to carry emotional pain throughout our lifetime, but many of us need help knowing how to be released from it—just as I did. The percentage of counselors who were abused is much higher than the general population. It is our recovery from it, and the help that we received by the counselors who went before us, that makes us believe in our profession.

Abuse is not the only source of deep psychological pain. Perhaps an even greater pain than abuse is the pain of being ignored and unacknowledged. Babies can die from that alone, even if they receive all the physical care they need. Adults may not die from such lack of acknowledgement, but some do. Besides this, there are other sources of pain—many of them even self-inflicted. Many people suffering from psychological disorders, bring pain into their lives every day by their self-

Counselors Are Survivors:

- **Most counselors have become sensitized to human pain and suffering by having a good deal of their own, prior to deciding to become a counselor.**
- **Not only does your counselor believe in the healing power of counseling, he or she has likely experienced it from the client side.**
- **Many counseling clients develop an interest in becoming a client after recovering from their psychological problems.**
- **They become better able to help their family and friends.**

In many ways, every person that I counsel is seeking some kind of relief from pain in their life.

rejecting thoughts, their projections of a difficult or scary future, and by behaviors that bring out the worst in others toward them. Getting help from counselors is about stopping that. In many ways, every person that I counsel is seeking some kind of relief from pain in their life.

Physical Pain and It's Relationship to Our Conscious and Unconscious Mind

Mood and pain are not entirely distinct. They are, in fact, interactive. What happens in our environment makes our pain seem better or worse.[7] Likewise, physical pain impacts our energy level, moods, thoughts, and emotional well being. If you are experiencing physical pain, you need to seek medical treatment because there may be a serious problem that needs to be medically taken care of. Psychotherapy is not used to treat physical injuries, although it can help people to cope with the emotional impact of those injuries. Do whatever you can to physically take care of your condition, before seeking help from psychotherapy with your physical pain management. Pain is a mental interpretation of signals from the body. As such, physical pain is both a physical and psychological phenomenon. It only makes sense to get help with both parts. Some psychologists specialize in the psychological management and reduction of pain that originates from physical problems.

As an example of the psychobiological nature of pain, consider that a paralyzed person will feel no pain in the paralyzed part. This is because no signal reaches the brain, where the pain is actually "felt." Another example is the phantom limb pain that people can experience "in" an arm or leg which has been severed from their body. The person can seem to feel pain in a part of them which is no longer there. That's because the brain believes the signals to be coming from the missing limb. Our experience of pain is mediated by our brain and affected by our beliefs.

Another characteristic of pain is that it is an experience of the conscious part of our brain. When we are unconscious (for example, when we are asleep), we don't experience pain. Because pain is experienced when we are conscious, it is impacted by thoughts that are *under our conscious control*. Think one thing and it intensifies the pain, think another and it dulls the pain. Some people have such good control over pain that they have had surgery without anesthesia. Hypnosis has been used instead of anesthesia to influence a person's thoughts in order to reduce or eliminate pain. People who have been repeatedly abused, particularly when they were young, often develop an ability to dissociate from their pain—to go somewhere else in their mind while the abuse is taking place. This is basically a reduction in conscious awareness that reduces not only physical, but also psychological pain. The more deeply we study either physical or psychological pain, the more the distinction becomes blurred. This holds great promise both for the healing of physical pain with psychological methods, as well as the healing of psychological pain with physical methods. Acupressure, acupuncture, and massage therapy are only a few of the physical techniques which are used to treat both physical and psychological pain. Since this is a book about counseling, the remainder of this chapter will be concerned more with the psychological management of physical and emotional pain.

The Purpose of Pain

Pain intensifies when we focus on it, and becomes less intense when we focus on something else. So, when people try to ignore, deny, or evade things which cause them pain, it makes perfect sense. And, if you get an emotional injury from a stranger in passing, or stubbed your toe on the curb, I would agree that the best thing to do is to move on. It's a different story when the source of the emotional pain is a family member, a coworker, or even an intense memory. Because these causes of pain are a regular part of our lives, ignoring or evading them is not helpful.

Recurrent Pain

Just as with recurrent anxiety, recurrent pain is not something that will go away if we ignore it. And, like temporary pain, It has a purpose—to tell us that something emotionally or physically damaging is happening. When we are

Whatever Reduces Psychological Pain Also Reduces Physiological Pain:

- **Relaxation**
- **Feeling Happy**
- **Focusing on the Positive**
- **Finding Meaning in the Suffering**
- **Seeing the Pain as a Challenge Rather than a Handicap**

Pain is a Warning System

- **Like the smoke alarm in an apartment.**
- **Like a burglar alarm at a bank.**
- **Like a friend who shouts "Look out!" when a car is coming at you.**

burning our finger on something hot, pain gets us to remove our finger and to put something on it to make it feel better. The pain gets us to move our finger away from the heat source very quickly, to minimize injury. Without being able to experience pain, our lives would be pretty short. As much as people hate pain, it has a protective and informative purpose. If we had the option to somehow turn off our perception of pain, it would a very foolish thing to do.

On the following page is an inventory for you to do a self-analysis of your emotional pain.

An Optimal Amount of Pain in Life

There are times when we must endure some pain, rather than immediately escape from it, in order to bring about a greater good. For example, you may need to get a tooth drilled or pulled in order to prevent further dental complications. Exercise is another example. When you are exercising, you will experience pain to the extent that you tax your body beyond what it is used to. Exercise that did not tax the body at all would also not strengthen the body. There is an optimal amount of desirable pain. Tax your body a little and you will become sore, but with regular exercise, you will get progressively stronger. Tax your body too much and you could rupture a disk, get a hernia, have a heart attack, or some other dreadful thing. Pain is helpful to athletes to tell them how hard to push themselves, and to tell them when to stop. In this sense, *pain is both a signal of progress and a signal of danger.* There is an optimal level of pain for both physical and mental progress.

Athletes like to "feel the burn" when they are exercising. They interpret it as a requisite to becoming stronger. In this context, the pain is actually tolerable and enjoyable (mentally), although physically taxing. If the very same "burn" were to occur suddenly at the dinner table, however, it would be experienced as severe pain and be mentally distressing. The "burn" is expected while exercising, not while eating. Our expectation of pain influences how severely it affects us. If you have a chronic condition that causes pain, fighting the pain will

Exercise: Personal Emotional Pain Inventory

Check the answer(s) which corresponds to what you <u>actually</u> do and believe (not according to how you want to think and believe).

<u>How do I deal with emotional pain?</u>
☐ Suppress it?—actively avoid thinking/talking/dealing with it.
☐ Drug it/medicate it?—alcohol, cigarettes, prescriptions, cheesecake
☐ Avoid it?—excessive working, multiple relationships, TV, video games
☐ Use it to improve myself?—look for healthy ways to eliminate the source of the pain

<u>I believe pain is</u>
☐ Sometimes necessary for growth—no pain, no gain.
☐ To be avoided at all costs—all pain is terrible.

<u>My goal is to</u>
☐ Be pain free—to let nothing bother me.
☐ To respond in a healthy way to pain—to recognize pain and use it to identify areas for self improvement.

<u>Pain is</u>
☐ Avoidable—it is possible to go through life with no problems whatsoever.
☐ Inevitable—Problems are part of life.

<u>If I could take a pill to remove all my worries and pains from life, I would</u>
☐ Take it—it's ok to have problems if I don't care about them.
☐ Not take it—I want to be aware of my problems so that I can do something about them.

Now, repeat this exercise, **circling** how you <u>want to</u> behave and believe. Wherever your circled answers differ from your checked answers you are likely to experience resistance to counseling. These can be some of the most difficult places to work but also the most rewarding. Write below any change(s) that you need to make:

My OLD belief/behavior: (e.g., "It is better to avoid pain")

_____

_____

My NEW belief/behavior: (e.g., "It is important to deal with painful issues")

_____

_____

How this change will benefit me: (e.g., "I will be happier in the long run")

_____

_____

intensify it. Expecting the pain and telling yourself that the pain is normal and that you can tolerate it, will make it more tolerable and less painful. Expecting pain, just like expecting any problem, makes it more bearable when it happens. The more you experience it and have success in dealing with it (like a boxer or martial artist), the less detrimental its impact. You will still feel it, but you will begin to experience it differently.

Managing Pain Is About Improving Function, Not Becoming Pain Free

Beginning martial artists ask, "Doesn't it hurt when you break a board with your hand?" Experienced martial artists answer, "Yes, but the secret is not to mind it." The more acceptable the pain is to you, the less it will interfere with your daily activities. It is not a matter of willpower or being strong. It is a matter of thinking differently about the sensation that you are experiencing.

A dull chronic pain will be easier to manage with changes to your thinking than sudden, sharp pains, which occur unpredictably. If you whip a person once in a while, they will experience severe pain each time. If you whip them regularly, they will build a tolerance to it. It will still hurt, but not as much. This is not because the body has lost its sensitivity, but because the mind begins to expect it and adjust for it. In extreme (and unhealthy) cases, a person can even come to enjoy pain as is seen with masochistic behavior like cutting and self-flagellation.

The basic thought that will help the chronic pain sufferer is, "I have pain in my ____. It is normal for my condition, I will feel it each day, but I don't need to focus on it. I can do many things even though I have this feeling, just like I am doing now." There are many people who live with chronic pain so severe that it would instantly debilitate us if we were to experience it suddenly. Yet they function, and have a variety of activities, including work and socialization. They have few choices. They either can live a life focused on the pain, or focus on other things despite the pain.

Pain is Experienced More Intensely When We:

- Focus on it.
- Are stressed.
- See it as awful rather than inevitable.
- Give it control over us.
- Predict that it will get worse.

106

Avoiding Pain Is Debilitating

Although pain is to some extent manageable by medications or changes in thinking, seeking pain seems a little crazy. Yes, we may do good things that cause pain (like sports), but we don't do them in order to feel pain. The other extreme though, of avoiding doing things in order to avoid pain, can actually cause us a great deal of injury. To put it another way—the seeking of comfort and avoidance of all that is uncomfortable cheats people out of better health (prevents them from getting stronger), better relationships (prevents them from risking rejection at the cost of intimacy), and better peace of mind (for example, working through and letting go of previous injuries done by others).

Pain Is a Helpful Signal

If you ever work with a physical therapist, you will quickly learn that getting well means doing some things which initially cause pain, but which result in greater strength and mobility. When you work with a psychotherapist, the process is very similar. The experience of emotional pain is an indicator that important and necessary changes are being made that will result in long term peace and stability.

Why do we say "pain" for emotions although our brain doesn't hurt? Although emotional pain is not the same thing as physical pain, it shares some of the same characteristics. Emotional and physical perceptions of pain are both indicators that something is wrong or damaging and needs our immediate attention. That is, they serve the same purpose, much like a flashing yellow light. The experience of emotional and physical pain are both influenced by how we interpret it. Some people are more disturbed by the thought of emotional pain than they are of physical pain. They will, for example, stay in a relationship with a physically abusive person in order to avoid the emotional pain they would experience if the relationship were to end. The greatest impediment to working with abuse victims is not their fear of physical harm, but their fear of the loss of their partner. They become caught between two types of

The seeking of comfort and avoidance of all that is uncomfortable cheats people out of better relationships , and better peace of mind.

emotional pain—the fear of loss and the fear of abuse. To deal with one, you have to also deal with the other.

People most often enter counseling because of some pain in their lives. It can come in many forms such as anxiety, depression, relationship problems, low self-esteem, etc. Often people want to get rid of the pain (the warning system) without taking care of the underlying cause. This is like taking the battery out of a smoke alarm in a building prone to fires. This is the potential danger of sedating drugs. If a medication makes you feel better to the extent that you are not motivated to work on the cause of your problems, your problems will continue. It would be like taking pain killers for a broken leg without setting the bone.

Your pain, emotional or physical, is not what is crippling you. It is the condition or situation to which the pain points. That is where the therapist must help you work. When the only way a person copes with a stressful situation is by using medication, it is no more useful than alcohol to a person who can't hold a job. Drinking may make them feel better, but will not help them to maintain a job. If you take a pill because you have social anxiety disorder, but then spend your time sitting at home (rather than socializing), the pill has done you no good. You will have turned off the alarm without doing anything about the fire.

Often therapists, including me, will refer their clients for antidepressant medication or anxiety medication. But, the therapist does not want the medication to be so effective that the person no longer experiences *any* anxiety or any depression. The goal is to reduce the amount of emotional pain to the level where it doesn't overwhelm the client, but where it still provides motivation for treatment. A person with mild anxiety or depression would not be referred for medication because further reducing the symptoms (the emotional pain) would decrease the desire for therapy and the client's willingness to work on the cause of the symptoms.

Two of the top reasons people drop of counseling prematurely are: 1) feeling good, and 2) feeling bad. The

---

Usually people seek treatment for pain (anxiety, depression, family conflict, etc.), but what actually needs to be treated is the source of the pain. Pain is more often the symptom than the problem.

Attempting to remove all psychologically caused pain by the use of drugs or medication makes people less functional, creating even more psychological problems. This is why drugs and alcohol can viciously spin a person's life out of control.

People are less likely to become addicted to pain medication when it is used legitimately to treat a physical injury.[8]

problem of dropping out of counseling when a person feels good is that the person's new ways of thinking and behaving may not have stabilized yet. In such case, the person will soon return to their prior level of distress and difficulty as old habits reappear. The problem of dropping out of counseling when a person feels bad (emotional pain) is that their problems remain unresolved. Often, therapists are wrongly blamed for being the cause of the pain. This is no more true than a medical doctor is the cause of pain for someone with a broken leg. In order to provide effective treatment in counseling, therapists help you to use your pain to identify the source of the problems. Pain helps us to be aware of the source of the problems so that we can do something about them.

Therapy Isn't Supposed to Be Painless

Emotional pain during counseling (e.g., sadness, anxiety, stress) often comes as a surprise to those who are new to counseling. The normal sequence of treatment in counseling is: 1) problem identification, 2) goal selection, 3) treatment, and 4) problem resolution. Pain is most intense in the first part of therapy, meaning that you will feel worse before you feel better. It's not until you get to the fourth stage, problem resolution, that you will have *consistently* good feelings. But, just as a child may get a lollipop after receiving an injection, you can also make the difficulty a little more bearable during the process. One thing you can do is to make yourself a "Rainy Day Box" (see the exercise on the next page).

Anytime during these four stages other problems may be identified, bringing with them renewed emotional pain. Although this may seem like an endless and complicated process of finding new problems and having more emotional pain, actually it is relatively short and straightforward. This is because the first problem is always the hardest to work through. As you work on it, you learn a lot in the process. After that, progress is made more quickly and easily for other problems. It's like the difference between a rookie paramedic and an experienced one. The rookie can be overwhelmed with relatively minor problems, but the experienced one may not be overwhelmed even with very severe ones. The more you fight

Two of the top reasons people drop of counseling prematurely are: 1) feeling good, and 2) feeling bad.

Exercise: Rainy Day Box

Pain is useful. Pain is no fun. Pain is inevitable. As you are learning, pain prompts us to take care of important issues in our lives. Doing so however, doesn't immediately remove our pain.

For example, in my work with clients I often teach them not to get really needy when their partner retreats into an emotional cave, and also not to walk on eggshells to prevent their partner from doing so. Even so, they need a way to take care of themselves as they are making these important changes.

One way to make such changes easier is to create a "Rainy Day Box " full of emotional self care items. What goes in the box? Anything that helps—poetry, chocolate, gift certificates for the movie theater, phone numbers of friends, etc.

The next time you do something really hard, but really healthy, you can reward yourself from your Rainy Day Box.

fires, the better firefighter you will become, and the less you will be afraid of fires. In counseling, you learn how to handle problems. Finding new problems becomes less of a sad thing, and more like an opportunity to improve even more. You can even get to the place where you get excited about identifying problems! Therapists like identifying problems because they know how to help people with them. You can become the same way, both for yourself and for others.

An Optimal Level of Pain in Counseling

To be successful in counseling, you must have an optimal level of emotional discomfort that will provide motivation for treatment. You must then be able to tolerate the discomfort of working on the problem long enough to get to problem resolution. The way to have such tolerance while in counseling is to understand that getting to the source of the pain is a normal and vital part of your treatment. An easy self-statement in this regard is, "Things need to get worse before they can get better." This self-statement provides an explanation for the discomfort as well as the hope of progress. You will also be able to draw strength from your counselor who should be increasingly earning your trust with sensitive and helpful responding.

Sticking with Changes:

- **Telling yourself, "Things need to get worse before they can get better," provides an explanation for the discomfort as well as the hope of progress.**

A realistic expectation for counseling is that you will feel worse after one month of counseling than when you first started. These feelings come right after problem identification and exploration and before there is time for improvement. In this case, feeling worse is a signal that you have made the right decision to enter counseling. It is not a signal that you should stop your counseling. This statement bears repeating—feeling worse in the early stages of therapy is a signal that you have made the right decision to enter counseling and is *not* a signal that you should stop counseling.

The person who drops out of counseling during this initial increase in emotional pain is most often worse off than the person who never entered counseling at all. This can be compared to people who marry with the expectation that they will never experience conflict with their spouse. When conflict arises (as it will, even in the best of marriages), they become distressed and wonder if they made a mistake in getting married in the first place. Couples are better off knowing that the normal way a marriage develops is first with a honeymoon phase (typically less than a year), followed by an adjustment phase (two to 3 years, depending on how different the couple are), followed by a long period of stable, but less intense loving. Just knowing this can help a lot in the adjustment phase, which is inevitable. When conflict is seen as a normal part of human relationships, and when people have the skills to successfully resolve such conflicts, they need no longer be feared. They are instead opportunities for growth. In counseling, your great advantage is that your counselor knows how to help you with all those painful things that you could spend years trying to deal with on your own.

When you have successfully made it through the cycle of temporary emotional pain to problem resolution in counseling, you will acquire a greater appreciation for pain. You may even learn to look and listen for other pain in your life because you will have a way to deal with it. When you can effectively cope with pain, it will no longer be an enemy but an ally in your quest for a happier and more fulfilling life.

The person who drops out of counseling during this initial increase in emotional pain is most often worse off than the person who never entered counseling at all.

Case Example: Emily

Emily was a single woman in her late 30's who had difficulties making friends and who had not had a boyfriend beyond a few dates. Despite her social isolation, Emily claimed that this did not bother her "at all" because she had a good career that took up most of her time and she couldn't be "bothered with" relationships. She was having difficulty with her coworkers, however, and was growing increasingly impatient with their lack of diligence in their work. Although her work was separate from theirs, she often tried to help them to see their mistakes and so improve their performance. She thought them very ungrateful for not appreciating her help.

I noted that Emily's predominant emotion was anger. Since

112

belonging and relationships are fundamental human needs which were not being met for Emily, I guessed that she was using her anger to mask her underlying sadness at not having relationships. Anger is often more tolerable than sadness because it allows us to blame others. If Emily could have a relationship, I thought it might go a long way toward resolving the underlying sadness and her preoccupation with her coworkers' supposed poor performance.

I worked with Emily to examine the relationships that she had had with other people since her childhood. Although she had learned to live without relationships, in the early years she had been quite hurt by rejection and mistreatment from others. Emily disliked talking to me about those times and could not see its relevance to therapy.

As we continued to work, Emily's demeanor began to change and she was looking more decidedly depressed than angry. I saw this as progress while Emily saw it as a sign that therapy was making things worse. I sensed that Emily would soon quit coming to therapy and label me as another incompetent (as she did with her coworkers). I pointed out to Emily that as she became more sad, she became less angry. I also empathized with her about how difficult it is to struggle alone in life without the help of others who could really help. I pointed out to Emily that she could certainly quit therapy and go back to being angry, or she could work on overcoming her loneliness and fear of rejection and so have some happiness in life.

Emily canceled her next two appointments, but then returned to therapy. I'm not sure that Emily agreed with me, but she did see I was someone who really cared. I may have been the only one who talked nicely to her. From then on, the focus of the sessions was no longer on the coworkers, but on grieving lost relationships. Eventually, Emily learned to treat her coworkers differently and got a better response from them. Therapy had helped her to stop running from her loneliness and to face it. It had been really hard for her in the beginning, but was a major turning point in her life.

I guessed that she was using her anger to mask her underlying sadness at not having relationships.

113

Emily's initial expectations about counseling kept her from getting help on her own. They also almost derailed her best chance to make her life better—something that wasn't happening by itself. On the next page is a quiz you can use to assess some of your own knowledge about the realities of therapy.

Summary

Therapy can sometimes be an Alice in Wonderland kind of experience. It can take you places you never wanted to go, and show you things that you never imagined you would see. But, they are all things which you are bringing into counseling with you. Your therapist just helps you to see them and to deal with them. Trust needs to develop, so you need to give your therapist a chance to earn your trust. When you do sense that your therapist really does care, then it will be time to gradually let out your real hurts. They are no longer a burden that you have to shoulder all alone.

Once the problem is gone, the pain disappears.

Exercise: Quiz on the Realties of Therapy

Match the corresponding statements (answers are on the next page):

1. Talking about anxiety

2. Talking about depression

3. Avoiding talking about problems

4. Dropping out of counseling

5. Continuing with counseling even when it is difficult

a. Makes problems worse

b. Temporarily relieves pain

c. Temporarily increases depression

d. Temporarily increases anxiety

e. Provides long-lasting improvement

Answers are on the next page.

Answers to the Quiz on the Previous Page

1. (d) Talking about anxiety temporarily increases anxiety. When an anxious person begins work in therapy, he or she initially fills the therapist in on the things that are making him or her feel anxious. Bringing all these things to mind often makes the anxious person more anxious. And, because people with anxiety disorders usually avoid anxiety provoking situations, they often do not return for the second session. This is unfortunate because not only will each session become easier, but they will also learn to be less anxious with continued treatment. People with anxiety disorders need to expect a temporary increase in anxiety and be determined to stick with counseling.

2. (c) Talking about depression temporarily increases depression. This is for much the same reasons as answer #1. Talking about the reasons for the depression in a short period of time makes things seem worse. It is necessary to get out these issues, though, so that the therapist can help you to not be depressed.

3. (b) Avoiding talking about problems temporarily relieves pain. That is why many people who have emotional pain avoid talking or doing anything about it. In relationships also, people will often avoid talking about problems because of the stress involved. The problem with avoidance is that it prevents problem resolution and leads to unnecessary long term suffering.

4. (a) Dropping out of counseling makes problems worse. People often drop out when they either don't like the discomfort of therapy, or when they feel relief from their problems. As noted above, discomfort is an important part of the healing process. Feeling relief from problems is a good sign of progress, but it is not a sign of *lasting* progress. You should stick with therapy long enough to make sure the improvements are stable. It is ok to reduce the frequency of attending therapy once you are satisfied with your progress, but you should not stop entirely until things have been going well for three months.

5. (e) Continuing with counseling even when it is difficult provides long lasting improvement. In fact, the most progress is often made just after the most difficult part of counseling. The ability to "push through" the most difficult part of working on any goal is what accounts for success. Many people who are experiencing difficulty do not realize that they are nearing the crest of the hill and things will be much easier if they will just continue a little more.

CHAPTER EIGHT

8. WORKING WITH YOUR THERAPIST

Unlike other people you hire, the bulk of the work of therapy will not be done by your therapist. When you get your car repaired, you drive it to the repair shop and wait passively while the mechanic works on your car. When the repairs are made, you pay and drive away. This is also the model for many human services such as getting your hair cut or a medical exam. While getting your hair cut, your job is to stay still while the barber or stylist cuts your hair. When the stylist is done, you pay and leave. When you go to see your medical doctor, the doctor does not ask you to put on some latex gloves and help out. Instead, you are passively led from room to room by a nurse. Then you patiently wait for the doctor to arrive (the reason you are called a "patient"). You answer some questions. Perhaps the doctor examines you in some way, you pay and leave.

The "cure" in psychotherapy never comes from the therapist. It comes from inside you. The therapist just helps you to find it in yourself, or create it in yourself.

A Different Model

It is no wonder that when clients arrive at a therapist's office, they have the mindset that the therapist is going to apply some kind of mysterious technique to fix them and that all they have to do is show up, answer some questions, and receive the cure. Psychiatry makes sense to people—the doctor prescribes a drug which changes something in the brain so that people feel better. Psychotherapy, where you pay to do most of the work, is not a model that people are used to.

Psychotherapy is also not like a classroom. You don't need to take notes and you don't memorize anything. The therapist

117

is also not imparting wisdom to you. For that matter, studying psychology also is not going to provide all that you need. This is because therapy is not a learning process—it is a collaborative discovery process.

One way to think of a therapist is as a guide who helps you see things, *you already know*, in a different way. The therapist does not know what those things are because you bring them with you and each person is different. Working together, you talk about what you know and the therapist helps you to organize this information and show you how it's impacting your life.

You can also think about psychotherapy as being like putting together a jigsaw puzzle. All of your life, you have spent your time looking at the individual pieces of your life, not realizing that it all fits together. Not only will your therapist help you to see how it all fits together, but your therapist can help you to rearrange the pieces to make an entirely new picture—one that you would not have known how to make without your therapist's help.

Passive Learning vs. Active Learning

The mindset of passivity is pervasive in Western culture. The educational system is a passive one on the part of the students. Students listen to teachers who impart knowledge to them. The religious institutions are much the same. People go to church, mass, or synagogue to have the pastor, priest, or rabbi perform a service for them.

Unfortunately, what is passively learned is also passively forgotten. Real learning only occurs when people put into practice what they learn. Vocational education, technical schools, internships and practicum, apprenticeships, residencies, and on the job training all involve active participation in learning. People in these programs learn by doing. Having had experience, and not just knowledge, they can use their skills even many years later with few recall problems. Would you want a surgeon to operate on you who had passed written tests on operating, but had never actually

Real learning occurs when people put into practice what they learn.

Regardless of the type of therapy, most of the work is done by the client.

118

cut into someone or at least assisted someone who has cut into someone? "Don't worry about a thing Mr. Smith, I read 10 books on heart surgery and scored 95% on the final exam." If I were Mr. Smith, I would be hoping very much that the 5% the surgeon missed on the exam had nothing to do with my heart!

Working and Participating in Therapy

Therapists work together with their clients. Clients actively participate in their own treatment. This makes it different from other types of treatment and service. Regardless of the type of therapy, most of the work is done by the client. While what the client desires is answers, what the therapist desires for clients is the ability to solve their own problems. That is, unlike other professions, the therapist is helping you to be able to independently take care of yourself. The good therapist works himself out of a job by making you less, not more, dependent on him. Psychotherapy is one of the very few professions which promotes healthy, independent functioning. This can only occur if clients actively participate in solving their own problems. It is also one of the very few professions which attempts to get at the answers by looking for them inside of you.

The exercise on the next page will help you to discover something you know better than anyone else—what you need for your difficulties. The answers are there, although you may need help drawing them out.

Work in Insight Oriented Therapies

For insight oriented or psychodynamic therapies, the primary method is for the client to talk (not the therapist) while the therapist listens and directs. The therapist directs and guides the client by the choice of questions she asks. Therapists using this style of therapy are in a sense like orchestra conductors, using subtle questions as their baton. In this way, they lead clients to talk about things they have never talked about, in ways they never have before. Because of this new experience, clients start to see connections where previously they did not. These connections are called "insights." It's like

Insights are new understandings which create new meanings, purposes, and direction from old information. They are "aha" experiences with the power to change your life.

119

Example: The Power of "If"

We often put limits on our creative problem-solving and personal growth by deciding, in advance, what is and is not possible for us. Using the word "if," we can remove the limits so we can accomplish more.

Whether or not you think the following are possible, answer "as if" they are:

1. If my therapist could help me to do anything, I would like help to do...

2. If my therapist could help me to feel anything, I would like help to feel...

3. If my therapist could help me to think in a certain way, I would like to think...

4. If my therapist could help me to understand something about my past, I would like to understand...

5. If my therapist could help me to forgive someone, I would like to forgive...

6. If my therapist could help me to connect with someone emotionally, I would like to connect with...

7. If my therapist could help me solve my biggest problem, I would like to solve...

8. If my therapist could help me to undo emotional damage from something that happened, I would like to undo damage from...

9. If my therapist could help me to change one thing about myself, I would like to change...

10. If my therapist could help me to accept one thing about myself that I cannot change, I would like to accept...

Although you may have gone to your therapist to get answers, it's probably more important that you get the right questions. Then, you can identify both the source of pain within yourself, and what you need to heal that pain. You will find that your therapist asks a lot more questions then he or she gives answers. This is because an answer found is always more valuable than an answer given.

coming to therapy with a box full of puzzle pieces. The therapist, who is an expert on putting together puzzles, helps you to line up the pieces until you mentally say "aha" as you see how to join the pieces, making more sense out of your life. The therapist cannot give you insights. You must experience the "aha" for yourself. This "aha" occurs because of your active participation and observation of yourself. Seeing more clearly, you no longer need to amble as blindly through your life, but can make new, better choices, based on your insights. Choices appear which you have never seen before.

Work in Cognitive Therapies

Cognitive and cognitive behavioral therapies require more active participation from the therapist who may talk half of the time. Rather than guiding clients to make insights, cognitive therapists actively instruct clients in skills they don't already have. Clients then practice these skills both in and out of their sessions. One of the most important skills taught is to examine what you say and think to yourself. The way we think about ourselves, our future, and the world greatly influences our feelings and choices. By helping you to talk or think in more positive and realistic ways, you will feel happier, more confident, and make more realistic choices.

Cognitions are your conscious thoughts—the internal dialogue you have with yourself. People with psychological disorders have many cognitions which don't match reality or which overemphasize the negative.

Case Example: Roger

Roger was not at all nervous on his first therapy visit. He was, however, very depressed. He had very strong doubts about how a therapist could help him. His depression, after all, was in his head. Other people had tried to "cheer him up" off and on for years with no success. He had his mind made up before entering my office that nothing I said was going to make any difference.

Much to Roger's surprise, I did not try to cheer him up. I asked many questions but not once ever suggested that the depression was all in his head and that he just needed to snap out of it. I told him that the only way he was going to get better was if he was willing to work on changing his thinking. I pointed out that even if he had the power to change the world around him, that he would still be depressed until he was willing to change his way of thinking about things. But, the decision was Roger's. If he wished instead not to work, but to just stay depressed, he did not need to schedule another session. Who was I to tell him how to live his life?

Roger was at first very surprised that I was giving him responsibility for his treatment and his participation. I was not telling Roger what to do, but clearly expected that if Roger wanted to change, he would have to work with me to do it. He could quit at any time if he just wanted to stay depressed. As a result, Roger became less resistant and more curious about how he could work on changing. Over the next few sessions, I helped him to see how he was creating his depression and what was needed to change. Then we got to work on making small changes. Roger had homework assignments that were not hard and which helped him to keep working between sessions. He learned that he was the key to recovering from depression. I would teach him how, but he was the one who had to do most of the work. He could count on me to help him, but he couldn't count on me to cheer him up. That was his job.

————

Improvement in Therapy Depends on Two People

Improvement in cognitive behavioral therapy depends on: 1) the therapist selecting the right skills to teach, and 2) the client practicing the skills. Improvement in insight oriented therapy requires: 1) proper guidance by the therapist, and 2) the client to be open and honest with the therapist. In all psychotherapies, both the client and therapist have a role to play. If either the therapist or the client does not do their part, little or no progress will be made. Expecting to improve in counseling without active participation is like trying to satisfy your hunger by collecting recipes.

Working in Behavioral Therapies

Behavioral therapies involve the therapist leading the client through a series of exercises which deal with the very situations that the client is having trouble with. If you have a fear of

I was not telling Roger what to do, but clearly expected that if Roger wanted to change, he would have to work with me to do it.

elevators, the therapist may very well go with you to an elevator and have you practice being near it, watching the indicators, touching it, and so on, until eventually you are riding it. The therapist often will also teach relaxation techniques so that you will have something calming to do while in the elevator (or near it). If your problem is communication, the therapist will direct you step by step through communications with other people while you are in therapy until you are good at doing it on your own. You could think of behavior therapy as the apprenticeship model of therapy. The therapist, who is a master in whatever it is you are wanting to do, teaches you to become a master through hands-on experience. Behavior therapy is very effective in bringing about positive change in a short period of time. Some problems don't lend themselves to the methods of behavior therapy, however (e.g., dealing with past loss or trauma).

Working in Other Therapies

There are many types of therapy, but they mainly entail some combination of insight, cognitive, and behavioral therapies. According to research, the skill of the therapist and your participation are more important than the particular style of therapy.[9]

In actuality, few therapists adhere strictly to one type of therapy and will vary their techniques according to a client's needs. Nevertheless, therapists do tend to gravitate more toward one style more than another and will tell you which one—if you ask.

Which model of therapy is the best is a question that is impossible to answer. Research psychologists will debate the merits of particular kinds of therapy, but practicing therapists use whatever they are skilled with and believe will most benefit you. If you have gone a full course of therapy and were not satisfied with the results, then you may consider trying a therapist with a predominantly different style. To insist on a certain style at the outset, however, probably doesn't make sense.

Behavior:

- **What you do that would be possible for other people to see, hear, smell, or feel physically, if they were with you.**
- **Only our behaviors can influence others and get positive results from the world.**
- **The end result of all therapies is a change in thinking, feeling, and behaving.**

To insist on a certain therapy style at the outset, probably doesn't make sense.

Independence

- The *ability* to do for oneself.
- Independence doesn't mean being detached from others.
- People can be independent and still have a close relationship.

Dependence

- An inability to do, think, or feel a certain way without the help of someone or something else.
- We all depend on air, food, water, and shelter, to be able to live. These are healthy dependencies because they lead to good outcomes.
- Some people depend on drugs, alcohol, or certain behaviors from significant others. These are unhealthy dependencies because they lead to poor outcomes.

You Are in Charge of Your Progress

Whatever style of therapy your therapist uses, you will be expected to be an active participant. Your life will improve or not depending on whether you apply what you have learned in therapy. If you gain valuable insights, but ignore them in your day to day interactions, you will not benefit. If your therapist teaches you how to change your thinking to help you feel better but you only do it in the therapist's office, then you won't feel better. If you and your therapist practice the very skills that you need to be successful, but you follow old habits when you are alone, then you will not succeed. Therapy is an active process. Progress is directly related to the amount of time you spend in new habits rather than old. Therefore, progress is not something that the therapist can do for you or give to you. To use the mechanic example, therapy is like taking your car in to be repaired and instead of waiting while the mechanic does the work, the mechanic takes you into the repair area, helps you to identify the problem, see how to fix it, shows you how to use the tools and then says, "go for it." "But," you say, "I've never done this before—I might mess it up." The mechanic nods and agrees that you might. "But," the mechanic says, "How will you feel when you fix it by yourself? And, after you fix it, what will you be able to do it if happens again?" You then bravely take the tool and reach under the hood.

Your therapist will help you to identify many hidden obstacles to your progress. That's great because you can then do something about them so that your progress is not blocked anymore. On the next page is an exercise that you can do to find some of your own mental blocks.

Dependence on Your Therapist Should Decrease Over Time

If you believe that the only way for you to get better is to have the help of a therapist—that is not a bad thing. It is much like believing the only way you can screw in a screw is with a screwdriver. Using the proper tool for the proper situation is not a sign of dependency or weakness. It is a sign of

Exercise: Finding Your Mental Blocks

Mental blocks slow us down or stop us from doing the very things that would help us to get ahead. Although we can make great long and short term goals, set priorities, and create daily to do lists, we can still be prevented from working on our goals. Having mental blocks is like driving with the brakes on. We can struggle against them, but it takes more energy to get things done. Mental blocks result when we want two incompatible things. For example, we can both want to be single and want to be married. This will take away from our efforts and desire to be with our partner and to have a good relationship.

Step 1: Get 3 sheets of lined paper. Title the first page, "What I want to do." Title the second page, "What I have to do." Label the third Page, "What I should do." (You may have some of these lists available from other exercises in this book).

Step 2: On the first page list all of the things that you want to do. Don't list things that you wanted to do in the past. List things you want to do now or in the future (thus, it will include long term goals as well as other things). The list should include everything you want without regard to whether it is proper or possible. You are limited only by your imagination. Don't censor anything that comes to mind. Be specific. "Have a happy life" is not specific. "Drink a big cup of coffee" is specific. "Be a good father," is not specific. "Spend one hour a day with the kids," is specific. "Be in good shape," is not specific. "Be able to swing through the trees like Tarzan," is specific. You should have a list of 100 or more things. Keep coming back to it until you have your list complete.

Step 3: On the second page list all of the obligations that you have to do. Be specific. "Take care of my wife and kids" is not specific. "Mow the lawn" is specific.

Step 4: On the third page list all of the things that you should do in order to be healthy and successful. (Don't list what you should not do). For example, "save money for retirement, eat healthy food, go to church," etc. Some of these things you may be doing already; list them anyway.

Step 5: Look for contradictions between the three lists. For example, if you want to have multiple romantic partners, but have obligations to your spouse/family, circle both of these items. If you want to go shopping every day but should save money, circle each of these items.

Step 7: Share the areas of conflict with your therapist. Even desires that may seem inappropriate are important because they speak to underlying needs. For example, if you have a family, but desire solo exotic vacations where you meet exotic strangers, this probably represents a need for excitement and independence. Your therapist can work with you to help you get more excitement and independence while still maintaining your family and values. The desires of the heart, although they may make us feel embarrassed or ashamed, reflect real needs. Only by examining these desires, can we figure out what those needs are. It only becomes inappropriate when we act on those desires which are destructive to ourselves or to others. Fulfillment comes when we learn to satisfy those needs in appropriate ways.

intelligence.

If, on the other hand, you believe that you will never be able to get along without your therapist, you will have an unhealthy dependency. It would be like using the screwdriver at the dinner table to eat your peas and to turn pages when you read a book. The longer you work with your therapist, the less you should need your therapist to manage your life difficulties. However, just as you may need to take your car to the mechanic again for a new problem, you may need to return to therapy in the future. Can you imagine, if every time you took your car to the mechanic, you and the mechanic worked on your car together? After awhile, you would not only be able to fix any problem with your car by yourself, but you would be able to help other people with their car problems. Likewise, many counseling clients report that they have become better able to help their friends and family with their life problems.

Lack of Progress in Therapy

It is possible to be in therapy for a long time and not make progress despite your best efforts. At times like these, you need to evaluate with your therapist the reasons for the lack of progress. It may be that the therapist has not correctly identified your problem (for lack of information), that the therapist does not have sufficient skills to address your particular problem (just as medical doctors can't treat every type of problem and must refer to other doctors at times), or that you and your therapist have not chosen the most important goals to work on.

> *Some clients have a tendency to blame themselves for their lack of progress, while other clients have a tendency to blame their therapist. The truth usually lies somewhere in between.*

Some clients have a tendency to blame themselves for their lack of progress, while other clients have a tendency to blame their therapist for their lack of progress. The truth usually lies somewhere in between. Do not be afraid to discuss these concerns with your therapist. By the time you bring them up, your therapist is likely to also have the same concerns and will be relieved that you are addressing them. If your therapist brings lack of progress up first, your tendency may be to get defensive. It is important to realize that the therapist is bringing this up at the risk of losing his working relationship with you. For therapists to take such risks requires courage on their part as well as a great deal of concern about their clients. Count yourself fortunate to have found such a therapist.

On the next page is an exercise that may help you to identify some ways to get more from your current therapy.

Summary

Your progress in counseling depends on a number of factors. Any one of these factors can delay or prevent progress. It is important that you do your part by actively participating in counseling and by following through with self-help assignments. By doing so, you will be maximizing your chances for success.

Exercise: Getting More Out of Therapy

Name three things that you are skilled at (e.g., golf, knitting, neurosurgery, reading, etc.):

1

2

3

You got <u>skilled</u> at those things by (circle your response):

1) Listening to advice
2) Letting someone else do it for you while you watched
3) By practice

What are you currently learning in therapy?

What practical things can you do to apply what you are learning?

List the things you have done so far to help yourself with your current problems (e.g., go to therapy, change the way I communicate, think, behave, etc.)

What is likely to happen if you stop doing these things?

Is there something that you can do that would make your therapy more effective (e.g., doing homework, bringing someone else to therapy with you, taking notes, recording your session, etc.)?

9. UNHEALTHY DEPENDENCIES

There is a lie that is often taught to children—"Be nice to others and they will be nice to you." While therapists agree that children should be taught to be nice and to play nice, they also need to know how to deal with other children who are not nice. The fact is, whether you are a child or an adult, some people won't be nice to you, whether you are nice to them or not. This is because people will react to you more according to their personality than to anything you say or do. That is, when you are nice to nice people, they are nice to you in return. When you are nice to bullies, they bully you in return. When you share with a sharing person, they will also share with you. When you share with a selfish person, they will take what you have and want more, then blame you for not giving them enough.

Were You Taught To *Always* Be Nice To Others As A Child?

- **If you were, do you still believe that is a good rule to follow?**

Old Beliefs Die Hard

Unfortunately, many adults continue to operate under an old false belief and conclude that if someone is treating them badly, then they must not have been nice enough to that person. "Surely," they reason, "if I were nice enough, they would be nice to me—I must have done something wrong." Of course, sometimes it is the case that others treat us badly because we have done something wrong. It is also true that some of the nicest people that have ever lived have been treated brutally, and were even killed, despite their niceness. It certainly wasn't because they did something wrong.

We Can Learn Many Things From Having Healthy Role Models.

- **Do you have a role model (parent, famous personality, Jesus, Martin Luther King Jr., a teacher, etc.)?**
- **Do you think your role model always is (or was) nice to everyone?**

It can be hard to sort out personal problems and weaknesses from those of the people we are in relationships with.

Unhealthy Dependency— being physically or emotionally dependant on something or someone which harms you.

How Can We Know If the Problem Is In Us or Those Around Us?

In marriage and family counseling, therapists often help their clients to identify who "owns" the problem. For example, an alcoholic husband may blame his wife for his drinking, saying that she is a stressful nag. The wife is just as likely to blame her husband's drinking as the reason why she nags. So, who is the owner of the problem? Is the wife responsible for her husband's drinking, her nagging, or both? And how about the husband?

One way to sort this out is to look at the choices people have. Generally, the person with the choice is the owner of a problem. Does the husband have a choice about drinking? Is there any other way that he could deal with his wife's nagging besides drinking? Because there are other choices, such as walking away, talking to a friend, or working on his marriage, the problem of drinking is his. His wife is not to blame for the drinking, because he has other good choices (in fact, better choices).

And, does the wife have to nag? Does she have other choices for how to deal with her husband's drinking? In fact she does. She could separate from her husband or get help from other family members in doing an intervention, for example.

So, the wife would be the owner of the nagging problem and the husband would be the owner of the drinking problem. In improving relationships, each person needs to work on the problems that they own.

Another way to figure out whether it is our behavior that is upsetting others is by seeing how many people *of good character* get upset with us. If most people of good character react favorably, but a few others do not, then we can assume that the few who treat us poorly have some personality defect that we can't take personally. If, on the other hand, most people of good character get upset with us or don't like something about us, then we really need to take a long, hard look at our own behavior. We could be right—a kind of revolutionary or visionary like Martin Luther King Jr. or Gandhi. A therapist is helpful when you are really not sure.

Without judging you, a therapist will help you determine if you need to make some changes or not, for your own good as well as that of others. This is a very valuable service, especially for those of us who grew up in dysfunctional families with a lot of negative or confusing messages. My father, besides being physically abusive, repeatedly told me and other people that I was "mentally retarded" (not a term we use today, but the one he used). I was lucky in my case to be able to find out that I wasn't.

Developmental delays are not hard to check out and the evidence is clear. But what about people who grew up with other messages that are harder to check out? Like, "no good," "ugly," "unlovable," etc.? It can be hard to sort out personal problems and weaknesses from those of the people we are in relationships with. But, a therapist is not family, and therapists see clearly enough to help you to see clearly enough. If you are like the rest of the world (and there is a good chance you are), then you probably have some things about yourself that you need to work on and there are some things about other people that you need to learn how to deal with. Therapy makes sorting that out a lot easier.

There is also work that you can do to contribute to your understanding of where your own unhealthy dependency may have come from. The exercise on the next page will help you to explore that question.

The "People Pleasing" Problem

There are a certain group of people that we can think of as "people pleasers." They always try to do what other people want. Their usual motivation is to keep others from being angry with them. Others recognize their willingness to help and come to depend on them to do many things. They will be called on to volunteer in various capacities, to take phone calls

People Pleasing vs. Altruism: Was Mother Theresa a People Pleaser?

- **Mother Theresa was not a people pleaser.**
- **Her main concern was helping people who really needed it.**
- **She was not concerned about whether her actions pleased people or not.**
- **She was a person of principle (i.e. she was driven by inner values).**

The Heart of the Problem:

- **People who live to please others come to resent others.**

Exercise: Where Did It Come from?

Our fears of rejection can cause us to have poor boundaries, worry constantly about how others are reacting to us, and to frequently seek reassurance. This condition is known as "dependency" and often results in broken relationships.

To gain insight into how you may have become this way, you can write about each experience in your life when you felt abandoned or rejected. Writing them out will help you to objectively process them rather than just emotionally reexperience them.

After you have finished writing, answer these questions:

1. What is it about the other people in your life that contributed to the fear of rejection/abandonment? Did they have personality characteristics that made it more likely that they would reject or abandon you no matter how you were?

2. What behaviors did you have that contributed to the risk of rejection/abandonment?

3. What advice would you give to a person who is in the same situation that you were in before?

4. What advice would you have for people who choose to behave like those who threatened to abandon or reject you?

at any time of the day or night, to lend money, and to give rides whenever needed. All this would be fine if they *really* enjoyed doing these things. Secretly, they often feel like martyrs—sacrificing themselves for the sake of others. They begin to feel worn out and used. Eventually, people pleasers bite off more than they can chew. The number of demands from different people become so numerous that there is literally not enough time in the day to do them. People pleasers do try, however. In addition, people pleasers can't continue to please because they run out of energy and become ill.

Although some people can continue to play the martyr role for a lifetime, most people pleasers will become resentful in much less time. They come to see that although they are putting out a lot of energy and time for the sake of others (mainly family and friends), they are not being treated any better, and they may even be treated worse. When treated worse, they will initially try even harder to please since they believe that if someone doesn't like them, it is their fault. When that doesn't work, they will start to avoid contact with the demanding people. After all, if you don't talk to someone, you don't have to say "yes" to their requests. By avoiding others, or by avoiding talking to others, people pleasers also avoid directly refusing others' requests. Unfortunately for the people pleaser, this strategy of avoidance does not work well because the avoidance leads to increased feelings of guilt. Constantly doing for others creates resentment while avoiding others produces guilt. Psychologists call this an avoidance-avoidance conflict (avoid doing for others and avoid avoiding others). This internal conflict is very stressful. At this point people pleasers enter therapy—if they are lucky. Some develop chronic illnesses, while others turn to drugs, food, alcohol, or affairs to try to soothe their feelings, all the while digging a bigger hole for themselves because they know that what they are doing is wrong and causes harm to others.

How does a therapist help a people pleaser out of this trap of overexertion, resentment, avoidance and guilt? The first step, as mentioned earlier, is to undo the old belief about others with a new truth—*people respond to you according to their*

There is a difference between doing for others so they will love you and doing for others because you care.

personality. The second step is to learn the difference between doing for others so they will love you, and doing for others because you truly care.

You can get started by identifying some of your own unhealthy beliefs about relationships. On the next page is a relationship quiz that will help you to identify such beliefs.

Working to Please Others Loses Respect Rather than Fostering Gratitude

When we are willing to do *whatever* another person wants in order to have them love us, it makes it *less* likely that they will love us. The reason for this is that instead of winning their gratitude, we lose their respect. It's hard to love someone you don't respect. You can only earn respect when you live consistently, according to a set of standards, and when you stand up for what is important to you.

When we see someone doing something that is counter to what they say they believe or which contradicts what they did earlier, we perceive them rightly as hypocrites. This is true even if they are doing it for us. If someone says they value give-and-take in relationships, then just continue to give without taking, we respect them less. We don't see them as nice—we see them as needy, dependent, and passive. When someone acts according to their beliefs and it doesn't benefit us, we may not like it, but our respect for that person increases. A parent who always tried to please his or her child, even when something less pleasing was called for, would get less and less respect from that child. The same is true of friends, partners, siblings, coworkers, and even employers.

Pleasing Others and Loving Them are Two Very Different Things

People pleasers often need a lot of help figuring out what standards to live by. They have too long lived like a feather blown by the wind as they try to meet the demands of various people in their lives. Sometimes they are still trying to "mentally" please parents long gone. Sometimes people try to justify their people pleasing behavior with their religious beliefs

134

Exercise: Relationship Quiz

Circle "True" or "False" for each of the following statements. Check your answers with the answer key that follows on the next page.

1	If someone is upset with me, I must have done something wrong.	True	False
2	People will only love me if I do what they want.	True	False
3	The way to earn respect is by being stern and direct.	True	False
4	If people respect me, they will love me.	True	False
5	I can love someone I don't respect.	True	False
6	Consistently loving people is hard.	True	False
7	Avoiding short term conflict is easier than making changes.	True	False

Answer Key to the Relationship Quiz

1. If someone is upset with me, I must have done something wrong.

False. You <u>may</u> have done something wrong. But the other person <u>may</u> have a problem or personality trait that is causing them to be upset.

2. People will only love me if I do what they want.

False. People will initially enjoy your unconditional giving to them, but they will gradually lose their respect for you and even resent you as they become dependent on you.

3. The way to earn respect is by being stern and direct.

False. Being stern and direct can cause people to disrespect you. The way to earn respect is by consistently living according to your beliefs and by setting healthy boundaries.

4. If people respect me, they will love me.

False. Maybe, maybe not. It will be much easier for them to love you. Most people are repulsed by people they don't respect. We can respect those who hold very different positions from ours, but may choose not to have a relationship with them.

5. I can love someone I don't respect.

True. We can show love to others by doing what is in their best long term interest. It is always the best course of action, even when others don't love us in return. Revenge just leads to a loss of self-respect. Then, we won't be able to love ourselves.

6. Consistently loving people is hard.

True. We will sometimes need to ask forgiveness because, being a human being, we will mess up. We must be determined to love even when we don't feel like it.

7. Avoiding short term conflict is easier than making changes.

False. It is easier <u>for a short time</u>. But, failing to work things out can cause a recurring cycle of broken or empty relationships. It may be less painful not to remove a sliver from your finger in the short term, but in the long term can lead to infection and amputation.

What you have believed until now is a result of your particular experiences. You have the power to choose to believe differently and to create better relationships for yourself.

about loving others. But doing whatever others want is not at all a loving thing.

Loving others means that sometimes we stand up for them, and sometimes we stand up to them. "I love you so damn much that I won't let this happen to our relationship," or "I can't agree with you on that," or "I have to help you stand on your own two feet," turn out to be a lot more loving than "Whatever you say," or "I'll do anything you want—just don't get mad."

For many people, it's a new discovery that pleasing others and loving others are two different things. With this new perspective, they begin to see why others can't respect them. It also helps them learn to say "no" without feeling guilty. Therapists teach assertiveness, not aggressiveness, and not passivity. Assertiveness is the best foundation for taking care of yourself, others, and your relationships with others.

Besides learning how to earn respect, the people pleaser needs to learn what real caring or loving will mean with the people who are in their lives now. They need new behavior to replace dependent, passive, passive aggressive, or resentment building behaviors. Real caring will mean doing for others what is in their best interest, regardless of what that person desires. For example, to give an alcoholic a drink is not a caring thing, no matter how much the drink may be welcomed. Driving the alcoholic to the alcohol rehab program, on the other hand, may not be welcomed, but is very caring. Parents don't give candy to their children just before dinner even if it would make their children happy. They know that it is healthier for their children to wait and eat dinner. The children may not be happy about not getting the candy, but their respect for the parent grows and the child benefits. Agreeing to have no friends in order to help your partner feel secure would damage your relationship, even if it quieted your partner's jealousy. Choosing between making a person temporarily happy (or avoiding conflict) and doing what is best for the other person is usually the hardest step for the people pleaser to make. It is an essential step, however, to having healthy relationships and a happier life—free from irrational guilt.

Loving Others:

- **Doing what is best for them,**
- **Even if they don't like it.**

137

Learning New Ways to Make Decisions Means Better Decisions and Fewer Problems

Often the people pleaser will ask, "How can I know what is the best thing to do at the time I am asked or expected to do something?" That is, they want to know when they should say "yes" to someone's request. As the therapist helps them to learn, the key to making good decisions is to look at the long-term consequences of the decisions. A decision is bad if it has bad long-term consequences. A long term relationship will be doomed by behaviors which would be detrimental in the long term, even if they would avoid short term conflict. Giving in to friends, spouses, children, in-laws, and others, may be toxic to our relationships in the long-term.

Resentment Is a Self-Inflicted Injury

We create our own resentment when we do for others what we don't want to do, or when we expect some kind of payment although payment was not promised. Expectations of gratitude or obligation change our positive expectations to feelings of resentment when the person receiving our help is not grateful and does not reciprocate in kind. When we then continue to do things that make us resentful, we emotionally distance ourselves more and more from the other person. Doing things that make us feel resentful is a hateful, not helpful, thing to do because over time it destroys our relationships. Many a people pleaser has had a spouse divorce them or has left their partner for another. This has resulted because of the distance created by people pleasers trying to create a loving reciprocation in their partners. "I did everything to make him happy, but he never appreciated it. Finally, I couldn't take it anymore and had to get out." Deciding for the long term initially increases short term conflict, but reduces long term conflict, so people can grow closer. Respect and love, not pleasing and expecting, are the key components of a long-term, healthy relationship.

Other People Often Don't Welcome Our Healthy Changes

For a people pleaser, making these sorts of changes is a

The key to making good decisions is to look at the long-term consequences of the decisions.

When We Stop Over-Pleasing People, They Will Become Angry

- The anger response is a normal part of adjustment.
- We can tolerate it.
- We can learn to deal with it.
- It will stop resentment.
- It will lead to better relationships.

138

challenge because of the anger that other people will have when they are no longer freely benefitting from the people pleaser. Very healthy people will react very favorably to the change, but the people pleaser usually doesn't have such people in his or her life. The people she has formed relationships with usually match her willingness to give by their willingness to receive. The people pleaser's friends and family don't care what the therapist says and will try to convince the people pleaser to quit therapy. They will point out that these new changes are bringing more conflict into their relationships and that they don't like it. The people pleaser needs to be meeting with her therapist often at this point, to get support and to repeatedly come back to the reason for making the changes.

Losing People Who are Not Real Friends Is Not a Big Loss

Making this kind of change without the help of a therapist may be almost impossible for a people pleaser. The therapist will also normalize the conflict by predicting it and by telling the client to expect it. Temporary increased conflict is actually a sign of improvement and positive change. Although others will initially be angry (as a child may tantrum for not getting candy just before dinner—especially if she is used to getting her way), *in time* their respect will grow and so will the opportunity for a healthy loving relationship. The people pleaser will discover that not only can people get by without her help, but that she is less stressed and enjoys being with other people more. After her family and friends readjust to her, she will be closer to them because her resentment will be gone. Those who were merely using her to get what they could will reduce and stop their contact with her, allowing her to spend her time with people who truly care about her.

Knowing Is Quick, Becoming Takes Time

This process may sound easy, but can take many months of therapy with a skilled therapist. The people pleaser needs to stay in therapy and continue to receive support while she is criticized and rejected by those who are using her. Depending on how committed she has been to sacrificing herself for

The people pleaser needs to stay in therapy and continue to receive support while she is criticized and rejected by those who are using her. Depending on how committed she has been to sacrificing herself for others, there may be quite a few such people.

others, there may be quite a few such people.

This need for support through change is true for all types of therapy. When we change, we must endure the adjustment process of others in our lives. For example, the addict often loses his group of addicted friends when he recovers, until he can make healthier friends. The loss of the original friends is not an indication that it was wrong to overcome the addiction. It is simply an indication of the unhealthiness of the original group of friends. Other people, already in the alcoholic's life, will become friendlier, but not until they are sure the alcoholic has changed. Support from the therapist is necessary to help clients bridge this difficult time and be patient with others during this process.

So too, many people pleasers lose friends and even family as they become healthier. This is a difficult event which creates a kind of psychological pressure for the people pleaser to return to his old and unhealthy ways. Given the choice, would you rather remain passive and resentful in order to keep someone in a relationship with you? Or, would you rather be more assertive and feel more at ease at the risk of losing some relationships in your life? This turns out to be a very hard question for most people and it is not unusual for a person to decide to remain unhealthy in order to keep their present relationships the same (alcoholic friends, physically abusive husbands, critical parents, ungrateful children, etc.). Perhaps you have seen people in such relationships and wondered why they stay in them and put up with them. Some people would rather have abusive and ungrateful friends and family than to be alone. They don't see the possibility of different ways of relating or the possibility of good relationships with other people. When you consider this, it becomes apparent why therapists often include making new and healthier friends in their clients' goals. Having new and healthy friends makes it easier to sustain new, healthy behavior. It also makes losing unhealthy friends easier.

Fortunately, it is also true that many dependent, addicted, abusive, and/or critical partners decide to get help themselves when their significant other or friend gets healthy. After all,

Do You Have a Fear Motivation or a Success Motivation?

- **Some people are motivated by fear to sacrifice long term happiness to keep what they have.**
- **Others are motivated to sacrifice in the short-term in order to get something that they don't have.**

140

they risk losing the relationship if *they* don't change. It must be remembered that other people who need to adjust have not been in counseling, do not yet know how to change, and still fear change. When we become healthy, we must be patient and supportive of others who are just beginning this process (and usually without the help of a therapist).

When we become healthier, we create motivation for those we have relationships with to become healthier. That's why the most powerful way to change a relationship for the better is always to work on yourself.

Case Example: Mary

Mary was a very kind and giving woman. Everyone who knew her would remark how thoughtful and helpful she was. Many people in her church could give examples of how she called on them when they were sick, asked about things that other people had forgotten, and how they could always count on her.

Mary's children were involved in many activities after school and on the weekends. She always took them where they needed to go no matter how busy she was and even if her husband was available. She had tried asking him before for more help, but he had gotten angry, so she did as much as she could by herself to avoid upsetting him.

When other people asked Mary how she was, she would always tell them she was fine even if she was very stressed and tired. She never wanted to "bother" other people with her problems. She also noticed that people tended to call her only when they wanted something and never just to talk. People treated her nicely when they wanted something, otherwise they did not talk to her at all. Even her family members seemed to only come to her when they wanted something.

Mary was becoming more stressed and burned out. She was overcommitted to other people and had no time for herself. She couldn't get the rest she needed because of all the things she "had

She had tried asking him before for help, but he had gotten angry, so she did as much as she could by herself to avoid upsetting him.

to" do. More and more she felt like she was doing for others and no one was doing for her. She began to find reasons not to go to church, and to avoid answering the phone. She felt like little more than a servant for her family (including her parents and in-laws) and she was becoming more and more emotionally distant from them. She felt trapped and stretched thin.

Mary went to counseling to deal with her stress. She thought that if she were less stressed, then she could enjoy her family more and be more helpful for others instead of "selfishly" thinking about her own problems. She felt a victim of everyone's demands and didn't think she could continue to cope although she didn't know what that would mean, exactly. She had some fleeting thoughts about divorcing or running away, but knew she would never do it. Still, something had to be done.

Mary found me to be a sympathetic and caring listener—something she got little of from other people. I helped Mary to consider things she never had before like whether doing so much for others was really in their best interest and hers. I also helped her to consider why other people, who did not do so much for others, were less stressed and had good relationships. In fact, even better than hers. Mary did find that really puzzling.

Mary started to see that some of the beliefs she held for years were not actually true. Being extra nice to others brought stress, not closeness.

Mary started to see that some of the beliefs she held for years were not actually true. Being extra nice to others brought stress, not closeness. She also began to see that it was her beliefs, actions, and expectations that were stressing her and not other people's demands. She had trained others to depend on her and had raised her children to treat her like a servant They were only doing what she had taught them to do.

Mary learned to take little steps toward saying "no" to some people who were not likely to be so upset with her. The first time she turned down a church committee member's request to bake cookies was hard for her, but she found that someone else made the cookies and that no one was upset at her about it. She felt a little freedom and the ability to start to control her life just from this one action. This also encouraged her to continue her counseling.

As Mary's counselor, I taught her to focus on relationships rather than reactions. She learned that although others may initially be upset with her, that if she just continued to sacrifice for them, she would cheat both herself and the other person out of a relationship with her. Had she not started to say "no" to some church requests, for example, she would have very soon quit going to church altogether. That would have hurt her relationship with church members far more than saying "no" to a few requests.

As Mary and I both predicted, her husband became irritable with her as she learned to share the job of parenting with him. But she knew that either she had to face his irritability or end up losing her relationship with him altogether as she grew to despise him. She had already traveled part of the way down that road. Mary knew that his irritability was part of his adjustment, a positive adjustment, that gave her marriage a chance. Her children also had some initial irritability. I was proud of her new thinking and behaviors and encouraged her. She needed that support as she continued to make changes while experiencing pressure from her family to be her "old" self.

Mary also made some new friends who did not ask things of her, but who wanted to do things with her. Sometimes they even did things for her! Mary was discovering a whole different kind of relationship and that she didn't need to continually do for others in order for them to like her. In fact, those she continually did things for liked her less than her new friends.

Mary's beliefs about needing to please others in order to get their affection changed. Her stress level decreased and she enjoyed her family more—after they got used to doing some things for themselves. She lost some people she had considered friends but told me that she realized that they had never really been her friends and that she didn't need to worry about them. She decided that it was ok for her in-laws to be dissatisfied with her new "share the responsibility" behaviors because she wasn't married to them. If they wanted to be her husband's servant, they were welcome to, but that was not her job.

Mary was discovering that she didn't need to continually do for others in order for them to like her.

Mary continued to enjoy doing things for people, but only when she chose to and because she wanted to. Like many clients, her biggest regret was not entering counseling earlier.

———

Summary

Working with your counselor is bound to help you see the world, and yourself, in some new ways. The benefit of that is that you will have new options you can select for better outcomes in your life. What you have believed until now is a result of your particular experiences. With a little learning and self understanding you will have the power to choose to believe differently and to create better relationships for yourself.

CHAPTER TEN

10. USING THE PAST TO MOVE FORWARD

One thing that Hollywood seems to have gotten right about therapists is therapist's interest in the past. Our past makes sense of who we are now. It answers the question, "How did I get this way?" Understanding exactly how we came to be the way that we are now helps us to feel less crazy. After all, the more we can see our problems, our real problems, the less crazy we will really be.

"There But for the Grace of God, Go I"

How does a therapist sit across from someone who has messed up their life and possibly someone else's without becoming judgmental? By realizing the truth that however the client is, or what he or she has done, the therapist may have done even worse given the same background or experiences. One possible supportive and honest statement a therapist can tell his client is, "If I grew up in the same environment as you and was faced with all the same problems that you had, I might have even more problems than you. In light of all that you have been through, you may be doing very well." When your therapist says such things to you, it is not just to help you feel better. Your therapist is telling you that he is sensitive to what you have been through, does not blame you for your problems, and is able to see that you have some strengths that you may not see yet. Although things may seem bad, you may have done better than most people would because of your strengths. Many therapists have troubled pasts of their own that they have worked through in their own counseling. They know how easy

Why Look Into Our Past?:

- It helps us to understand how our problems developed.
- It helps us to see patterns which are continuing to affect us in the present.
- It helps us to see the influence other people have had on us, and perhaps continue to have.
- It helps us to see our strengths, and how we overcame our difficulties.
- It helps us to make meaning of how we came to be the way we are, so we feel less crazy.

Although you may have been hurt in the past by your parents, your peers, or others, it is not necessary that you continue to hurt because of them.

it is to mess up, how hard it can be to forgive yourself (and others), and how hard it can be to like the person you see in the mirror.

Although you may have been hurt in the past by your parents, your peers, or others, it is not necessary that you continue to hurt because of them. That old saying about words never hurting is wrong—words do hurt and can continue to hurt for years. Verbal abuse is as real as physical abuse and can do as much or more damage. People who have been physically abused are usually suffering from the effects of both. Even if you were not abused, old messages may be getting in the way of your progress.

The avoidance of pain can influence the choices you make. Just as we can be burned by a hot stove, we can also learn to avoid stoves altogether. The exercise on the next page will help you to become aware of how pain, and the avoidance of pain, shapes your decisions and the results you are getting in life.

The Work of Letting Go

In order to move forward with your life goals, it is often necessary to close the open wounds from the past. Depending on the style of therapy that your therapist uses, this work can come in many forms, but essentially the goals are the same. Sometimes the bulk of work in therapy consists in healing the old wounds. This is often true for victims of abuse and for people suffering from other unresolved past trauma. Sometimes the open wound is unresolved grief from the loss of someone very important—even if that loss occurred long ago. There is no statute of limitations on pain. Time does not heal all wounds.

Some people seem to go through a natural grieving process and move on with their life while others continue to grieve (or fail to grieve) for years. Unresolved grief can make emotional and physical problems worse, damage or destroy relationships, and take energy and pleasure away from everything a person does. People with unresolved grief may not walk around in pain, but they find it very hard to find joy in anything.

Exercise: The Role of Pain in My Life

Pain is supposed to teach us important lessons, like not to touch a hot stove. But, sometimes we learn the wrong lesson—that stoves are bad, dangerous, or scary. So it is that many people come to fear relationships, taking reasonable risks, and even being positive. "I better not get my hopes up...," "I better not try...," "I better not say anything...," etc. These beliefs just create another kind of pain.

Complete the following statements:

1. I am particularly sensitive to ... (criticism, rejection, failure, loud noises, being alone, etc.)

2. Because of that, I avoid ... (meeting new people, eye contact, leaving my house, letting myself feel happy, speaking up when things bother me, etc.)

3. I have been hurt in this area in the past by ... (e.g., a critical teacher, boyfriend, mom, financial problems, etc.)

4. Although I am trying to protect myself, my avoidance is hurting me because ... (e.g., I don't have friends, I'm not close to my partner, I'm living below my potential, my chances for many desires are passing me by, etc.)

5. This makes me feel (lonely, sad, scared, regretful, etc.)

6. If I didn't have that painful experience in the past, I would (meet new people, be outgoing, speak my mind, try new things, etc.)

7. Rather than avoiding or being scared, I can learn (how to handle rejection, how to take small risks, how to be assertive and get respect, etc.)

8. Learning to do that will help me to (not be lonely, have a close relationship, find a new job, do things that I enjoy, etc.)

9. If I don't learn, but just continue to live according to my fears, later I will regret (not having had friends, wasting my life in a meaningless job, having been too afraid to either improve my relationship or get out of it, etc.)

10. The part of this that I most need my therapist to help me with is ...

Others may have hurt you in the past, but you are the only one who can keep those wounds open. Overcoming them will allow you to be successful in more areas that are important to you, and to stop being a victim. Our lives should not give more power to the actions of those who have hurt us.

Therapists know the importance of resolving grief and how to help you with that.

It is also possible that you were the one who did the harm to someone else and that you need to move on. On the next page is an exercise to help you to deal with guilt in a productive way.

Trauma, victimization, and guilt are all products of the past, but we feel their effects in the present. Although we cannot change the past, we can change its impact on our current life and our future.

Digging Up the Past Is Temporarily Painful

What many people don't realize when they are going through the process of healing past wounds is that their pain will initially *increase*. People who need help the most seem to sense that getting into the old issues is going to dredge up a lot of pain from the past, and because of that, seek to avoid the counseling process altogether. Trying to avoid the pain of grieving just spreads it out over our lifetime, just as a film of dirt covers a shiny car.

Perhaps the worst situation is someone who begins the process of healing the old hurts, but because of the increase in pain, drops out of therapy. People who do this are worse off than before they entered therapy. It is like quitting in the middle of a dental procedure. After the dentist has drilled the tooth, but before the filling can be put in place, the patient runs out of the office. Not only would the person still have a tooth problem, but they would have a big open hole in their tooth that they did not have before. Life would become even more difficult and the patient would find it hard to focus on anything except their tooth pain. Until the patient returns to the dentist to complete the treatment (getting a filling), the pain would continue. Digging up the pain from your past and then quitting counseling before you get through and past the pain would be like that.

Often people consider medical treatment to be necessary regardless of how much pain is caused by treatment. They

Example: Coping with Rational Guilt

Therapists distinguish between rational and irrational guilt. *Irrational guilt* comes when we *feel* responsible, but actually were <u>not</u> the direct or indirect cause of others suffering. *Rational guilt* comes when we have done wrong and we need to make amends. Rational guilt is deserved.

How to Deal with Rational Guilt

1. If it will not be harmful to the person(s) you hurt, approach them with your desire to make restitution.

2. Make restitution and ask for forgiveness.

3. Forgive yourself, whether they forgive you or not.

"What if restitution is not possible because the person can't be contacted, is dead, etc.?"

1. Make a proxy restitution to someone else who has similarly been hurt. For example, by giving to or working for a church or organization, helping with a project at the woman's shelter, etc. You must decide, concretely, what restitution would be fair.

   a. For example, if you have abused someone, they may not want you to approach them. But, you can help out other abuse victims by work, donations, advocacy, etc. You will, in effect, be making restitution for someone else. And that will help.

2. Forgive yourself by reminding yourself that your debt is paid. Regret is good, but forgiving yourself means that you are no longer going to withhold happiness, or opportunity from yourself.

"Wouldn't it be fair if I just continued to punish myself?"

1. Although self punishment may help to temporarily relieve your guilt feelings, it is not "fair" because it in no way makes restitution. Harming yourself never helps another.

know that not to have the treatment would be worse and would make it more difficult for them to continue to care for themselves and for others. I have had six surgeries and not because of my love of doctors or because I wanted to be the unconscious center of attention in an operating room. Although I knew that recovery from the surgery would be worse than the surgery itself, I had them because of my desire for a better future with a body that allowed me to function as well as possible. I may not be in great shape compared to someone with a naturally healthy body, but still I want to be the best that I can. If I have to face some temporary pain to do that, then so be it. Let's have done with it.

Unfortunately, many people don't consider that failing to get counseling for an emotional problem also risks their health and ability to care for themselves and others. People heal from medical treatment. People also heal from therapy. To avoid either of these treatments, when they are needed to heal a chronic condition, is unwise.

Your Openness will Help the Process Along

One thing that you can do to help with the healing process is to fully cooperate with your therapist. Experienced therapists tend to be very good at knowing what past areas to probe because they see the same patterns of problem causation in many of the people they treat. Therapists may ask directly about painful experiences that you have had in the past. The natural temptation that people have is to lie to their therapist in order to present a good image or to avoid facing a problem.

When a therapist sees that you have a strong emotional reaction to something in the present, it is a good guess that you have had similar difficult experiences in the past. When your therapist asks you about them, admit them. If the therapist does not ask, then bring them up. For example, "When my boss criticizes me, I get scared. That happened to me in my old job, too. Come to think of it, I used to get scared when my dad criticized me as a kid too." You may not think of the past occurrences right away, but if you remember them some time later in the session, feel free to bring them up then. This kind

When a therapist sees that you have a strong emotional reaction to something in the present, it is a good guess that you have had similar difficult experiences in the past.

150

of introspective detective work will help you to make mental connections. The mental connections will help you (and your therapist) to make more sense out of your life. It is not enough just to think of these connections. You need to say them out loud. The additional mental processing that occurs when you say things aloud accomplishes much more than thinking alone does. And the more you say these things aloud, the easier it becomes.

A Way to Decrease the Level of Pain So that Therapy Is More Tolerable and So that You Still Like Your Therapist

Pain occurs when you talk about painful past events—especially when you talk about them for the first time, or when you talk about several past events in a short period of time. If working through old memories seems too much for you to bear, stay on the same painful topic for a longer period of time before moving on to another painful topic. The more time you spend on a single painful topic, the easier it will become—hard at first, but then easier. I have had many injections and blood tests in my life. The way that I was able to tolerate that is I got them one at a time (usually). One time a nurse stabbed me five times trying to hit my vein. I still think it's a wise decision for that nurse to stay out of my path. What I learned from that is to not go beyond my limit. Nurses get one shot at my veins, not two, not three, not four, and not five. I am in control of that. You are also in control of how many difficult things you want to talk about at one time. Regulating that for yourself will help your therapy to go a lot better (and you won't mind running into your therapist in the grocery store).

Putting Desensitization to Good Use

Research has shown that the more we are exposed to a traumatic event, in fact or in thought, the more desensitized we become to the event. Many teens today happily gobble popcorn as they watch people being beheaded and cut apart with chainsaws at the movie theater. The more they see that kind of stuff, the less they are bothered by it. Someone in their 50's or older is much more likely to be bothered by it since they

Is Your Pain Too Much To Deal With?:

- **Break it down into separate issues.**
- **Only deal with one of those issues at a time.**
- **Don't move on to a new issue until you have fully taken care of the last one.**
- **Many small fires are easier to put out than one big one.**

have had less exposure to it. When today's teens hit nursing home age, they will be showing chainsaw massacre movies in the nursing homes. "Why don't you relax grandma, and watch this nice old movie about chopping people up in the woods?" Although it makes me shiver, this process of desensitization not only accounts for the increasing grotesqueness of the media (in order to get the same emotional response), but it also offers clues about how to take the pain out of painful memories.

One way to think about a painful memory is as a mini horror movie that you see in your head. Each time you "see" it, it brings back all those bad feelings that you had when you first experienced it, so you try not to think about it. When you try not to think about it, what you actually do is to continue to think about it, but less frequently. That is, you can put it out of your mind for awhile, until something reminds you of it. These reminders of bad memories are called "triggers" because they trigger the bad memories. Avoiding triggers is hard because the smallest thing associated with the memory can act as a trigger. If it was a cloudy day when you had the traumatic experience, then another cloudy day could trigger the memory.

Learning from the Treatment of Trauma Survivors

One method to help people with post traumatic stress disorder (PTSD) is to ask them to talk repeatedly in detail about their experiences. For example, a person may have witnessed a horrible traffic accident. The therapist will have the person talk about what they experienced—the sights, sounds, smells, feelings, etc. The first time the person talks about it will be the most difficult and stressful. When the client is done telling about it, the therapist then has the client tell about it again immediately after the first time—again with the sights, sounds, smells, feelings, etc. What the client discovers, to his or her amazement, is that the second time he tells it isn't as hard as the first time. It is still stressful, but less so than the first telling. The therapist may have the client schedule 10 sessions in which he does nothing but repeatedly tell about the incident in detail. By the time the person gets to session five, he is usually starting to get bored (rather than upset) while talking about the incident (what a change in feelings!). By the

> *Reminders of bad memories are called "triggers" because they trigger the bad memories. A trigger can be literally anything—a key ring, a belt, a certain kind of man's voice, a smell, or even a cloud.*

time he completes session 10, he is completely desensitized to the memory. Ten sessions to get over a bad memory is not much compared to the years that people can torture themselves trying to suppress a memory. This kind of therapy for painful memories is initially very difficult, but in a relatively short time produces lasting relief. I have used this procedure with post combat marines, police officers, and other emergency responders, as well as family members who have witnessed suicides and severe abuse. These methods work. No one has to be stuck with their trauma.

Your memories may not evoke the same kind of strong response as a person suffering from PTSD, but the same principle will work. By repeatedly telling your therapist in detail about the painful events, you will desensitize yourself to the memories of the events. In post-traumatic stress work, one memory is desensitized at a time so as not to overwhelm the client. Sometimes clients think that they continually need to be telling something new to their therapist. There often is a reluctance to rehash the same material. As you can see from this example, however, it may be very important for you to tell your therapist the same thing every week until it is no longer an issue for you. You might spend two months talking about the same thing every week, but then, suddenly be ready to move on.

To move on to something else before the pain is resolved can open wounds without closing them. Too fast a pace will either make you feel overwhelmed from opening so many wounds, or make you feel frustrated because you only feel worse with little sign of improvement. Pace and repetition are important aspects of counseling. That is true for every style of therapy.

I Feel Good, I Feel Good, I Feel Bad (Two Steps Forward and One Back)

Therapy goals work the same as other goals in your life. You need to finish one before you move on to the next or else risk not reaching any. No pain, no gain, is as true in therapy as anywhere else. Therapy is a process of moving two steps

Self-Help with Past Trauma

- **One way to do this kind of post traumatic stress desensitization is to repeatedly write about what happened to you.**
- **It is more effective to write this out with a pen or pencil than to use a computer.**

Some Past Trauma is So Painful that a Person will Emotionally Fall Apart (decompensate) with Desensitization Work

- **The best thing you can do for such people is to help them to get professional care, without trying to open up the old wound yourself.**

Resist the urge to move on before you have completely processed a painful memory. By doing so, you will improve the long term effectiveness of counseling and reduce relapse.

forward and one step back. Knowing that the one step back is an essential part of the process can help you not to get discouraged with your therapy. When you find yourself taking one step back, be encouraged that you are making progress and that the next two steps will be forward (on average). When you take one step back, your therapist is not disappointed in you—it happens in every successful therapy. When you watch an infant just beginning to walk and she falls on her bottom, you don't shake your head, think "What a klutz" and figure the infant is never going to learn to walk. You know that falling is part of the process of learning. Skiing works almost the same way. So does singing, public speaking, teaching, learning to read, and therapy (as well as a few other things). We must be prepared for initial failure, stress, and pain when seeking to become more than we are. This knowledge is being lost in our society and is resulting in a discouraged, avoidant generation that seeks easy, short-term solutions. To fear pain and difficulty is to fear success and change. We don't learn much from failing, but failing is part of learning.

Have Realistic Expectations

You can increase the successfulness of your counseling by expecting increased short-term struggles and by hanging in there until you achieve the goals you set out to achieve. Your counselor will never ridicule you, blame you, or shame you about your past. Take advantage of this helping relationship by being open and honest about your past. Resist the urge to move on before you have completely processed a painful memory. By doing so, you will improve the long term effectiveness of counseling and reduce relapse.

Case Example—William

William was a young, 20 year old marine who was identified as needing counseling when he was having difficulty readjusting to his return to the United States following an overseas deployment. His girlfriend described him as very moody and irritable at times while at other times he seemed to be shut down and unaware of what was going on around him.

In counseling, William was hesitant to talk about what was going on in his thinking when he was "out of it." I was able to help William understand that what was happening to him was his mind's attempt to cope with something that was very traumatic. Although he was no longer exposed to the same traumatic event in real life, he was repeatedly being exposed to it in his thinking and in his dreams. I helped William to see that his irritability was not an indication that he was crazy or a bad person, but that it was understandable given what he had gone through.

I also helped William to see that although he did not want counseling, his military career, relationship, and happiness were in jeopardy unless he did work in counseling. I worked within William's value system and helped him to see that a marine's strength comes from being part of the team and not from suffering alone and in silence.

William decided that he did want to get on with life and leave his combat memories in the past where they belonged. At first he tested me by talking about some graphic things he experienced in combat, but found that none of this was new to me and that I was not shocked or disturbed by it. Because I was comfortable even hearing about graphic things, William was more comfortable and somewhat relieved in being able to talk about his experiences (it should be noted that I was accustomed to working with marines and combat imagery).

After William had talked about a particularly harrowing experience in which he had watched a friend die in an automobile fire, I asked him how he was feeling and how hard it was to talk about that. It was extremely hard for William and although he remained in control (an important consideration for this type of counseling), it made him feel sick to talk about it.

I gave William a lot of credit for the strength he was showing in talking about it and asked him to continue to be strong by talking about the experience again, from the beginning, and in as much detail—just as though I had not heard about it already.

William's irritability was not an indication that he was crazy or a bad person. It was understandable given what he had gone through.

William learned that he didn't need to forget his memories (which is impossible), but that he could take the pain out of them.

William was reluctant to retell about the incident, given how he was feeling. After the second telling, however, he was surprised to discover that it was much easier to talk about it the second time and that he didn't feel as sick. I used this experience of immediate, detailed retelling, to teach William how memory desensitization works. William learned that he didn't need to forget his memories (which is impossible), but that he could take the pain out of them. Then he wouldn't need to spend a lot of energy avoiding them or dreaming about them. Just like many other things that had happened in the past, the memories didn't have to intrude on his current life, such as his relationship with his girlfriend.

Over the next 10 sessions, he continued to tell and retell in detail about what he had experienced in his deployment. William became less irritable at home, drank less, and had fewer bad dreams, although he still had some. He was well on his way to recovery and grateful for my experience and expertise in treating trauma survivors.

———

William was having difficulty coping with his painful memories. He had thought that nothing could be done about them since the events happened in the past. What he learned is that the events are in the past, but the memories are really thoughts that we are having in the present. He learned that although we can't change the past, we can change the way we remember it, and so be able to move forward again—both for the sake of ourselves and our loved ones.

On the next page is an exercise to help you examine whether you are unnecessarily burdening yourself by not dealing with your memories of the past.

Exercise: Coping with Painful Memories

Part I: Are my memories affecting my happiness or effectiveness?

I often think about things in the past that I would rather not remember.	True	False
I have recurrent bad dreams about past events.	True	False
I am not as happy as I could be because of what has happened to me.	True	False
There are some people that I will never be able to forgive.	True	False
I have fantasies of revenge.	True	False
I have difficulty paying attention because of thoughts about the past.	True	False

Part II: How effectively am I healing myself from these memories?

I just try to put them out of my mind.		
I drink, smoke, eat, or use drugs to feel better or calm myself.	True	False
I sleep to avoid thinking about things that happened to me.	True	False
I constantly keep busy, and never relax, so that I don't need to remember.	True	False
I have fully grieved the losses of past events.	True	False
I have learned how to make what happened less personal.	True	False
I have taken responsibility for my current emotions.	True	False
I have learned how to change my feelings by using relaxation techniques.	True	False
I have given up expecting others to make-up, or un-do for a past event.	True	False
I have used memory desensitization techniques with my therapist.	True	False
I have found positive meaning from my past experiences.	True	False

Healing memories does not involve forgetting the past—that is not possible. It involves taking the pain out of them (although they are still unpleasant to remember), and being set free from them. Dealing with painful memories is like having a heavy pack taken off of your back. You will feel lighter and freer. Don't hesitate to bring up painful memories with your therapist. There is a lot that can be done about them.

Summary

Never assume that because you don't think there is anything that can be done about a past experience, that there is actually nothing that can be done about it. Although the actual event is in the past and cannot be changed, the "pain" of painful memories is in the present. Psychologists and counselors are trained to help you modify your current thinking so that you don't need to continually recreate the pain of a past experience.

CHAPTER ELEVEN

11. PSCHOTHERAPY IS JUST ONE PART OF YOUR ANSWER

Some people pin all their hopes for their happiness or their relationships on the effectiveness of psychotherapy. While psychotherapy has helped a lot of people to become happier and to improve their relationships, it is not essential for success. Therapy is at best a tool and therapists are advisors. They will be helpful to the extent that you need them and use them, for the areas in which they have expertise. There will still be other parts of your life which will require work, and other people from whom you will need help.

If therapy is like a tool, then you are like the carpenter who uses the tool. Many people who work in therapy do not make good progress because they are not active participants. They go to their therapy sessions, but don't work on themselves during the time in between sessions. That's like a carpenter expecting the tools to do the work. "I think I'll just sit back and wait for my tools to build this house." Pretty ridiculous picture, isn't it? No tool ever built a house. And, no therapist ever fixed someone's life for them.

On the other hand, it is very hard to build a house without tools. When we use just the right tool for the situation, our work is easier and we can make progress faster. If the tool breaks or doesn't quite do the job, then we need to get a new one, a different one, or an additional one. Therapy, being just a tool, will not help you with every situation. You need to regularly evaluate the effectiveness of therapy and your therapist. If things are not quite going the way you would like

Carpenters Have Many Tools With Which to Make Things.

- **Likewise, your therapy is only one of the "tools" you need to make your life the way you want it to be.**
- **In therapy, you will do most of the work, using your therapist as a guide and resource.**

Just as the carpenter needs a plan to build a house, you need to have a plan to build a good life. You must see with your mind's eye the person that you want to become.

them to, there are still other possibilities for improvement and change.

Therapy Is Not Your Last Hope

Clients who tell themselves that therapy is their last hope really don't understand that therapy is just a tool. It's much like a carpenter saying, "If this hammer doesn't work, then there is no way I can build a house." If a carpenter has a bad hammer, he will get a new one. If he lacks the skills necessary to complete the house, he will learn those skills and try again. He would be stuck only as long as it took for him to figure out what he needed and to get that. If your therapy wasn't very helpful for some reason, you could get another therapist or try a different approach such as medical treatment, natural healing methods, or coaching.

Even if your therapist is very helpful, therapy may not be all that you need to achieve your goals. Of course a carpenter doesn't only use a hammer to build a house. Cutting through boards with a hammer or installing wiring with a hammer is just not going to work. Getting a better hammer is not a solution to this either. A carpenter needs other tools in addition to a hammer to build a house. A saw, a level, and some nails would be a good start. Most importantly, a carpenter needs to have a plan that he can follow while using the tools. He can't just keep nailing boards together until it looks like a house. The finished product must already be in his mind's eye. He has a clear idea of what he intends to build from the beginning of the job.

A Haphazard Approach Is Only Effective by Accident

Just as the carpenter needs a plan to build a house, you need to have a plan to build a good life. You must see with your mind's eye the person that you want to become. To have a plan, you must know what you want from life. When you have such a plan, you can see how the counselor fits into the picture and that the counselor is only one important step along the way. Your plan might include such things as getting out of debt, and getting more job training, as well as overcoming your depression. These three things complement each other nicely, but you can't get them all from your therapist. Your therapist would be most helpful with the overcoming depression part.

Once you know what you want, you can begin to assemble the knowledge and list the skills that you will need in order to have a good life or to reach your life goals. If, for example, you want to be financially secure, you could buy a book on money management. That would be one way to gather information. Or, you could take a seminar on money management. You could hire someone to manage your money for you (if you could afford it), or you could hire a consultant to advise you on how to manage your money. Each of these options has associated costs and benefits. Some people learn a lot from books, while others benefit more from a one on one approach. You are free to use as many or as few of these tools as you like. We must all start somewhere, so start wherever you can. If your source of knowledge is good, it should guide you toward more steps that you can take. Those steps will then help you to get a little further, and so on, until you reach your goal. No one needs to figure it all out at once.

Have a Reasonable Timetable for Success

No matter which source of help you choose, unless your goal is very simple, you will not be successful right away. Building anything worthwhile takes time. You will be able to monitor your progress by comparing where you are to where you were when you started (always plan forward but compare backward).

For the goals you have which are related to mental health or relationships, you have similar options—buy a book, take a course, attend a seminar or retreat, or hire a consultant (a therapist or coach). Besides this, there are many lifestyle changes that you could make that will help your mental health or relational goals. Some examples of such changes are getting a new or different job, making new friends, joining a gym, or going on a spiritual retreat.

Some Resources to Consider:

- **Self-help books**
- **Therapists**
- **Spiritual Retreats**
- **Marriage Retreats**
- **Life or Relationship Coach**
- **Seminars**
- **Clergy (Pastoral Counseling)**

The Internet Has Many Kinds of Information of Various Quality:

- **Make sure the person you are taking advice from on the internet is qualified to give it.**
- **Avoid personal advice from forums and "answer" sites. Although it may be well meant and sincere, it could actually end up harming you or your relationships.**
- **Remember, what works for one person or relationship won't necessarily work for another.**
- **Everyone is different, which is why therapists gather information from you over two or three sessions before they really start to help you know what to do.**

Never depend on a therapist, a partner, or anyone, to do the work to make you happy or successful.

Measure Success by Progress, Not by Effort

As helpful as therapy is, it is but one tool among many. To really enhance your life, you will need to use several tools. To measure the usefulness of any method, you need to compare your progress with that method against your starting point. Simply doing something new does not indicate progress—even if you have put a lot of work into it. It is possible to read 20 books on a subject without making any progress on it. To measure success by the number of books you have read or the number of therapy sessions you have attended makes no sense. While success is related to work, it is not true that hard work alone will get you what you want. The work you do must actually move you toward your goals, no matter how important it seems or how good it feels. Focused approaches, rather than general ones, tend to result in the most progress. Trying to improve ourselves in every way or all at once seldom results in any lasting improvement at all.

No One Can Do It for You

Even when you decide on counseling, your progress will be related more to what *you* do in therapy (and between therapy sessions) than to what the therapist says or does. Never depend on a therapist, a partner, or anyone, to do the work to make you happy or successful. With a dentist, we can sit back and let the dentist do the work. But sitting back and letting the therapist work is no more helpful than it would be in a marriage. Can you imagine someone thinking, "Well, I'm married now, so I can just take it easy and let my spouse make me happy?" Anyone who believes that needs more than therapy—they need to get in touch with reality.

Happiness and success at anything requires our participation. Spending 45 minutes a week talking to a therapist will not change your life. Likewise, buying and reading a stack of self-help books will not change your life. Going to seminars will not change your life. Going to church will not change your life. Would you expect to become a good skier simply by watching a movie on skiing? Or by regularly visiting a ski lodge? Even if you watched one skiing movie per week and stayed overnight in the lodge, you still could not get good at skiing that way. Reading books on skiing also would not make you a good skier. While you could learn some important things about technique and pitfalls to avoid, you won't become a good skier without getting out there and practicing your skiing. So it is with everything in life, from relationships to careers. And, it's no less true for psychotherapy.

Life Is Not a TV Show, Your Participation Is Required

This in no way minimizes the importance of self-help books, therapists, seminars, retreats, marriage partners, or going to church. Just as the carpenter can't sit back and wait for the tools to build the house for her, she also cannot build a house without the tools. To be successful, you must interact with the tools (the resources) at your disposal. If you participate in therapy you must also make changes in your life *between* therapy sessions. If you read self-help books, you must *apply* the methods taught in them before you can expect any success. No matter how good you feel reading a self-help book, you will not change at all if you don't apply something from the book to your life. Likewise, just reading a Bible or attending a church does not make someone more spiritual; neither does simply reading a book (or 20) or meeting with a therapist make someone more healthy. A cookbook can guide you to cook many dishes that you could not prepare otherwise, but it does not cook the meals for you. No matter how much money you spend on cookbooks or how much time you spend reading them, they will do nothing to fill your belly.

Medication Is Also a Resource

Medication also is a tool. But, it is only helpful to the extent that you need it and take it as directed. It will directly affect your biology and can affect your mood and energy level. But, it cannot make you healthy or happy. There is a difference between feeling good and being happy. A crack addict feels good at the time she smokes crack. At least she feels "less bad"

Plants don't grow at the time you water them:

- **They grow during the night, while you are sleeping.**
- **Likewise, you get "watered" in your therapy sessions, but most of your growth will happen between sessions.**

Would I take medication if I needed it and it helped me to function better?

- **Absolutely.**

Anything that creates "instant happiness" does not create lasting happiness. Long term happiness comes from the inside out. But, the little joys along the way are nice bonuses. Seek both for maximum gain.

than she does when she is not smoking it. The crack does nothing, however, to make her life better in any way. She feels better, temporarily, but she is actually deteriorating more and more with each hit of crack. Prescription or nonprescription medication can also be abused (anything can be abused), like crack, to make one feel better without making one better.

Of course there are many legitimate and good uses for prescription medication. Medication, when used to eradicate or to reduce the effects of an illness or a disorder is a very good thing. But, eradicating a disorder does not make someone healthy or happy. Healthiness requires good lifestyle choices. And, happiness is the long-term result of making meaningful life choices. If you ask happy people what it is that makes them happy they will talk about the things that give meaning to their lives. Life, lived on purpose, for a purpose, creates life satisfaction. Anything that creates "instant happiness" does not create lasting happiness.

Why Temporary Joys Don't Last

Suppose that you suffer from very poor circulation in your feet and that the only shoes you have are two sizes too small. Whenever you go somewhere your feet hurt, get tingly, and then become numb. Sometimes they make you stumble and fall down. After a while, it would be hard for you to focus on anything except for your hurting feet. Then suppose that someone gave you a pair of shoes that fit perfectly—neither too big nor too small, with just the right amount of cushion and support. You actually would feel better in the new shoes than you would without them. Because your feet would no longer hurt, you would enjoy life more than before. The first few days with those new shoes would be great, but then you would just be used to comfortable feet and they would not be the focus of your attention anymore. What would you start to focus on then?

Suppose again that before you started to have foot problems, you were lonely and sad. Getting foot problems added to your misery. It's even possible that you would become so focused on your foot pain that you were really not feeling that lonely or sad anymore. It may sound ridiculous, but people hang on to all sorts of problems because they help them avoid facing other kinds of problems. People often "mask" sadness with anger, for example.

In the shoe example, getting new shoes relieved the foot pain, but they did nothing to take care of the original problems of sadness and loneliness. If the source of our immediate pain is dealt with, sometimes we find more pervasive problems underneath. Happiness and life satisfaction always go deeper than removing our immediate problems.

We are always happiest when we have something to live for—beyond ridding our life of problems. However your therapy helps you with pain in your life, you will still need to work on increasing *meaning* in your life. Your therapist may help you identify ways to get started with that or you may already have some ideas. Take care of the pain first, so you can get to that even more important issue. But don't despair when you find deeper problems—they are your opportunity for rich and rewarding growth—not a setback.

Happiness:

- **Is not achieved by removing problems.**
- **Is achieved by adding meaning to our lives.**
- **We are happiest when we live life on purpose, for a purpose.**

Without the help of a close friend, family member, or therapist, It's only as life goes on and we live in different situations and face different struggles that we become aware of some of the things we really need to change. It is in our best interest to catch as many as we can now. Use the psychological self care checklist on the next page to identify your weakest area (we all have one), and then work on it in therapy and out. Rather than try to work on all things at once, it is more helpful to work on the weakest link in the chain. More than any of the others, it's working on that weakest link that allows us to pull a bigger load.

Medication May Also Help you to Relieve Symptoms so that You Can Get to What You Need to in Therapy

In the best case scenario, taking medication is like new, comfortable shoes for aching feet. It helps restore you to the condition that you were in before you had the illness or

Exercise: Psychological Self Care

Instructions: Here are listed some of the self care skills that will help us to feel better, think better, plan better, love better, and be more at peace. None of them will prevent life struggles, which are essential for growth, but by identifying and working on your weakest self care skills, you will be better able to handle struggles and help others with them as well. They will also help you to identify the most important areas to work on in psychotherapy. Rate yourself from 1 to 5 for each skill. A "1" means you have very poor self care skills in that area, a "5" means you have excellent self care skills in that area, and a "3" is somewhere in between.

SKILL	SELF RATING (Circle)
Sleep enough	1 2 3 4 5
Proper Nutrition	1 2 3 4 5
Exercise Daily	1 2 3 4 5
Manage Stress Effectively	1 2 3 4 5
Use Problem Solving Methods	1 2 3 4 5
Give Love to Others	1 2 3 4 5
Receive Love from Others	1 2 3 4 5
Love of Self	1 2 3 4 5
Show Emotions in Nondestructive Ways	1 2 3 4 5
Avoid the Creation of Regrets	1 2 3 4 5
Have a Purpose in Life	1 2 3 4 5
Continue to Learn and Grow	1 2 3 4 5
Have Long Term Intimate Relationships	1 2 3 4 5
Live in a Safe and Secure Environment	1 2 3 4 5
Grieve and Let Go of Past Hurts and Grievances	1 2 3 4 5
Have Appropriate Boundaries	1 2 3 4 5

Another way to think about medication is to imagine that medication is like reading glasses. They can help you to see the letters, but they won't teach you to read.

If you need more and more of something just to stay where you are:

- **Look for healthy ways to supplement what you are doing.**
- **For example, exercise can often supplement the effects of medications.**
- **Either therapy or medication can be seen as a "supplement" for the other.**

disorder. Pills can fix ills, but they don't teach skills. Pills for depression, for example, may help you to feel more motivated or hopeful, but they won't get you new friends. You will need to use skills to make friends. Medication helps to restore you to the point where you have the energy to learn the skills you need to change your life. Medication alone cannot change your life. Another way to think about medication is to imagine that medication is like reading glasses. They can help you to see the letters, but they won't teach you to read. Both the glasses and reading skills are required.

Start in the Most Logical Place and Be Consistent

Although a therapist can teach you skills, if you get an infection you need medication and not 45 minutes in a therapist's office. Therapy is not a cure all, pills are not cure alls, and books are not cure alls. The solution to your problems rests in your choosing and using the appropriate resources and skills you need, on a regular basis, to increase meaning and effectiveness in your life.

If you feel like you are on a medication or therapy treadmill—always getting more but getting nowhere, then you have become dependent on those things to work for you when it is you who must do the work. You will have bought into the myth of the miracle cure. You will have become like the junk food junkie who depends on diet pills to help her to lose weight, the perfectionist who relies on coffee to keep her awake to do "just a little more," and the arm-chair athlete who substitutes watching action for taking action. Something else will be needed, in addition to, or instead of, what you are doing if you are going to make any more progress. For example combining exercise with either therapy or antidepressant medication will help you to make more progress in overcoming depression than either therapy or medication alone.[10]

Case Example—Robin

Robin was a 27 year old single woman who lived alone in a small Pennsylvania town. Since graduating high school she had several jobs that required minimal education such as being a waitress and delivering pizza. At the time she came for counseling, she was working in newspaper distribution—transporting bundles of newspapers to delivery routes of paper carriers at 4:00 a.m. each morning.

Robin had no friends. In elementary school she had been teased a lot for her appearance and in high school she was mostly ignored. She had not been able to excel academically or socially and had looked forward to the time when she became an adult and could change her life.

Unfortunately for Robin, her life had not changed much as an adult. She still believed that others looked down on her and that no one wanted anything to do with her. She entered counseling at the recommendation of her mother.

In counseling, it became apparent that Robin blamed others for her lack of friends, often saying how stuck up and unfriendly people were. She said that she had given up on being friendly with people other than when she had to for the sake of her job. She was unsure whether she wanted a friend or just to be left alone. Loneliness and rejection were both painful ideas for her, but she had become used to loneliness.

We spent the initial part of her counseling reviewing her childhood relationships as well as what she had learned in her family about socializing and getting along with others. This helped Robin to see that she had been trained by others to behave and think in such a way that led to social isolation. It made sense that Robin had no friends, given her training in avoidance of social interaction. Robin admitted that a few people had tried to be friends with her but that she knew they "didn't really" want to be her friend, so she had acted indifferently toward them until they gave up. Then she used their giving up as evidence to confirm that they had not really wanted to be her friends. She had a recipe for loneliness and followed it well.

Gradually, Robin began to see that making friends was an interactive process that depended as much on her behavior as on others. Unfriendly people will always be unfriendly, but friendly

It made sense that Robin had no friends, given her training in avoidance of social interaction.

people will also be unfriendly if you aren't friendly with them. It was also apparent from her behavior with me that she used a "don't bother me" body language.

Now that Robin could see that what she did was important if she were to befriend anyone, I asked her what she imagined her life would be like if she and others continued to do things the same way as in the first 27 years of her life. Robin said that if others don't change and she doesn't change, then she would become an "old maid," a term that her mother often used with her.

The next step in helping Robin was in helping her to give up her strategy of waiting and hoping that other people would change. Also, Robin needed to learn that rejection is not a sign of failure, but rather a sign of effort. No rejections meant no effort to make friends and, as a result, no friends. Trying to make friends would surely result in some rejections even for popular people. In her case, trying to make friends would mean a lot more rejections because she was not very good at it. But, if she was willing to learn some social skills and to give up some anti-social behaviors, then she would have a lower rate of rejection. She decided that having one friend was worth having some rejections.

Learning to make eye contact, smile, and to say "hello" was tough for Robin, but she found that people reacted much better to her than they had in school and it encouraged her to continue. She looked at fashion magazines for clothing ideas in her price range and let the sales lady at the store help her pick out clothes that were attractive for women her age.

As time went on, Robin got help from more and more people, mainly sales clerks at first, and then by learning to ask advice from people she liked. She became more confident about herself and her ability to make changes in her life. When she tried to credit me for her success, I asked her what I had done and what she had done that were responsible for her success. Robin saw that although I had helped her to see things in a different way, it was what she did that helped others to see her in a different way.

The next step in helping Robin was in helping her to give up her strategy of waiting and hoping that other people would change.

What one thing can you think of right now that would help you to:

- **Feel better?**
- **Understand something that puzzles you?**
- **Be perceived more positively by others?**

Summary

Your decision to attend therapy was an excellent one, but therapy must not become an end-goal in itself. To have lasting change will require personal life changes. What further changes do you need to make in your life in order to get what you want? Who is the only one that can make those changes (hint: it isn't your therapist)? What resources (tools) besides the ones you are already using do you need to help you?

What is the next step you need to take to get those resources?

CHAPTER TWELVE

12. PUTTING ANXIETY TO GOOD USE

Anxiety is essential to our everyday lives although we often don't think of it that way. Let's imagine that you had no anxiety at all—none. Your alarm clock goes off in the morning and you feel like sleeping some more. Without anxiety what do you do? You sleep some more of course. Perhaps you are late for work or school and the boss is angry. Because you are not anxious about that or other consequences, it doesn't bother you at all. Your boss is stressed out at your lack of concern, but you are cool as a cucumber. On your way out to the parking lot you don't bother to check to see if a car might run you down—you are not worried about it. You can see that life without any anxiety would be devastating to our careers, relationships, and health. In fact, without the protective component of anxiety, our lives would be in grave danger.

Anxiety Helps Us To:

- **Avoid dangerous situations**
- **Protect others**
- **Protect our valuables**
- **Establish helpful priorities**
- **Anticipate future problems**
- **Prepare for future problems**
- **Make back up plans**

-

It is my hope in this chapter to teach you to look at anxiety in an entirely different way. I want you to learn to use anxiety as a tool to help you achieve your goals. Far from being a curse, anxiety is a blessing when we use it to benefit ourselves and others.

The Functions of Anxiety

Anxiety has two important functions: 1) to protect us from harm: and 2) to prepare us for necessary tasks of living. Anxiety is an internal prompt to action that will prevent us from being harmed. Anxiety does not tell us what to do—it just makes us feel like we have to something. Once we make a definite choice about what our actions are going to be, our anxiety is greatly reduced. We may, for example, not go hiking if we are worried about being bitten by a snake. That is an action of avoidance. We may also put off applying for a job or making friends because we are afraid of rejection.

On the other hand, we can use our anxiety to prepare us for something that we fear. We can learn to identify snakes, their habits, how to be safe on the trail, and what to do in case of snakebite. We can also use anxiety about rejection by putting together a nice resume and doing practice interviews before applying for a job. We can use our anxiety about social rejection by learning social skills.

When our anxiety prompts good coping behavior and preparation, our anxiety helps us to grow and have more of what we want.

Our Level of Anxiety Is Proportional to Our *Beliefs* About Danger

Some things are more dangerous than others. Accurately evaluating how dangerous a situation is results in an appropriate amount of anxiety that prompts us to take an appropriate response. A poisonous snake in your path would likely be evaluated as more dangerous than forgetting to return a library book. The snake would get your immediate and prolonged attention until it was dealt with or successfully avoided. The book might be quickly forgotten. Our beliefs about how dangerous or how "bad" something is will determine how much we focus on it, how long it stays on our mind, and how much we experience anxiety. The more important or dangerous we believe something to be, the more anxious it will make us feel.

Individual Differences

Although everyone experiences anxiety, people differ in their evaluation of the actual dangerousness or importance of a situation. Because of these evaluation differences, different people experience different amounts of anxiety *in the same situations.* For example, often young drivers underestimate the dangerousness of driving a car. As a result, they have minimal

Anxiety is a result of a mental interpretation

- **The fact that we can feel anxious about something that is happening in a movie is a good demonstration of the connection between thinking and anxiety.**
- **The more important or dangerous we believe something to be, the more anxious it will make us feel.**

172

anxiety and are less likely to drive carefully. They could actually use a little more anxiety to make them be more careful and improve their driving. On the other hand, some people become so anxious about driving that they refuse to drive at all. Like everything else, there is an optimal level of anxiety for driving.

Another example is people with agoraphobia, who may become so anxious about leaving their home that they imprison themselves in their home. People with such high levels of anxiety believe that their only cure lies in getting rid of their anxiety, but as illustrated above, that would be both dangerous and impossible. Having a more appropriate level of anxiety, on the other hand, will help them to deal more effectively with everyday life and anticipated events while still allowing them to leave their home comfortably. I can't honestly tell an agoraphobic that it is safe to go outside. There are dangers outside the home. But I can show that it may be safer to go out than to stay at home. While they have overestimated the danger of going out, they have neglected the much higher probability of social isolation, emotional and physical illness, and loss of life quality, which they are already experiencing. More realistically appraising the danger of both going out and staying isolated can help the agoraphobic to make a greater effort to fight their disorder.

Reducing Anxiety with Medication or Drugs

In efforts to reduce their anxiety to a manageable level, people often take medications or sedating drugs (such as alcohol) to temporarily reduce their anxiety. The more severe the anxiety, the greater will be the need and the desire for the medications or drugs. Both medications and drugs bring their own set of problems such as side effects, financial expense, as well as legal and social costs (as with addictions). Even when people manage to use prescription anti-anxiety medication in a controlled way, the medication only temporarily relieves the anxiety. It does nothing to permanently resolve the anxiety. There is also the danger that the medications or drugs will

Counseling and Medication:

- **Optimally, medication should remove enough anxiety to allow you to work on it.**
- **Having too much anxiety relief from medication would lower your motivation to work on anxiety, and is much more likely to create a dependency.**
- **Some of my clients have carried an anti-anxiety pill with them, "just in case," for more than a year. Having the medication available helps them to enter more challenging situations.**

173

You have probably known some people who did not take their problems seriously enough, or were too reckless in their behavior. This is the problem of having too little anxiety.

relieve the anxiety so well that people will lose their motivation to find healthier ways to reduce their anxiety, even if it would decrease their dependence on drugs.

A Good Way to Use Medications for Anxiety

The use of medication in a controlled and responsible way allows many people to get to the place where they can have enough focus to be able to work on their anxiety. So, for extreme cases of anxiety (as for depression), medication may be the first step in managing the disorder. For moderate or mild anxiety, the use of medication as a first order treatment is debatable.

The goal of counseling is never to directly or completely remove a person's anxiety, but rather to promote a *realistic evaluation* of the importance or dangerousness of situations. Then, the side effect of exaggerated anxiety will not appear. With realistic evaluations, people's anxiety levels will be both appropriate and helpful (medical doctors also don't want people to become too relaxed by anxiety medication as it would put them in danger). Whether drug treatment or psychotherapy is used, the goal is never the elimination of anxiety, but rather a more realistic level of anxiety.

The Ideal Level of Anxiety Is Related to Functioning

In some cases, a more accurate evaluation of present life events will raise a person's anxiety, while in others it will lower it. There is no such thing as a constant, optimal level of anxiety. Different situations demand more or less anxiety for good decision-making. Consider a marital situation, for example, when a spouse has very little anxiety about the effect of his or her behavior on the relationship. After becoming more aware of the negative impact and risk to the relationship, an increased amount of anxiety may result which will make it easier to commit to new and better behavior. A man may realize that his behavior may cause the end of the relationship, making him both more anxious, and more willing to change his behavior. In such cases an increase in anxiety results in an improvement in the relationship. Although people usually enter counseling for levels of anxiety which are too high, anxiety levels that are too low can also create serious problems. You have probably known some people who did not take their problems seriously enough.

People with very high levels of anxiety feel very uncomfortable and have overly restricted behavior. Such people tend to overestimate the dangerousness of some situations, while completely ignoring the dangerousness of others. They are focused on their anxiety and the problems it causes. At the same time, they may be oblivious to the damage that is being done by their lack of concern for something else. For example, the agoraphobic who is afraid to leave her home may well recognize the dangers in the environment (e.g., becoming ill in public or having a car accident), but not be aware of the dangers of staying at home. Aside from the fact that most accidents happen in or near home, the loss of career, relationships, and self-esteem from isolating oneself at home can be more devastating than anything that could happen in public. Actually becoming more anxious about staying at home can help to level out the anxiety playing field and increase motivation to leave the house.

In another example, anxiety about one spouse's possible infidelity can result in frequent questioning and distrust by the other spouse. Although reassurances from the first spouse temporarily relieves the anxiety, the continual distrust and interrogations can themselves drive the first spouse away. That is, there is an *overestimation* of the danger of the spouse's infidelity while there is an *underestimation* of the danger of repetitive interrogations. The distrust and interrogations may present the greater risk to the marriage.

Therapists help people to see more clearly *all* of the dangers associated with a behavior and to more accurately assess the risks and benefits involved. If you suffer from an anxiety disorder, one thing you cannot trust is your ability to realistically appraise danger. Your evaluation of reality is out of whack. Anxiety is a good guide only for those with already good functioning. Your therapist can help you to become more realistic in your appraisal of dangers so you can become more

Anxiety Can be Self-Perpetuating:

- When our anxiety causes us to create problems (for example as the result of jealousy or suspiciousness), our lives can become more difficult, resulting in even higher levels of anxiety.
- Either reducing the anxiety directly (as with medications, or relaxation methods), or changing the behaviors can help to stop this negative spiral and make life easier—resulting in even lower levels of anxiety.

175

functional (i.e. make decisions that benefit your life more than the ones you make now).

The Benefit of Realistic Anxiety to Our Future Goals

Realistic anxiety preserves us and also prepares us. *Realistic* levels of anxiety are a blessing and not a curse. Anxiety is a very useful tool for anyone who wants to have success reaching goals. Without anxiety, our natural inclination is to do whatever is easiest for the short term. This could be eating junk food, staying up all hours, being promiscuous, spending all our money shopping, running up big debts, criticizing and nagging our partner, and so on, without any concern for the future. While these activities can bring a certain amount of immediate, pleasurable feelings or results, they will not help us to reach any worthwhile long term goal. In fact, they will promote long term losses rather than gains.

Anxiety helps us to reach goals by providing motivation to take *appropriate* action. Consider, for example, college students at midterm exam time. Before midterm exams two major shifts occur on campuses: 1) students become more anxious; and 2) most students study more. This is not a coincidence. As students become anxious about their grades, they study harder. This both improves their grades and reduces their anxiety. This is exactly how anxiety is designed to function. Feeling anxious prompts us to take actions (like studying) to prepare or prevent a perceived danger (such as getting a poor grade). Our actions reduce the danger and our anxiety level drops. In a healthy individual, there will be a continuous pattern of briefly increased anxiety followed by effective coping behavior.

When people do not have effective coping behaviors and don't take effective action, problems escalate. For example, not all students will study more before exams. Some will study less. Now that you know something about anxiety, you can see that one of two things is responsible for these students' behavior: 1) they either underestimate the danger of not doing well on the test (have too little anxiety); or 2) rather than reduce their anxiety by preparation, they reduce their anxiety by distraction

In a healthy individual, there will be a continuous pattern of briefly increased anxiety followed by effective coping behavior.

(e.g., games, sex, TV) or sedation (e.g.. drugs and alcohol). For students who use avoidance, their level of anxiety is appropriate, but their actions are not effective in reducing the risk of poor grades.

The key to helping the *low anxiety* students is to help them to realistically evaluate the risk of not preparing for the exams and so increase their motivation to study. The key to helping the students with *normal anxiety but ineffective action* is to help them to use the strategy of preparation rather than distraction and sedation.

Sedation and Distraction Interfere with the Normal Process of Preparation

You can see that both sedation and distraction reduce anxiety but actually interfere with preparation. Whenever you are feeling anxious, the key questions to ask yourself are: 1) "What am I imagining could go wrong?" 2) "How can I help to prevent that?" and 3) "What is a good back up plan, if that bad thing does happen?" Then, immediately get to work answering these three questions. You need to answer all three to become less anxious and more effective. The time to consider anxiety reduction methods (e.g., relaxation, distraction, sedation, medication, etc.) is when you are taking effective action yet still have debilitating anxiety. Such might be the case with students who are effectively studying for their tests yet have such a high anxiety level that it interferes with their actual test performance.

Level of Skill and Anxiety Level

Another example of the need for anxiety reduction methods would be a skilled surgeon who is too nervous to concentrate when operating. This example, though, is very unlikely. We might expect it from a new surgeon, but not from a highly skilled one. This is because people tend to have low anxiety in areas in which they are highly skilled. This actually teaches us that preparation or training is an effective coping method for anxiety. If your partner's behavior makes you feel anxious, you can learn to become skilled in handling your partner's

Become Skilled in the Use of Anxiety:

1. Anticipate possible setbacks and dangers,
2. Prepare for them, rather than just thinking about them, and
3. Make a backup plan in case your preparation does not work out.

Expertise and Anxiety:

- The more expertise someone has, the less anxious they feel when dealing with problems in that area.
- Becoming an expert in what scares you is a very healthy way to reduce excess anxiety.

behavior (or your boss's, customer's, mother-in-law's, or anyone else's). Then you will be more effective and less anxious. Each day, there are tens of thousands of people receiving personal training and coaching to become less anxious and more effective in a variety of areas. You can, too.

Anxiety and Sleep

Have you ever noticed that anxiety can interfere with sleep? You are trying to sleep but your mind just keeps going over the same "what if" situation again and again? It can seem like your mind is broken when actually your mind is not broken at all. At bedtime you are less distracted than in the day, and so you are more aware of the concerns that have been there all along, but have been drowned out by your busyness. Since it's difficult to be busy and fall asleep at the same time, distraction is not a good way to cope with anxiety at bedtime. (Some people do manage to do this, however, by watching television until they fall asleep). Even if you do use distraction to get your mind off things while you fall asleep, it won't help you to prepare for the future event you are worrying about. Your anxiety will just be postponed until the next day (or the next night). Until that dreaded future event has occurred, or until you prepare for it, the anxiety will not go away.

When you are having difficulty sleeping due to anxiety, rather than attempting to distract yourself from your anxiety or drug yourself (sleeping medication), you can work *with* your mind (which is not defective) to reduce the anxiety and go to sleep. One very good way to do this is to get out of bed and draw two lines on a piece of paper to divide the paper into three vertical columns (see the exercise on the next page). On the left side, make a list of things you are worrying about and number them. In the middle column write two or three action steps that you can take to deal with each problem. The third column is for contingency plans, should your action steps prove ineffective.

For example, let's say that in column one you write that you are worried about an exam. In the second column, work out a study schedule that you can follow to prepare for the exam. In

Forcing yourself to consider the possibility of failure and prepare for it is the key to overcoming anxiety.

Exercise: Three Steps to Managing Anxiety

MY WORRY/PROBLEM	ACTION STEPS I CAN TAKE TO PREPARE FOR THIS PROBLEM	WHAT I CAN DO IF THIS ANTICIPATED PROBLEM OCCURS (at least 3 things)
1. doing poorly on my big test next Tuesday	make a study schedule ask previous students what is the best way to prepare	1. get extra help 2. ask for extra credit work 3. ask the prof if I can retest 4. retake the course in the Summer
2. I might have an illness	get a medical exam blood tests eat, sleep, and exercise enough to maintain my health	1. follow MD orders 2. take prescriptions as prescribed 3. research treatment options, then get on with my life

"Worry" occurs when we are anxious about something and are unprepared to deal with it. Everyone has anxiety, but not everyone worries. You can be someone who does not worry if you use your anxiety as a signal to make a plan of action along with backup plans. The backup plans help you not to worry about your plan not working.

Which of the following do you think would be the best way to deal with anxiety before a school exam?

- Take anxiety medication
- Get psychotherapy
- Try not to think about it
- Study

Preparing for a problem is not the same as solving a problem

- We cannot solve every problem, but we can have a helpful response to every problem.

the third column, write down an action you can take if you don't do well on the exam. This third column answer is actually the answer to the "what if" question that was interfering with your sleep. "What if I flunk the exam?" may be the persistent thought interfering with your sleep. It is possible, of course, that you can fail an exam even when you study a lot for it. Well, what if you do fail the exam? Will it be the end of your life? What could you actually do? As difficult as considering the bad possibility might be, it is essential to realistically appraise the danger of the situation. Forcing yourself to consider the possibility of failure *and prepare for it* is the key to overcoming anxiety.

Simply trying to be positive ("I know I will do well on the test") will not be helpful because your mind will remind you of the possibility of failure once you let your guard down ("but what if I fail?") Typical third column answers (to the question "what if I fail?") that clients in this situation write include: "I could ask the professor for extra credit work," "I could repeat the course during the summer," and "I could get a tutor." Having a plan for the possibility of failure (a "backup plan") along with effective coping (how to prepare) will calm your mind. You will have worked with your mind to effectively deal with your concern. This is the *healthy reason* your mind created the anxiety in the first place. Your subconscious has no interest in simply interfering with your sleep. Your therapist can help you to become better at realistically appraising situations, deciding on good actions, and making backup plans.

Let's consider another example problem: "What if I have a serious illness? (column one)." What would your action steps be? Most likely you would list getting a physical exam as a first action step (column two). The second would be to consider what you would do if you do have a serious illness (column three). Again, your own answers will be the most meaningful to you, but clients have said things such as, "I will get treatment for it and follow the doctor's recommendations," "I can go on short-term disability," and "I can pray and trust God with the results." When the ideas come from the therapist, they can seem pat, but when they come from you, they will have more meaning.

Preparing for a Problem Is Not the Same as Solving a Problem

We cannot *solve* every problem, but we can have a *helpful response* to every problem. One thing you can be sure of in life is that you will have problems. This is part of the human condition and is neither a disease nor a disorder. Problems cause us anxiety, but they also help us grow. Having an effective way to cope with, if not overcome, our problems is the challenge that brings growth. A therapist will never be able to help you have a problem free life (how boring would that be!?). But, you can learn from therapy effective approaches for managing problems.

With the three column problem list, mentioned above, if there is a problem in column one for which you have no action steps in column two, then the action step should be to get a professional consultation. This is because there is no problem that you have that has not been successfully dealt with by others, although you are not experienced in dealing with it. If you don't know what to do (column two), then get help from someone who does. Make an appointment with a financial manager, clergy, counselor, physician, or whoever is appropriate. Taking actions to rid yourself of anxiety is not a good goal. *Using* your anxiety as a prompt to realistically evaluate situations and prepare for them is a good goal. Then, when you have anxiety, you will not think you have relapsed and become even more anxious. Instead, your anxiety will prompt you to take effective action. Rather than avoiding anxiety, you can use it to propel you toward success. Indeed, you will never have success without it.

There is no problem that you have that has not been successfully dealt with by others. If you don't know what to do then get help from someone who does.

Case Example—Miriam

Miriam came to therapy at the urging of her husband, although she admitted that she needed help. She had been so worried that she was "crazy" that she previously had avoided coming to counseling.

Although Miriam recognized that these tragedies were not likely to happen, this realization did not calm her because they remained possible.

Miriam found herself increasingly worried about things. For example, she worried about one of her children being in a sports accident or her husband coming home in a bad mood. When she had these worries, she exaggerated them to catastrophic proportions. For example, she thought if her children were injured playing sports, then they could become infected, get gangrene and require an amputation that would forever alter their lives. If her husband came home upset, they might have conflict which would lead to greater and greater conflict and the eventual demise of the marriage. Needless to say, Miriam was always on the alert for any signs of trouble.

Although Miriam recognized that these tragedies were not likely to happen, this realization did not calm her because they remained possible. The newspapers were all the proof she needed of all the terrible things that can go wrong. Only if such things were not possible would she be calmed. Thus, if her children did not play sports, then they couldn't get a sports injury. If her husband did not go to work, then he would not be able to come home upset from work. If he did need to work, Miriam did all that she could to be pleasant and to make sure that everything was in order for her husband's return. This too would not reduce her worry because it was still possible that he would be in a bad mood.

With Miriam's permission her husband had a private session with me. Her husband admitted that he had become frustrated with needing to "tip toe" around and to "constantly" reassure Miriam that things were alright. He was becoming increasingly dissatisfied with the marriage, and in a very emotional state said that he might eventually not be able to deal with his wife's anxieties. I helped him to understand a little about the treatment of anxiety and also to make a backup plan for marital counseling if progress wasn't made in his wife's individual treatment.

I did a cost-benefit analysis of Miriam's anxiety with her. Together, we listed all of the benefits of worrying about things, as well as all of the costs that her worry brings. This helped Miriam to see that her worries did not actually prevent any bad things from happening, but actually made it more likely that bad things would happen. For example, her worrying about making her husband upset was stressing the marriage more than if her husband did get upset. Preventing her children from taking sports did not really keep them safe, since they could be injured elsewhere, but did cause more family conflict and caused social difficulties for her children. There was also the risk of them becoming overly fearful as Miriam was. Miriam admitted that her mother had been such a worrier and that she probably learned this behavior from her.

I taught Miriam the three column method for putting worry to good use. She learned to turn her worries into challenges for effective action, to list actions she could take, and how to make back up plans should those actions turn out to not be effective. Miriam got some information about sports injuries and how to care for them. She learned some ways to deal with her husband's moods that were better for him and for her. By preparing for injuries and moodiness and by knowing what to do if they occurred, she was less anxious about them happening.

As Miriam learned to use her anxiety she became more confident of her ability to manage difficult situations. Although she still had worries, she learned not to worry about having worries, and so lessened her overall anxiety. With practice, she found that she could answer the "what if" questions that arose in her mind, as she had them. For example, "What if my son is injured in today's game?" would prompt her to tell herself that the coach would be sure that she was called and that her son would get any necessary medical treatment. The thought, "What if my husband comes home upset?" would prompt her to tell herself that it's ok if he is and that they could talk about things or go to counseling if it got beyond their ability to handle. With such skills, Miriam was able to focus more on things she enjoyed rather than things she feared.

Miriam's husband was very grateful for the change in his wife, and this too, helped Miriam to worry less. Miriam was ending a family tradition of worrying and was hopeful that her children would not become worriers as she had.

Although she still had worries, she learned not to worry about having worries, and so lessened her overall anxiety.

Summary

Not everyone can manage anxiety without medication, but everyone can benefit from the addition of effective coping skills. Using the methods you learned in this chapter to supplement your counseling, you can put your anxiety to good use.

13. OVERCOMING PERFECTIONISM

One thing is certain—you will be no more perfect when you finish therapy than when you began it. I would also say that you will be no closer to perfection when you die than when you were born. Perfection is such an elusive characteristic that it is not to be found in the domain of mortals. Every person has not just one, but many flaws. To some people this is painstakingly obvious. Yet there are scores of people who strive to perfect themselves and others to the detriment of their loved ones. The *compulsion* to continually correct yourself and others is a mental illness, and the fear of making mistakes is a major obstacle to growth.

Perfectionism is Far from an Admirable Trait:

- **It cheats people of relationships.**
- **It cheats people of happiness.**
- **It cheats people of lifetime.**
- **It's a kind of anxiety disorder.**
- **It keeps people focused on the worst aspects of themselves and others.**

Perfectionism Doesn't Lead to Improvement

Perfectionism can be a monumental problem in a person's life. Although the goal of perfectionism is improvement, it actually brings loss of productivity, isolation, anxiety, and sadness. You often hear that we should try to do our best at everything. Superficially, that sounds like good advice. But, how many things can you say that you have done to the best of your ability? Where you have given 100% and couldn't have given just 1% better? If not, then why didn't you? Did you intuitively know that good enough is good enough? Did you feel guilty afterwards?

Children are often asked if they did their best. Although they most often say "yes," they most often hear, "I think you could have done a little better if you tried harder." The message is, "If this is your best, then your best is not good enough." This message can be internalized and replayed endlessly throughout one's lifetime.

Perfectionism Lowers Productivity

With perfectionism, productivity is *decreased* because in the effort to be perfect, great care has to be taken not to make a mistake. This requires an absolute thoroughness. It may seem noble, until you consider some real world examples. How would a perfectionist approach raking leaves for example? Every leaf and every part of a leaf would have to be raked up in order to reach perfection at raking leaves. The amount of time required to rake up 80% of the leaves would be about one fifth of the time required to rake up absolutely all the remaining leaves. So, if it would take 1 hour to rake up 80% of the leaves, it would take 5 hours to rake up all of the leaves—a 6 hour job. Would the lawn look better with 100% of the leaves raked up than with 80% of them raked up? Sure. But, what will have gone undone while the lawn was raked to perfection (in those 5 hours that were used to achieve perfection)?

Sometimes perfectionism prevents people from even getting started on task. For example, in working on their doctoral dissertations some students get so overwhelmed thinking of all the things that they need to do in order to complete their dissertation, they avoid getting started. What should take a few months can take a few years for such perfectionistic students. In the meantime they continue to have to pay tuition and are delayed starting their career—which is the greatest expense, although a hidden one. The things that we don't get to do often cost us more than the things that we do. On the next page are some exercises that can help perfectionists to get started on large tasks.

While the perfectionist will succeed at getting some things done very well, the time used will take away from many other things that could have been done in the same time period. In essence, perfecting one thing means failing many other things by default. Even a delicate task like open heart surgery would not benefit from a perfectionist's approach. While, of course, the major components of surgery must be done correctly and

With perfectionism, productivity is decreased because in the effort to be perfect, great care has to be taken not to make a mistake.

186

Exercise: Ending Perfection Blocks to Action

Do you delay working on a project because of all the steps that are necessary to do a good job? If so, you may be falling prey to perfectionism. The idea that we must do everything well stops many people from learning new skills and taking on projects. In their mind, success has become linked to excellence and preventing mistakes. In reality, success is most often linked to productivity, not excellence. Ten seeds planted imperfectly will yield more fruit than one seed planted perfectly.

Lower the mental threshold for action with these self-questions:

1. If someone offered me a million dollars to get this project done, and quality did not matter, could I get it done? If yes, how would I do it?

2. If I needed to get this job done by a certain deadline in order to save a life of a loved one, could I get it done? If yes, how would I do it?

3. How important will the quality of this job matter in ten years? Will anybody care about it anymore? Or is it more important just to get a "passing grade"?

4. Is it more important to do this job perfectly, or to get the rewards that come from getting this job done?

5. Is this just a draft or model that I can improve on later if I need to? If so, I can focus on getting this job done "sloppy and quick," since that's what a draft is anyhow.

Examining the cost of extreme thoroughness before beginning:

1. What is delay costing me? Is it preventing me from doing something else well? For example, what could I now be doing if this present task were out of the way? Is that something more valuable than this task?

2. Is my time as valuable as this project I need to do? If so, how can I excel at protecting my time? Does delaying on this project corrupt my time by keeping worries and burdens on my mind?

Getting motivated to action by using role models:

1. Who do I admire for this kind of work? How would he or she go about getting it done?

2. What advice would my role model give me about this project? (For example, if your role model is Mark Twain, what do you imagine he would say to you about starting your book?)

3. Would my role model have done better to wait and try to get everything to be perfect before beginning? Or, would that have been a losing strategy for my role model? (Successful people value action over perfection and so become famous despite making many mistakes).

without accident, an attempt at a perfect procedure of any kind would leave the patient cut open so long as to present more risk than good. There comes a point where the leaf raker or the surgeon must say "good enough" and move on.

You can use self-directed questions to assess your tendency to perfectionism. The questions need to help you assess how much you are losing in some parts of your life by spending too much time in other parts. The next page has some questions you can start with. Sometimes we do need to sacrifice some part of our life for the sake of another, but we should avoid sacrifices that will only bring regret. To do that, we need to be aware of our losses now, because later will be too late.

Perfectionism Brings Isolation

Perfectionism also brings isolation because intolerance of mistakes in oneself (and often in others), distances the perfectionist from others. Perfectionists are experts in detecting flaws because of their constant practice of looking for them. Other people will also hesitate to ask the perfectionist to do something because of the amount of time and stress involved for all parties. People will not understand why the perfectionist just can't "lighten up."

Perfectionists Have Excess Anxiety

For the perfectionist, limited time and limited energy both conflict with doing a perfect job. And, conflict always brings anxiety. The perfectionist, then, cannot enjoy doing a job because of the stress caused by this conflict ("I'm too tired, but I have to..." or "I have too, but I don't have enough time"). The best the perfectionist can hope for is a relief from anxiety once the job is done. Doubt, though, usually limits the relief.

The observation that the finished product does not match the perfectionist's image of the way something should be is the source of another anxiety provoking conflict. It is actually impossible to do anything perfectly, so there is always a flaw that can be found. Even if no one else can see the flaw, the perfectionist can. The resulting imperfect product also acts as evidence for the perfectionist that she didn't try hard enough

> In most of us, there is a set point that lets us know when it's time to stop:
>
> - **For the perfectionist, that set point is too high,**
> - **Recovery from perfectionism requires the use of a different set point.**

> Every time a perfectionist corrects someone else, he is losing a little more of his relationships.

Exercise: Perfectionism and Priorities

Perfectionism is not about doing things perfectly because perfection can neither be conceived nor achieved. Perfectionism is an attempt to reduce anxiety by doing more than is necessary to do well, without enjoyment, and at the expense of doing something else which is more important. Working more on long term priorities is a good way to reduce perfectionism. It also reduces anxiety by putting things in perspective (i.e. "the details of these reports won't really matter a year from now").

Answer the following questions to assess your own perfectionism and priorities. Do not be satisfied with simply "thinking" the answers. Write them out. Writing out our thinking gives us an objectivity that is not possible simply by thinking.

- Do you feel like your life is balanced among work, family, other relationships, and leisure activities, or are you spending the bulk of your time in a single area?

- In what areas of your life are you wasting time and losing out on other opportunities because of your perfectionism?

- If you are spending the bulk of your time in just one area, what are you missing out on in the other areas? What are you are sacrificing? Is it really worth the sacrifice? If so, why is it?

- When you come to the end of your life, do you think you will be satisfied with the way you have divided your time? Or, will you wish that you had spent more time in another area? Where do you think you will wish you spent more time?

- What can you do differently this week that would help you to have a more balanced life? (e.g., spend more time with my family, restart an old hobby, etc.)

and needs to try harder. "If only I had done this or that, things would be so much better," is the belief of the perfectionist. But it is a false belief. Guilt and anxiety result from this belief rather than any benefits.

Perfectionism Results in Loss

Perfectionism also brings sadness because of all the losses experienced by the perfectionist. The perfectionist will miss out on many opportunities because of the fear of doing poorly or because of lack of time. It would be hard to join a bowling league or golf club because of the fear of doing poorly. Self-criticalness and criticalness of others damages relationships and so the perfectionist loses the closeness that could have been had. While straight "A" students have an easier time getting into college, it is the "B" students who are often more successful after graduation. They know the importance of doing a good job, but tend to be less anxious and to have more people skills. This doesn't mean that everyone who gets all A's is a perfectionist, but you won't find many perfectionists among the "B" students.

Therapy Conflict's with the Motivations of the Perfectionist

Reasoning does not work very well in helping perfectionists out of the dilemma that they set for themselves (the necessity of doing the impossible). Often perfectionists will enter therapy not to try to overcome their perfectionism, but as part of their desire to do better. They don't fare very well at that in therapy, though, because they soon discover that their therapist is not perfect and also that rather than becoming more perfect, they are discovering more and more of the problems they have. The realization that they have more problems than they thought puts even more of a strain on their attempts to be perfect and therapy quickly becomes overwhelming. The client may go off in search of a more perfect therapist.

There are some people who realize that they are perfectionists, and are very tired and frustrated with being that way.

When Perfectionism Is Recognized as a Problem, Help Is Possible

There are some people who realize that they are perfectionists, and are very tired and frustrated with being that way. They want help. They know that they are wasting their time trying to be perfect, and that others like them less for it, but they don't know how to change. Often they enter therapy because of the damage that has been done to some significant relationship. Like most clients in therapy, they know what they are doing is unreasonable and they know what they should do, but they find themselves unable to do it. Trying to force ourselves to relax seldom works. They are also prime candidates for addictions ("medicating" either the anxiety or the sadness caused by losses), eating disorders (through attempts at body perfection or a way of gaining control), and other obsessions and compulsions.

Treating People for Perfectionism

Rather than giving advice or reasoning, therapists use several more helpful approaches. One possible approach is for the client to take anxiety medication so that they are less anxious about not being perfect. Their "mistakes" will be less upsetting. This allows them to spend less time doing things, make less effort "correcting" others, and be less upset with final results. This will help as long as the person is taking medication, but is not a cure for perfectionism as no skills are learned and the perfectionism returns if the medication is stopped.

Exploring the origin of the perfectionism may bring important insights and may give the person some freedom to be other than perfect. Early childhood fears of separation and loss may play a role. Many of our childhood lessons stick with us even when we don't benefit from them anymore. An internal message like, "I need to be perfect so that daddy and mommy will love me," may be protective for a child, but harmful for an adult. A genogram, or detailed family tree, may also reveal that perfectionism is a family trait, which may be

Paradoxical Techniques in Psychotherapy Refer to Prescribing the Symptom to Treat the Disorder

- For example, trying to stay awake can help people with insomnia to fall asleep (whereas trying to sleep would actually keep them awake)
- Having someone try to become anxious usually helps them to be more calm (whereas telling them to stop worrying actually makes them more anxious)
- Anxiety disorders, in particular, often respond well to paradoxical techniques

partly genetic and partly learned—a kind of family legacy.

A Paradoxical Approach to Perfectionism

Another approach is help the perfectionist to redefine "perfect" as something that has flaws. There is real world evidence that some flaws do create a better outcome. Flawed gems can be very valuable, flawed coins and stamps as well. And everyone values a flawed partner better than a perfect one. We've already talked about the importance of not being perfect even in surgery. Indeed, the best performance and relationship is always a flawed one. Doing one's best means leaving some things uncorrected.

To put this into practice, the person needs to intentionally make at least one mistake in whatever they are doing and preferably more. This will improve both what they do and their relationships. The only way to do anything well is to make at least one mistake. Any additional mistakes that the person makes are to be considered a bonus. In painting a wall, for example, one spot may be left undone or some paint intentionally dripped on the floor. Once perfectionists start using this technique, they find it very freeing. It allows them to bring projects to completion faster than they have before. "I did a good job raking those leaves, because, look—there are still some out there." In the past, completion could only be marked by perfection; with the new technique, completion can only be marked by evidence that the person quit early. Quitting a job before it's "fully" done is a nice mistake for perfectionists to make. It frees up a lot of time and energy for the perfectionist, while also improving relationships. It greatly increases productivity.

A person who is pressuring himself to give a perfect speech, will have a very high anxiety level. A person who stands up and gives a speech with some intentional "mistakes" (for example, by coughing or mispronouncing a word) will feel more at ease and will have more satisfaction with the results. When he makes a mistake, it will be what he expected and desired rather than what he wished to prevent. With this technique, perfectionists soon discover that the consequences of

The consequences of intentionally making some mistakes are far more pleasing to oneself and others than the consequences of spending all one's efforts trying not to make mistakes. People don't mind others who mess up, but they often can't stand others who don't.

192

intentionally making some mistakes are far more pleasing to oneself and others than the consequences of spending all one's efforts trying not to make mistakes. This technique has the advantage of not directly opposing the perfectionism. It goes with resistance rather than against it by redefining "perfect" to mean making some mistakes.

Case Example—Paul

Paul did not have obsessive compulsive disorder. He did not have persistent, repetitive, thoughts or behaviors that made no sense. But he did waste a lot of time working on things that should not require that much time. And, no matter how much time he put into his work, he was never satisfied with it.

For example, he would painstakingly type out reports for work that he admitted went mostly unread and were just a formality for his job. He would check them repeatedly for grammar and spelling errors as if he were working on a novel for publication. He reasoned that if someone did look at the reports, it would be a reflection on him since he wrote them.

Paul also monitored the stock market very carefully, checking stock fluctuations as many as thirty times a day. When he made a wrong buy or sell decision, he would chastise himself for days although no one can consistently predict the movement of stocks. He would also follow details of the businesses he was invested in so closely that he often knew more about them than the people who worked at those businesses.

Paul was always concerned about "saving for a rainy day" and became miserly with his money. Despite his stated desire to enjoy his life and to spend time with friends, he rarely had time for friends. When he did spend time with friends, he was ever vigilant to any kind of criticism. He tried very hard to make sure that no one had anything to criticize him about, ever, whether it was having a wrinkled shirt or a misspelled word.

Not surprisingly, Paul was both exhausted and lonely.

Paul was both exhausted and lonely. Although people were friendly to him, they did not talk with him beyond simple things like the weather.

With this new, healthier resistance, in place, Paul was freed to either use all of the time he was supposed to, or finish early by making an intentional mistake.

Although people were friendly to him, they did not talk with him beyond simple things like the weather. The two relationships he had had with women had been disasters. The women had a lack of concern for what Paul had thought to be important and they also complained that Paul was critical and "no fun." He admitted to me, his counselor, that they had been right.

I knew that reasoning with Paul would not be helpful, as he could already see the unreasonableness of his behavior. Encouraging Paul to try to make mistakes just made Paul feel more anxious. Instead, I recommended to Paul that he not resist his urge to be perfect, but to actually try to be even more perfect. If Paul spent two hours on a report and then felt "finished," he was to continue to spend another hour on it. (This is a procedure known as "overcorrection" and is sometimes used to treat obsessive-compulsive disorders).

By doing more than he felt like doing, Paul started to develop the desire to stop before he spent the time he was "supposed to" spend. His previous resistance to stopping a task early started to change to a resistance to continue a task. With this new, healthier resistance in place, Paul was freed to either use all of the time he was supposed to, or finish early by making an intentional mistake. He found himself choosing not to reread his reports, and thus leaving any mistakes that might be in them, without needing to make corrections. (Combining techniques, like overcorrection and paradoxical intention is one of the specialties of psychotherapists).

Although when he first came to therapy, Paul was unable to intentionally make mistakes, with the aid of his new resistance to spending an even greater amount of time on a project, he was able to start to make intentional mistakes. Although when he did that, he was anxious, he was also relieved at being able to stop. With praise and support from me, Paul was able to make intentional mistakes more easily and be less concerned with the outcome.

Paul and I also worked on plans for dealing with people who might criticize him. This was to replace his usual strategy of trying to prevent the criticism. By being prepared for such *instances, Paul was less anxious about them, able to be himself more, and even less anxious about making mistakes. He could "practice" his new skills by intentionally wrinkling a tie, or putting a piece of lint on his shirt. He learned though, that people didn't even notice these things. Although he remained a little eccentric, he was more comfortable with himself and others were more comfortable with him, too.*

———

Only God Has the Time for Being Perfect

Knowing many things well is better than knowing one thing perfectly; doing many things well is better than doing one thing perfectly. If we had unlimited time, it might be otherwise, but we are limited beings with limited time. We are mortals. Our lives require adaptation and flexibility, mixed in with a lot of acceptance and forgiveness. In therapy, you will have the chance to work on very few things compared to the great variety that life has to offer. It is not essential that you choose exactly the right goals to work on. In the process of reaching the goals that you have chosen, you will learn new methods and ways of thinking that you can apply on your own in a variety of areas.

Don't Try to Solve All Your Problems in Therapy

When you finish therapy, you will be nowhere near perfecting yourself. You will have made significant progress in some areas while becoming more aware of deficiencies in other areas. The decision to end therapy does not rest in reaching perfection, or resolving every little symptom, any more than graduation from high school means that you have mastered all the material you studied in your classes. Finishing therapy means that you have been through a significant process that has in some way transformed you from who you were before. The feeling of *completion*, rather than perfection, can guide us as to when to move on in our daily tasks as well as therapy.

Consider the landscape painter. How does a landscape painter know when her painting is done? When she has completely painted every leaf and tree in sight? No. When she

When Does it Make Sense to Stop (work, therapy, exercise, leisure activities, etc.)?

- **When continuing significantly impacts something else that is important to us,**
- **When what can be gained by continuing is not worth the time or expense of continuing,**
- **When continuing results in changes, but not in improvement.**

has used up all her paint? Again, no. A painter is finished with her painting when she looks at the painting, nods her head, and knows that she has something that she did not have before. Continuing to work on the painting would make it different, but not better. Five trees are not necessarily better than three trees. Of course there are many more paintings to be painted, but with this one it is time to move on.

When you get to that point in therapy, both you and your therapist will sense that although you could continue to work together, that essentially what you have come for has been completed. You won't be perfect by a long shot, but you will be done.

Summary

(Intentionally left out!)

CHAPTER FOURTEEN

14. PARADOXICAL TECHNIQUES

There are two types of clients who enter therapy. The first type are those that know how they want to be but not how to be it. An example is people who want to be happy, but have no idea what to do to be happy. Often, these people feel little hope because they have concluded there is nothing that they can do to be happy unless they fall into some kind of luck or someone else changes to make them happy. The people that fit this way of thinking are addressed in other chapters of this book.

The second type of therapy clients are those that know what they need to do, but are unable to bring themselves to do it. They are hopeful about change because they know that there are ways that other people, in the same situation, are able to have improvement. They may even have been able to have partial success, but then have come to a mental "block" where they just can't do anymore. This chapter is for just such people.

Which Type of Client Are You?

There is a simple test you can do to see if your happiness is being blocked by lack of knowledge or by subconscious resistance. Take a piece of paper and then list several things that you know would improve your health, happiness, and relationships if you did them (for example, making a budget, exercising, or meeting more people). Then ask yourself why, if these things would make your life better, are you not doing them.

If you weren't able to list anything that would improve your

Which is your biggest problem?

- **Not knowing what you want?**
- **Not knowing how to get it?**
- **Not able to get started?**
- **Not being able to be consistent?**

The answers to most problems are easy. it's their application which is difficult:

- **To lose weight, eat fewer calories than you burn.**
- **To be happier, stop worrying and focus on achievable goals.**
- **Treat others the same way you would want them to treat you.**

life, then you are at least lacking some good knowledge. You may have internal resistance once you find out what you need to do, but you need to begin by acquiring knowledge. You need to learn *what* to do. If you were able to list some improvements, but have no idea how to go about doing them, that also is a lack of knowledge. For example, if you listed "make friends," but you have no idea how to make friends, then learning social skills will give you a good start.

If you were able to list one or more ways to improve your life and you know *how* to go about doing them, then a lack of knowledge isn't your problem. For example, if you listed "make a budget," and you know how to make a budget, but just are not doing it for one reason or another, then your main problem is internal resistance. Although you may consciously tell yourself that you don't have the time to follow through, or that you are planning to do it, that is just a mental cover story for your lack of action. You are being blocked by forces in yourself that you don't have control over.

This chapter will help you learn how to work with and work around those internal forces to get unblocked and unstuck. Then you can get to work on those things that can really make your life better. You can do this as a supplement to your therapy, or with the guidance of your therapist. Either way, it is another way to enrich your life more quickly.

On the next page is an exercise you can use to help you take a closer look at your resistance. Often people do not take a look at these things because our internal resistance makes us avoid looking at. It's a mental blind spot. Therapy will help you to uncover your mental blind spots, but you can start to do some of the work on your own. Then, you can bring them into your therapy session to work on.

Knowing an Answer Does Not Solve the Problem

There are many times when people know what they should do, but are unable to get themselves to do it. There are likely to be some things that you can think of that you should do and that would make you happier or more successful if you did

When people know what to do and have the means to do it, but are unable to bring themselves to do it, they have run into an invisible wall therapists call "resistance." Regardless of what you call it, you need to deal with it if you are going to change for the better.

Exercise: Identifying Resistance

Resistance is an internal condition which prevents us from reaching our goals. Although we may not consciously feel like we are resisting anything, we can observe the unconscious resistance by observing our behavior. Identifying resistance is the first step in dealing with it.

Is there something that I should do, but can't bring myself to do no matter how many times or how hard I try? (e.g., listen calmly to my partner, trust in my abilities, be on time for appointments, make new friends, keep to my schedule, etc.):

_____

_____

_____

Do I keep forgetting to do things that would help me (e.g., forgetting your therapy appointment, forgetting to do your therapy homework, forgetting to work on priorities at work or home, etc.)

☐ Yes   ☐ No

What am I doing instead of what I should do? (e.g., argue, worry, isolate myself from others, procrastinate, play games, sleep, talk on the phone, etc.):

_____

_____

_____

What are the long term consequences of doing my typical unhealthy behavior? (e.g., bad relationships, stress and poor health, loneliness and regret, failure to reach my goals and achieve success)

_____

_____

_____

If I did make the changes that would be good for me, is there something that I would miss about my current lifestyle?

_____

_____

_____

Is there something I imagine about changing that I really don't think I would like?

_____

_____

_____

Is the best way to change someone's mind to argue with them, or to agree with them?

- **Arguing causes resistance, which makes the other person strengthen their resolve.**
- **Agreement makes them more willing to meet you halfway.**
- **The same is true of our own minds.**

I once had a Christian client who had the persistent and unwanted thought, "I can't do anything." Rather than oppose that strongly programmed message, I had him go along with it, but to also add, "without God's help." So, he ended up saying, "I can't do anything without God's help." It quickly ended a battle he had with his own thinking for years. He didn't resist the unconscious message, but worked with it. Maybe you can change some of your own internal messages by tweaking them a little.

them, yet you find that you cannot do them. Or perhaps you are occasionally able to do them, but can't maintain them. For example, you know that you should walk away when someone treats you badly, but argue instead. Perhaps you know that you need to do some relaxation exercises when you are stressed or worried, but don't. Or, you can do these things a few times, but then revert to your old behavior. Maybe you know you should pay off your bills and stop using your credit cards, but you just can't bring yourself to stop. Easy answers; difficult applications.

Resistance Revisited

When people know what to do and have the means to do it, but are unable to bring themselves to do it, they have run into an invisible wall therapists call "resistance." It stems from our subconscious, which is a giant in comparison to our conscious mind. This subconscious resistance can be as difficult to break through with sheer willpower as it is to walk through a brick wall with sheer willpower. There are, of course, times people deliberately and consciously resist making a change because they consciously don't want to change—a common condition that most anybody who has lived among people has encountered. But the kind of resistance that I am describing here occurs when part of us wants to change, but another part of us does not. It is very frustrating because we think, "I want to change and I need to change, but no matter how hard I try, I just can't get myself to do it."

Coming to therapy for help with such a problem can also be a struggle. The part that wants to change wants to be in therapy making life better, and the other part wants to quit therapy and avoid dealing with the problem. I am not referring to multiple personality disorder (MPD), although the concept is similar. In MPD, the different personalities are really just different aspects of the self, but have further individuated by other identifying characteristics (different names, pulse rate, personality traits, etc.). Sometimes we feel like we have MPD though, with a battle going on in our brain. It particularly happens when we desire two incompatible things at the same time. We can't both deal with a problem and forget a problem, for example. You can see this clearly when you are trying to distract yourself from thinking about something, but it keeps popping into your mind (popping into your consciousness that is; of course it's been in your mind all the time—it's not popping in from an alien influence!). Many people spend restless nights trying not to think about things.

One type of technique that some therapists use to help people with resistance (the part of us that doesn't want to change) is called *paradoxical techniques*. You saw an example of that in the chapter on perfectionism. Instead of trying to oppose the perfectionism, the perfectionist was given the goal of becoming more perfect by doing less. It seems like a really tricky thing to do, but especially with anxiety disorders, such tricky things (which psychologists call paradoxical techniques) often work. And, unless they present some kind of danger, they are worth a try.

Paradoxical Techniques are Not the First Method Your Therapist will Use

These techniques are considered paradoxical because you actually achieve your goal by doing the very thing that would seem to prevent you from reaching your goal. Because they are counterintuitive, or "unnatural" to clients, these techniques are likely to be rejected if used early in therapy. Paradoxical techniques are therefore usually used only after other methods have proven too difficult or ineffective. Having tried everything else, clients are more willing to try something that seems a little strange. It reminds me of when I used to suffer from migraine headaches. I would have tried just about anything people suggested to get rid of them, even if it meant tying a tuna fish sandwich to my head (if you try that and it works, please let me know).

Consider these examples of direct approaches that do not work: trying to sleep can keep you awake; trying to change someone's mind is likely to make them hold all the more tightly to their position; trying not to worry can make you worry all the more; trying to control others results in loss of control of the relationship.

Paradoxical techniques make little sense to most people in the short term, but have good long-term results.

- **You can keep trying it over and over.**
- **You can give up.**
- **You can use a paradoxical approach.**

There are many times when the direct approach does not work. Even though the direct approach is not working, people will continue to use it for years because it makes sense to them. It is as though they discard the fact they are getting poor results in favor of the logic of the technique. If you ask a person whether or not a bad habit they have has been helpful to them (for example, if you ask someone who argues a lot if arguing is helpful for them), they will tell you "no." Then if you ask them, "What is the long-term consequence of your continuing to do that?" They will say something like, "Yeah, I know, I shouldn't argue, but I just get so mad that I can't help it." Or, "I know I'll regret it later, but it makes me feel better at the time." Some will tell you that they plan to stop although they have been doing the behavior for years. They are stuck doing a behavior which makes sense to them at the time they do it, but which actually is unproductive or harmful in the long run. Paradoxical techniques, on the other hand, make little sense to most people in the short term, but have good long-term results.

Example—A Paradoxical Approach to Arguing:

THERAPIST: "You argue with your husband about how often?"

CLIENT: "I guess a few times a week."

THERAPIST: "And you've tried to stop and find that you just can't, right?"

CLIENT: "Yes, that's right. He does stupid things and I just can't let it go."

THERAPIST: "You've told me that if you continue arguing like this, you are afraid you will destroy your relationship—that every time it happens, you can feel the two of you becoming further apart."

CLIENT: (tearful, nods in agreement).

THERAPIST: "What do you suppose would happen if the two of you did split up? Would you continue to argue?"

CLIENT: "I don't like to think about it."

THERAPIST: "I know, but because of the way you are going, it is a real possibility so I think we should consider it."

CLIENT: "Well, if we split up, we wouldn't talk anymore, so there wouldn't be any more fighting. Actually, that's starting to happen now because he's coming home later and later from work."

THERAPIST: "Then, I think we have found your solution."

CLIENT: "(now curious) What's that?"

THERAPIST: "Instead of trying not to argue with your husband, which obviously does not work, I think you should try to argue with him more often. Really try to show him just how stupid he is. He really is stupid after all, as you've said. You could leave notes for him reminding him of his stupidity and be sure to bring it up every time you see him or talk with him on the phone. You're bound to convince him of how stupid he is, or if not, then he will leave you all the sooner— sparing you years of drawn out aggravation. It really is a win-win approach for you."

CLIENT: "I don't want to do that!"

THERAPIST: "You mean you would rather continue to argue only sometimes and gradually drift apart, becoming more and more miserable and wasting valuable time from your life and happiness?"

CLIENT: "(caught in a bind). You're saying that I should argue more?"

THERAPIST: "Absolutely. Your husband will either come to see that you are right or leave and spare you years of aggravation. You win either way."

You could leave notes for him reminding him of his stupidity and be sure to bring it up every time you see him or talk with him on the phone.

The Paradoxical Prescription

The paradoxical *prescription* is to do the undesired behavior in order to achieve an *unwanted* result all the sooner (in the previous example, breaking up with the husband). When she tries to do it intentionally (argue in order to break up), her mind reels against that behavior and allows her to stop. The old reason (proving that her husband was wrong) ceases to be important and is no longer a barrier to stopping her arguing. I honestly need to say that I have not seen this technique fail to work when clients have tried it. It is very effective.

This kind of intervention is best done toward the end of the session with the therapist virtually escorting the client out the door with the homework of doing the paradoxical prescription (arguing more in this case). The intervention is simple and elegant. Typically, the client comes back the following week and says that she didn't argue at all that week (after having been told to argue a lot). The resistance has been broken (previously she was resisting giving up arguing). On the other hand, if the client comes back and reports arguing less but still arguing, then the therapist continues to make the paradoxical prescription outlined above ("Good, just keep arguing in order to break up the relationship and get it over with").

Sometimes the client will say that she did the paradoxical prescription for a few days (in this case, arguing much more), but then decided it wasn't worth it. "I just decided that it's not worth it to argue with him. If he wants to be stupid, that's his problem." Whichever way the client takes it, the result is the same—the client develops a dislike for arguing (she actually develops a healthy resistance to the harmful behavior). I won't blame you if you need to reread this section. It's a powerful technique, but it's different from what people are used to. So, it takes a little longer to understand.

It's Easy to Think Your Therapist Is Nuts

It is important to realize in this example that the therapist is making the paradoxical prescription in order to break the resistance to the good behavior and to achieve positive results

The paradoxical prescription is to do the undesired behavior in order to achieve an unwanted result all the sooner. This prescription often makes people stop doing the behavior altogether.

for the client. Previous attempts to reduce her arguing had not been successful although she knew it was destructive. When the client would try not to argue, resistance would occur (resistance to stopping) and prevent her from changing her behavior. She "couldn't help" herself. With the use of the paradoxical technique, the goal was to argue more. Her resistance to stopping arguing had no affect on this goal. Freed from her resistance, she could make the *choice* to stop arguing. It stopped being a struggle. A little confusing, I know. Let's look at another example.

A Few Easier Examples

I gave you the above example to help you respect the training it takes for therapists to be able to use these advanced techniques. But, here are a few easier examples from everyday life. Consider trying to go to sleep. The harder we try, the less able we are to do it. Trying *not* to sleep (although we want to), bypasses the unconscious resistance to sleeping and we often fall asleep.

You can also consider that trying not to worry will make us worry more, while trying to intentionally worry more will often stop the worrying. Paradoxical methods often succeed where direct methods fail, when something inside is holding us back from doing a healthy thing. Where direct methods succeed, however, they should be the treatment of choice.

Although paradoxical prescriptions sound bad on the surface (trying to do an undesirable thing), their intent is always the welfare of the client. Also, keep in mind that your therapist will never direct you to do something dangerous. Your therapist would never tell you to abuse someone or allow yourself to be abused, for example. The means don't always justify the ends.

Short of abuse, however some seemingly bad paradoxical prescriptions can be put to good use. An overly controlling parent, for example, could be encouraged to be all the more controlling so that his relationship with his child can be broken altogether and he no longer need to worry about it, as in the

Example Paradoxes from Everyday Life:

- **Trying to sleep keeps you awake.**
- **Trying not to worry will make you worry more.**
- **Running from our fears makes them scarier.**
- **Being patient usually delays progress.**
- **Loving someone too much bugs the hell out of them.**

following example:

Example—Paradoxical Technique Used with an Overcontrolling Father

THERAPIST: "It may be very helpful for you to prevent your teenage son from having any contact with his friends. Although it will destroy your relationship with him, it will help to keep him out of trouble. Trying to control him by degrees, is after all, just slowly destroying your relationship anyway without really keeping him out of mischief. This week, try to control his every move and watch him as much as possible. It may cut into your free time, but it will make sure he doesn't get into trouble. That's your goal, right?"

(Father returns the following week).

FATHER: "I know you said to be more controlling and to watch him more closely, but I decided it's not worth it. Why should I sacrifice all my free time just to keep him out of trouble? If he wants to get into trouble, that's his problem, not mine. He's the one who will have to live with the consequences."

THERAPIST: "Yeah, I see what you mean."

(The end result is that the father and son develop a better relationship, and the son gets in less trouble).

_____

We Can Do Paradoxical Techniques Even When We Know They Are Paradoxical

It is not necessary that you be "fooled" by the therapist using this technique. There is nothing secret about it. Even if you are fully aware that it is a paradoxical prescription, it will still be just as effective. What works in therapy is not always what makes the most sense. After all, if doing what makes sense

I know you said to be more controlling and to watch him more closely, but I decided it's not worth it. Why should I sacrifice all my free time just to keep him out of trouble?

206

really worked, then people wouldn't need therapy in the first place. In the case of paradoxical techniques, you need to decide if you would rather continue to use the common sense way that has not worked for you, or the paradoxical technique. The paradoxical approach feels risky, but it is actually the original, "sensible," behavior which carries the most risk since it is not working and is actually causing harm. Let me say that again—when doing the common sense thing is causing damage, continuing to do what makes sense is a risky behavior.

On the next page is an exercise you can use to make your own paradoxical prescriptions. Although they may sound crazy, they are not as crazy as continuing to do something which makes sense, but just doesn't work.

When It Makes Sense to Do What Doesn't Make Sense

Paradoxical techniques by their very definition do not make sense. Otherwise, they would not be considered paradoxical. For people who have poor coping skills, many of the more common techniques taught by therapists don't make sense. It takes time to trust your therapist enough to do something that does not seem to make sense. That is why therapists can't use paradoxical techniques early in treatment. Asking someone to do something that seemingly does not make sense requires a good working relationship where there is mutual trust. Also, waiting until later gives the therapist time to demonstrate to you the ineffectiveness of your current attempts to cope.

There are other techniques that don't seem to make sense, but do work. Paradoxical techniques are just a sample of the many possible coping strategies that your therapist can teach you. Of course, in your individual therapy, the coping strategies will be tailored to your individual needs.

Direct approaches to anxiety often fail where paradoxical approaches succeed. Probably the most common direct advice that a person suffering from worry and anxiety hears is, "relax" and, "don't worry." Of course, if the anxious person could relax, she would. The advice to relax is useless. Only a person

The only things that make sense to us are those that match what we already think. That means some of the things we think make sense are actually nuts, and some that don't make sense are things we need to learn.

Exercise: Creating Your Own Paradoxical Prescriptions

Our willpower is not always sufficient to overcome subconscious resistance. And, willing ourselves to have more willpower just digs a hole of guilt. Paradoxical techniques do not oppose subconscious resistance the way that willpower tries to. Instead, they get the subconscious to "switch off" the resistance. This is also known as "breaking through" the resistance. Basically, if we want to diet, but we crave donuts, we can stop this craving by eating only donuts for breakfast, lunch, and dinner every day. This is also true of habit thinking and behavior. When we do it to the point that our own habits become repugnant to us, there is no longer any subconscious resistance to changing them.

Step 1. Make a prescription that tells yourself to do the bad behavior as much as possible (but only for things that are not dangerous):

Example 1: (To quit arguing)
Prescription: Argue all the time, even if I really agree with what people are saying.

Example 2: (To stop worrying)
Make myself worry all the time about everything, no matter how trivial it is.

Example 3: (To overcome avoidance of people)
Isolate self from everybody; don't talk to anyone; don't answer the phone. Don't watch people on TV. Don't listen to people on the radio or music, etc.

Example 4: (To overcome procrastination)
Always procrastinate; even if something is important, put it off as long as I can.

Step 2. Follow through with your prescription until you cannot stand doing the unhealthy behavior any longer (i.e. until you have created a resistance to your original resistance)

Step 3. If you find that your original resistance is not breaking, then you are not following your prescription closely enough. Remember that you must *dramatically* increase the undesirable behavior in order to build a resistance to it.

Step 4. If you find yourself returning to your original resistance to improving, immediately start following your prescription again.

who knows how to relax can relax. As any brain surgeon will say, "It's easy once you know how." For the person with an anxiety problem, saying "just relax" is about as helpful as telling someone to "just do brain surgery." When you don't know how, doing something which seems easy to others (e.g., tying your shoes) is very difficult. It is part of the therapist's job to make it easy for you. You do remember that one time in your life, someone helped you to tie your shoes, don't you?

Paradoxical Techniques Are a Good Back Up Technique for Worry When Planning Doesn't Work

Learning to manage worry is also something you can master. Worry can be thought of as the mind's *continual* attempt to prepare for some possible future event. Although we may regret the past and suffer pain because of it, we don't worry about the past. It has happened already. Trying to put worries out of your mind by sheer willpower or by distracting yourself with other activities is a temporary solution at best. As soon as you stop being distracted, your mind will remind you of what some other part of your mind is trying to forget. Although it can seem like something is wrong with your mind, actually this tendency can be put to good use.

If you are a student and you are worried about how you will do on a test, your mind reminding you about it will prompt you to study. Without an ability to be anxious or worried, we wouldn't prepare for important events and we wouldn't be careful. We wouldn't look before crossing the street (preparing to cross the street), we wouldn't bother to be careful how we respond to other people (preparing for continued good relations), to obey traffic laws (preparing for a safe trip), to get out of bed if we were still tired (preparing to deal with daily responsibilities) and many other things too numerous to mention.

The ability to experience anxiety about the future is one of the best characteristics we possess and elevates us above the level of animals. Knowing that anxiety is an internal prompt to prepare is helpful to those suffering from anxiety. As I pointed out in an earlier chapter, the single best way to deal with

Worry can be thought of as the mind's continual attempt to prepare for some possible future event (if it weren't possible, we wouldn't worry about it).

anxiety is to prepare for the event you are anxious about.

Making plans in order to cope with anxiety makes sense once you understand the purpose of anxiety. Planning does not always work, however, because there are some things that we don't know how to plan or prepare for. And, even with a good plan, worry can still be a problem for some people. They can continue to have unwanted thoughts that interfere with their daily routines and their happiness. They may fall back into the use of distraction or sedation, which just reduces the ability to concentrate and also makes people tired. Before deciding to take or increase your medication, you might be willing to try a paradoxical technique.

Worry Scheduling

In cases like these, a non-common sense technique (paradoxical technique) is that of *worry scheduling*. Plan a time that you will worry sometime during the day. It needs to be at least half an hour, but no more than one hour. When that scheduled time arrives, you are to do nothing but worry. Think of every possible terrible thing that could go wrong. Say out loud how your life is ruined and how horrible things are. Add some drama, if possible such as rubbing ashes or dirt onto yourself. At the end of the scheduled time, schedule another worry time for the next day.

With this technique it is critical that you do two things: 1) schedule a definite block of time to worry; and 2) worry as much as possible during that time. Although it sounds nuts, it has the effect of satisfying the mind's desire to worry. After a few days of keeping your worry appointment with yourself, your mind will greatly ease up on you for the rest of the day. When you are doing something and you start to worry, just tell yourself that you will be sure to worry about it during the worry time. If, however, you do not keep your scheduled worry appointment, the technique will fail. You cannot fool your own mind. In *every* case that I have seen a person use this technique, it has worked well. The problem lies in getting people do it. Some people would rather do what makes sense, even it doesn't work, than do something that seems weird but

Worry Scheduling—A paradoxical way to worry less and enjoy your worry more:

- **Decreases worry by limiting it to certain, scheduled times.**
- **Giving your worry some time to be out of control helps you to be more in control.**
- **When you worry, you are less stressed by it.**

210

might work. Choosing to worry all day rather than use this technique for half an hour is something that really doesn't make sense to me.

Case Example—Wendy

When Wendy first came to counseling, she said that she worried about everything and that she couldn't relax. I helped her to learn some relaxation techniques which brought her some relief, but not a cure.

Since Wendy's worrying was not confined to a few specific fears, and was intruding on her daily routine, I helped Wendy learn how to put limits on her anxiety by doing worry scheduling. Wendy would schedule a 30 minute block of time in the afternoon and then again in the evening when she was to worry. During those times, she was to go to a private place and try to worry as much as possible—exaggerating her worries far beyond what she had been.

During her "worry time," she would use a list of worries that she had made throughout the day on an index card. One item, for example, was from the morning when she worried that someone would think her a slob for wearing a wrinkled blouse. During her worry time, she exaggerated this, as instructed, by telling herself that she would end up on the nightly news as the "city eyesore" or get a national award for worst dressed woman.

For her worry time, I had encouraged her to wail, rub ashes in her hair, or anything that really exaggerated the calamity that could happen and how terrible things were. She was to play it up and really satisfy her mind's desire to worry, but only at these times. At other times, she was to tell herself that it was not yet time to worry, but to add the thought to her index card list for later. In this way, Wendy was able to structure her worry and limit it while reducing anxiety at other times.

Although Wendy had been hesitant to try this technique at first, she found to her amazement that she started to worry less

> *I helped Wendy learn how to put limits on her anxiety by doing worry scheduling*

> *Although Wendy had been hesitant to try this technique at first, she found to her amazement that she started to worry less after only doing her worry scheduling for a few days.*

after only doing her worry scheduling for a few days. She also learned, however, that if she did not keep her worry time appointments, her condition would worsen again.

Trying not to worry had never helped her, but using the paradoxical technique of intentionally worrying helped her to feel more normal and more in control of her own mind. By extremely exaggerating her worries, she also was able to see their ridiculousness, which often caused her to laugh at her own silliness.

Before long, she was able to reduce her worry time to once a day. By using a combination of relaxation techniques, worry scheduling, and planning for the worst, Wendy got her life back on track and took worry off of center stage.

———

A Combination Paradoxical and Retraining Technique for Sleeping

Here is a list of things to do in bed, for people who have trouble sleeping:

- **Sleep**

For people who have trouble sleeping, trying to sleep just brings aggravation and actually delays the time it takes to fall asleep. A paradoxical approach promotes sleeping because trying to stay awake is more effective than trying to sleep.

As with other paradoxical techniques, good habits must also replace the bad. For falling asleep in bed, this means not doing other things in bed. That means no eating, watching TV, reading, having sex, jumping, or any other activity in bed. Why? Because you need to teach your brain that getting into bed is a cue for sleeping. Cues are most helpful when there is one cue for each feeling or behavior you want to have.

Specifically, the paradoxical part of learning to sleep in bed is to get out of bed whenever you are tired, but are having trouble sleeping. Tossing, turning, and trying to sleep just leads to not sleeping. Instead, get out of bed and do a relaxing activity (e.g., read a boring book, listen to soft music). Do not do any stimulating activities like using bright lights, watching television, using the computer, listening to loud music, etc. When you feel sleepy, again go back to bed. *Don't try to sleep, though. Just continue thinking about that relaxing activity or boring book.*

If you have been doing things other than sleeping in your bed for a long time, then it will take a couple of weeks for this technique to work. But, once you have trained your brain to sleep upon going to bed, you should be able to maintain this pattern. Another bit of advice—if you are having trouble sleeping at night, do not take any naps regardless of how tired you are in the daytime.

Paradoxical techniques have many applications in our day to day lives. Always try the direct route first and if you find that you just can't make *necessary* changes, a paradoxical technique may help you to finally change. It takes creativity and expertise to create a good paradoxical intervention for a serious problem, but working with your therapist will give you the best chance to overcome even the most difficult of situations. Your therapist also may not be experienced with paradoxical techniques. Remember, there are many ways to peel a potato (skinning cats is too cruel).

Don't Worry if You Don't Want to Do This Stuff

If this chapter has made no sense for you—trying to argue more in order to argue less, planning to worry in order to relax, trying to stay awake in order to sleep, you are not alone. Suffice it to say that our minds are very complicated. Simply knowing what we should do and then doing it is really not simple at all. We find ourselves failing time and again to do what we know to be best. To make matters worse, the longer we have had a bad habit, the harder it is to break.

Summary

Hopefully this chapter has introduced to you the idea that your therapist is an expert on human behavior and thinking and has interventions that you may have never heard of. If someone else had written this book, they may have made this chapter about hypnotism rather than paradoxical techniques.

Resistance to Overcoming Resistance?

No problem. Just tell yourself you are happy with the way you are and that you like the way your life is heading. (Doing this may help you break through your resistance to overcoming resistance, even if you don't want to!).

You cannot make positive changes in your life by just continuing to do what you were doing before coming to therapy.

Paradoxical techniques just happen to be something that I'm good at.

What your therapist says will sometimes not make sense to you because it does not fit what you have learned or done so far. But, you cannot make positive changes in your life by just continuing to do what you were doing before coming to therapy. You want to learn better ways that work, right? Do what your therapist advises before deciding it won't work for you. Let your experience, rather than your common sense, be your guide.

15. A REALITY APPROACH TO SELF-ESTEEM

"Do you like yourself?" is a pop psychology question with little meaning. What does it mean to "like oneself"? A more meaningful question is, "What do you like about yourself?" And depending on your goals, another helpful question might be, "What do others like about you?" If someone tells us directly that they "like" us, we can be suspicious of their motives or wonder what they mean. However, when someone tells us something they specifically like *about* us—whether it is our necktie, our smile, our laugh, our eyes, the way we clean a window—anything, it helps us to feel good about ourselves, especially if we agree with their opinion. On the other hand, when someone tells us that we are a wonderful person or that they like *everything* about us, then either they don't know us very well, are lying, or are very needy (or some combination thereof). Likewise, self-esteem is not about liking everything about yourself. You can hate some things about yourself and still have good self-esteem.

Specificity, Sincerity, and Self-Esteem:

- **People are perceived as being more sincere when they compliment something specific about us (e.g., You have a nice butt, You're a really good listener, etc.).**
- **We value ourselves more when we are specific about what we like about ourselves (e.g., I have a nice butt, I'm a good listener, etc.).**

Being Liked by Others Doesn't Have to Do With Being Better than Them

We know that not everything about us is likeable. No matter how hard (or not so hard) we try to be nice and to do things well, we mess up time and time again. There are some aspects of ourselves that are better swept under the rug than displayed on the mantle. The people who know us well, know these things. Those who have accepted our faults and like us anyway are our friends and loved ones. We feel better about people who accept our faults and like us anyhow than we do

215

about people who think we have no faults. They give us. acknowledgement and acceptance. It helps us to feel important and to feel like we belong. These are real self-esteem boosters.

"Basically Good" Is Hard to Believe; Basically the Same Is Much Easier

Acknowledgement and acceptance are not only desirable from others, they are also keys for thinking about ourselves and improving our self-esteem. For many years, pop psychology has tried to convince people of their basic self-worth and inherent goodness. All the while crimes and wars rage on and moral decay is all around us. The people who try to believe that they are inherently good end up feeling even more unworthy in light of a lack of supporting evidence. The idea of basic self worth is an illusion that is too difficult to maintain. As soon as we try to raise our self-esteem by telling ourselves that we are basically good, we mess up and prove to ourselves that we are not. Just as standing in the cold and telling yourself that you are actually warm simply will not make you feel warmer, so repeatedly messing up and telling yourself that you are a good person will also not work.

Unless you are a narcissist, if I try to convince you that you are as good as everyone else, you will probably come up with examples of people you consider to be better than you. Even if you do believe me for the moment, the next time you mess up, it will remind you that you are not that good after all. I can pump you up with compliments, but I can't keep you inflated. If, instead of trying to convince you that you are basically good, I tell you that you are just as bad as everyone else, that will be much more believable.

Evidence that others are messed up is all around us and has been for all of recorded history. Usually we don't need to look any further than our own family. The idea that we are good and others are bad doesn't hold up to the evidence. People have rarely lived up to the moral standards they set for others. On the other hand, the idea that we are bad and that others are good also does not hold up to the evidence. Whether we turn on the TV, read the news, or observe people at the mall doesn't

The people who try to believe that they are inherently good end up feeling even more unworthy in light of a lack of supporting evidence.

matter. Unless we are watching reruns of Sesame Street, the reminders that we are in a messed up world are all around us. The fact is, we are messed up people living in a messed up world. Seeing this clearly is actually a good start for building your self-esteem.

Just Like Building a House, It Is Easier to Build Self-Esteem on Ground that Is Level

One of the successful ways to improve our self-esteem is to realize just how "bad" (imperfect, prone to mistakes and temptations, prone to act in ways that help us to momentarily feel better although we hurt other people, etc.) we and other people actually are. It is a real world approach to self-esteem because it fits the evidence. It is believable. The next time that you make a mistake, say to yourself, "There I go again, making mistakes just like everybody else," or "There I go again, doing stupid things just like everybody else." When you say, "just like everybody else," it accomplishes two things: 1) it keeps you from blowing your mistakes out of proportion, and 2) it levels the playing field. It is healthy because you are seeing reality more clearly. You are neither elevating others nor debasing yourself. You are putting yourself in the same situation as everyone else. You see yourself as more of a part of the human race. The recognition that fundamentally you are like others promotes feelings of bonding and acceptance—both by yourself and by others. After all, how easy would it be to bond with someone who thinks he or she is better than you? How about someone who says they are just as bad as you? Easier, isn't it?

People with low self-esteem find it easier to bring others down to their level than to bring themselves up to the level of others:

- **"I'm just as good as everyone else" meets heavy internal resistance.**
- **"I'm just as bad as everyone else" meets no resistance, but accomplishes the same job.**

Keeping the Field Level by Accepting and Acknowledging Others

This principle can also be used in reverse. When someone does something that we don't like—for example, telling a lie, we can say to ourselves, "There he goes, being dishonest just like I have been before." Or, in a more general way, "There he goes messing up just like I have many times before." It cuts down on the hypocrisy, levels the field, stops us from being judgmental, and helps us to see the other person as more like ourselves—again promoting bonding and acceptance. Self

217

esteem or self-love comes after self-acceptance. Love of others comes after accepting others. If others need to be perfect in order for us to love them, then we will be critical, angry, and lonely. We will find ourselves settling for our partners instead of enjoying them. Also, if we need to be "good" (always cheerful, competent, and loving) in order to accept and love ourselves, we will be self-critical and robbed of life energy. Self-esteem is based on self acceptance and not on being better than others. Our finest achievements will only temporarily impact our self-esteem, even if they build a marble statue to honor us in the middle of town.

Trade In Your Rose Colored Glasses for Clear Ones

You will never be able to prove that you are a good person, but you can prove that you are not a good one in only a few seconds. Positive thoughts about our "goodness" don't stand a chance. Therapy or any kind of self-improvement we make will also only be one piece of evidence about our goodness in contrast to a lot more convicting evidence. Part of the work of psychotherapy is to get you to be more realistic while at the same time being positive. But that does not mean trying to brainwash yourself to believe things that aren't true. Dealing with reality makes us more effective, and in turn, more positive. Being positive keeps us motivated and helps us to enjoy the process of life. Low self-esteem results from an unrealistically low self appraisal or an unrealistically high appraisal of others. Seeing ourselves and others realistically involves seeing both the bad and the good.

You're Not All Bad

Besides being realistic about your faults, it is important to see your good qualities and to learn to emphasize them. If you were a farmer with both good seed and bad seed, which would you rather plant? Would you say, "Well, I got both, so I'm darn well going to use both"? No, you wouldn't. You would plant only good seed because you would be interested in maximizing your crops, even if the bad seed went to waste. Likewise, when we emphasize our good qualities we yield better results for ourselves and for others.

Dealing with reality makes us more effective, and in turn, more positive. Being positive keeps us motivated and helps us to enjoy the process of life.

218

How Are Your Public Performances?

If you were good at singing, but terrible at dancing, which would you rather do in front of an audience? Which would they prefer? Although you may think that you would never do something in front of an audience, the fact is that you do something in front of an audience whenever other people are present. You also do things in front of an audience when others are not present. No one watches us as closely as we watch ourselves. We are a constant audience of not only our own behavior, but our thoughts as well. With all this continuous watching, we need to learn to put our best foot forward. The exercise on the next page will help you to identify small steps forward for some important areas of your life.

Putting Your Best "Parts" Forward

If you don't like the way you look, a good exercise to do is to stand naked in front of the mirror until you identify your *best* feature. Everyone has at least one best feature (not all parts are equally bad). Now, emphasize that feature to others (with makeup, grooming, jewelry, clothing, etc.) and to yourself. Let's suppose it is your arms. You can wear shirts and blouses which show them off. A nice bracelet or watch could help you to draw attention to your arms. Putting your best physical feature forward will actually make you appear more attractive to others and you will feel more attractive. Feeling more attractive, in turn, helps you to project your attractiveness to others. Starting with one good physical feature, we can create an upward spiral of attractiveness.

You can do the same with your personality. What do you like best about your personality? Your intelligence? Your sense of humor? Your ability to see details? Your creativity? If you are intelligent and humorless, don't try to wow people with your jokes. You have a sense of humor but are not so smart? Don't try to impress people with your intelligence. The point of course is not to impress others (people like you best if you are impressed with them—not if you try to impress them), but to feel confident in what you are doing. If you don't have any

The "Social Mirror":

- The way other people respond to us gives us a much better perception of our own attractiveness than what we see in the mirror or think about our abilities.

Exercise: Becoming a Better Person

Although you are just as bad as everyone else, that doesn't prevent you from becoming better than you are. Even small changes can make a big difference in the way we see ourselves and in the way others see us. Try to find one better choice you can make in each area. Some people will find it easier to complete the right hand column, "Better Choices," before completing the middle column, "Current Behavior."

Example Table

	Current Behavior	Better Choices
Work/Professional	Keep to myself	Be friendly to others
Health/Physical	Stay in all day	Go for walks
Intimate Relationships	Argue	Look for areas of agreement
Spiritual	Think nothing of it	Seek meaning; live for a purpose

My Table

	Current Behavior	Better Choices
Work/Professional		
Health/Physical		
Intimate Relationships		
Spiritual		
Hobbies/Activities		
My Home		
Personal Growth & Learning		
Friendships		
Financial		
Family		

good qualities or skills, then work on one. You need to be able to tell yourself, "I am a good _____." This acts as a buffer against all of those other things that we do so poorly. We may be a cracked pot but we can still hold water.

Suppose I bounce a check. I can say to myself, "I'm not good at balancing my checkbook, but I am a good therapist." To apply this to others, "She's not a good cook, but she sure is a good kisser." When you make these kinds of statements, always follow the negative with the positive and not the other way around. That is, don't say, "She sure is a good kisser, but she's not a good cook," or "I'm a good therapist, but I'm not good at balancing my checkbook." By admitting our faults (and the faults of others) and attending to our strengths (and those of others), we keep our perspective. We keep from seeing ourselves or others as all bad, which in turn promotes bonding and acceptance. Bonding and acceptance are keys to relationships. And life just doesn't feel meaningful without good relationships.

On the next page is an exercise to help you have some more ideas about how to put your best foot forward—both with yourself, and with others.

Helping Others and Ourselves to Build Self-Esteem

Our self-esteem cannot directly be built by others. It is only what we say or think about ourselves that influences self-esteem. But, what others say does influence how we think. And what we say influences others. Suppose your child comes to you with a bad grade. You can try to pump her up or you can help her to level the field. Trying to protect children from truths that are glaringly obvious to them does not help them any more than it does adults. On the other hand, pointing out the obvious while keeping it at a realistic level is very helpful. For children, it helps them to see their selves realistically. Here's an example of how you could put things into perspective for your child without damaging her self-esteem: "Well, Janie, you did mess up on that test—just like a lot of

Words Do Make A Difference.

Which one of these statements sounds more positive to you?:

- **She's sure a good kisser, but she isn't a good cook.**
- **She's not a good cook, but she sure is a good kisser.**
- **Putting the positive last shows acceptance and feels better to other people.**

Which way do you say things to others:

- **Negative first?, or**
- **Positive first?**

Which way do you think about yourself:

- **Negative first?,**
- **Positive first?, or**
- **Positive not at all?**

Exercise: Put Your Best Foot Forward

<u>Self-criticism does not lead to improved performance</u>. Actually, the more you criticize yourself, the worse your performance will become. You will not become more attractive by telling yourself you are ugly or more sociable by telling yourself you are shy. You won't become a better parent by telling yourself you are a lousy one or a better golfer by telling yourself that you stink at golf. On the other hand, water even the tiniest seeds of success/goodness in yourself to grow that part. Stop trying to reduce your bad qualities and start focusing on your good ones.   Here are some exercises to help you do that.

Appearance

No matter how bad you feel about your physical appearance, one of your features is better looking than the rest.

My best physical feature is:

People usually show that part off by:

A change that I could make to show that part off more is:

Personality

Just as with your body, there is some part of your personality that is better than the rest. That part can continue to grow and blossom and wow people (including yourself).

My best personality quality is:

People usually show that part off by:

A change that I could make to show that part off more is:

Talent

Everybody is more talented in one area more than in the rest. It can be a good basis for a career, for a hobby, for connecting with others, or all three.

My best skill is:

People usually show off this skill by:

A change that I could make to show off my skills more is:

<u>You can also help your kids/partner/friend to show off these parts , too. What a great gift!</u>

other kids." After that, you can help Janie to put her best foot forward by emphasizing the positives: "You seem to have real strengths in these other areas." With this approach, children don't feel singled out, they don't feel inferior, and they are less resistant to receiving help. Another example, "Well, Janie, you messed up on that test—just like a lot of other kids. So, just like a lot of other kids, you can do some things to improve." On the other hand, when your child does well, you can say, "Wow, Janie, you are super at that!" Be sure not to follow this kind of statement up with a negative comment. Positives should always follow negatives and not the other way around. Can you imagine saying, "You sure have strengths in these other areas, but you messed up here just like a lot of other kids"? Emphasizing the positive while acknowledging the negative will help to improve performance and self-esteem.

On the next page are some exercises you can do to improve your performance and self-esteem. They will help you to bring yourself down to the level of most people, where you can accept yourself better. Keep in mind that acceptance does not mean liking. It means not getting hung up on what is by pretending or wishing it was some other way.

When we give others a compliment about something they don't like about themselves, it does not make them feel positive about it. Rather it separates us from them and often makes the other person feel bad rather than good. Good intentions are not the same as good actions and we need to learn to say to others (and to ourselves) what is truly helpful. Better than false compliments is letting someone know that you see their faults, but that you accept them and love them anyway. How do you feel about others who really know you (warts and all) *and* who really love you?

Examples of Comments That Distance Rather Than Build Self-Esteem

"You are very beautiful," said to a woman who thinks she is ugly.

You Can Help Others by Normalizing Their Problems:

- When you point out someone's weakness, don't make it seem like their unique problem.
- If possible, offer a solution that is within their ability.
- For example, "Well, Janie, you messed up on that test—just like a lot of other kids. So, just like a lot of other kids, you can do some things to improve."
- Do the same with yourself.
- For example, "Well, I messed up on that just like a lot of other people do. And, just like them, I can get better at it."

Exercise: Promoting Self-Acceptance

As soon as we accept a reality about ourselves or others, we start to work to change things or work around them. We give up the blaming, complaining, and hoping, and instead get busy with things that really help. When we don't know what to do, we can always get help. Enough people have been in the same situation that we have, that we can learn from them how to cope, how to prosper, and how to move ahead with our lives. Here are two exercises to help you accept realities about yourself, in a positive and productive way. The next time you start to criticize yourself, try one of these exercises instead.

Part 1:   Write 5 sentences using this pattern: "I am/have _____, just like a lot of people. And, just like a lot of people, I can _____."

Example: "I am overweight, just like a lot of people. And, just like a lot of people, I can get help to lose weight."

Example: "I have relationship problems, just like a lot of people. And, just like a lot of people, I can get help to improve the way that I respond in relationships."

1.

2.

3.

4.

5.

Part 2: A Reminder Card

Write on an index card, the back of a business card, or any old piece of paper, *"There I go again—making mistakes just like everyone else."* Carry the card with you and every time you mess up, take it out and read it aloud to yourself (aloud is important). Convincing yourself you are just as mistake prone as everyone else shouldn't be hard. Then you can be easier on yourself and on them. Trying to convince yourself you are better than others will either make you a liar or arrogant. Neither is good for you or others.

"You are so smart," said to someone who thinks he is stupid.

"You are a wonderful cook," said to someone who can't even boil water.

"You are a great athlete," said to someone who just lost a competition.

Examples of Comments that Build Self-Esteem and Attract Others

(Said to the same people as in the examples above)

"I didn't see it before, but you have lovely hands."

"You don't need to be a genius to impress me. The way you treat me makes me feel special."

"Your best dish may be cold cereal, but I love you."

"You didn't win, but I am very proud of how hard you trained."

Which comments would you rather receive if you were these people? What can you learn about the way you should talk to others and to yourself? Honesty about our weaknesses can be tempered with our strengths. Honesty about other's strengths can help us to look past their weaknesses.

Summary

"Do you like yourself?" may not be such a bad question after all. But, just as being liked by others can be unclear, so can this question. It helps to know that everyone, including us, has faults. We can base our self- esteem on our relationships and on the frail humanity which is in others and ourselves. "Accepting" our weaknesses does not stop us from working on them. It does mean that they are no longer going to take center

"Your best dish may be cold cereal, but I love you."

With a level playing field, you can more easily love your neighbor as you love yourself.

stage in our attention. Weeds can choke out the flowers, but when we focus on growing the flowers, they can choke out the weeds. The more of yourself that you find to love and to grow, the less of yourself that there will be to dislike—both for yourself and for others.

As your self-esteem improves, so will your tolerance and delight in other people. Be sure to be honest with your therapist if you are struggling with low self-esteem. With your therapist, you can identify both negative and positive qualities about yourself and significant others in your life. Accepting both the good and the bad about yourself and others will help both you and the ones you love to accept each other. With a level playing field, you can more easily love your neighbor as you love yourself.

Part III—Ending Psychotherapy

16. GETTING INSPIRED BY LOOKING AHEAD

There is no doubt about it. Although we change in many ways without even trying throughout our lives, intentionally changing is hard. Clients who are new to counseling are often surprised that therapy is neither fun nor easy. Most of their ideas about therapy have come mainly from television.

Television has often portrayed therapists as wise sages that give wise counsel to patients who then have a new revelation and are immediately cured. From that moment on their lives are immediately better. Combine this with people's desire for instant gratification, and you get unrealistic expectations and disappointments about therapists and therapy. The truth is that although therapists do have all kinds of sage advice, people do not change upon hearing it. Never has the mere hearing of a solution been enough to effect change. One of the earliest examples of this is when Moses returned from Mt. Sinai carrying the stone tablets with the Ten Commandments. Although the Jews were a God fearing people, and believed the commandments to be the word of God, they continually struggled to follow them. Even when we agree with someone's advice and know that it is right, taking it can be very difficult.

Answers are Easy, Actions are Hard

The actual learning of what to do to improve your life is as easy as looking it up on the internet. For example the fundamental practices for being physically healthy are sleeping eight to ten hours per day, eating a healthy diet, and exercising daily. There is nothing complex about it. But, most people

There are answers to all human and environmental conditions. Most of them we already know. The challenge is their implementation.

- **The same is true for your life.**

don't want to hear that.

Imagine going to a medical doctor because you feel fatigued and irritable much of the time. The doctor says to you to sleep more, eat healthy food, and exercise daily to restore your energy and mood. Although the doctor would be completely correct (once illness is ruled out), you no doubt would say or think, "I already knew I should do that," and then go on being tired and irritable as you continue your same daily lifestyle. If, instead, the doctor says, "Here's a prescription for you that will help you feel better," you are much more likely to comply with the advice.

It is not knowledge that people are seeking, but shortcuts—some way to get the payoff without doing the work. Taking a pill is easy, changing a lifestyle is hard. Taking a pill is like magic, exercising is mundane. Sleeping eight hours means sacrificing our TV shows. Eating right means sacrificing our junk food habits and reducing our portions. There is absolutely no excitement in these types of lifestyle changes. Faced with the choice of doing hard work or continuing an unhealthy lifestyle, most people will continue their unhealthy lifestyle.

Get Off the Treadmill and Get on the Tractor

The tendency for people to continue doing what they always do is referred to as the "principle of homeostasis." The easiest thing for us to do today is the same thing that we did yesterday, and the day before that, and the day before that—year after year. It is an assembly line mentality that requires little thought and allows us to live life on autopilot. Intentionally changing requires a farmer mentality—we must toil and sow today so that we can harvest and enjoy tomorrow. Our behaviors must change as environmental conditions change. We can't continue to behave as children and expect our spouses and bosses to take care of us like parents. And we must be on the lookout for emotional and social pests, weeds, and diseases. It is up to us to make good decisions and to do the work which will bring the most success, however we measure it. The question is, "how can we develop this farmer mentality if we don't already have it?"

Even guaranteed solutions are hard to implement:

- **Eating fewer calories than you burn is guaranteed to result in weight loss.**
- **Finding ways to agree with others sincerely is guaranteed to improve your relationships.**
- **Exercising, eating right, and sleeping enough is guaranteed to improve your physical and mental condition.**
- **Seeing your problems as challenges rather than obstacles is guaranteed to raise your self-esteem.**

Going to a therapist is not about getting solutions. It's about putting them into practice.

Most Changes are Forced On Us

In our early years changes are forced upon us. What child ever really had the desire to use a toilet? Or get out of bed, put aside the toys and head off to school? Without a good deal of insistence from adults, kids would become no more than selfish barbarians. Even in the days when parents were encouraged to give their children the freedom to grow and mature with their natural inclinations, they were potty trained and sent off to school (whether they were inclined to or not). Parents did not wait until children's natural inclinations led them to it.

We Must Exercise our Willpower to Change

Our natural inclinations most often lead to time wasting or health damaging habits. If you are a parent or ever have been a child, you have probably noticed there are things that children like to do which need no encouragement at all. Watching television and playing video games is not something which ever needs to be taught to a child. And they will maintain these activities into their adult lives.

The things we are naturally inclined to do, do little more than ensure that we survive long enough to procreate. Our natural inclinations help us to survive—not to excel. To get beyond a minimum level of existence, we need to do what is uncomfortable and not our natural inclination. We've created police forces and laws for the most serious things. But to rise individually to a higher level of existence requires the free exercise of our will—willpower.

Four Groups of People

Growing up and not just growing older requires that we exercise our will. It also requires us to make good choices and to take responsibility for our actions. The more we do those two things—exercise our will and make good choices, the more grown-up we will be. Everyone grows older, but not everyone grows up. Some only make it to mental puberty. We can distinguish four groups of people.

To rise individually to a higher level of existence requires the free exercise of our will—willpower. Nobody is going to do it for us.

The Merely Surviving

One group of adults are not much different from children who need constant supervision and direction. They are marginally functional and can't hold long term relationships or jobs. Their lives are full of drama and chaos. They do not seek out help, but may need to be rescued. Many are in our prisons, which are overflowing. Many also suffer from mental disorders and addictions. They are poorly motivated to get treatment for more than a brief period when they decompensate or lose control. They much prefer escape or avoidance to dealing with problems.

The Maintainers

A second, still larger group, manage to make responsible choices with the result that they can hold down a job and take care of their families. Because they can maintain relationships and employment, long term, they are functional. Although there may be many days when they don't feel like going to work or taking care of their home and family, they do. Although capable of more, they do *just enough* to pay their bills and prevent divorce. But, they live on the edge. They have few friends, no savings account, and are uncertain if their relationship with their partner will last. Life is both risky and stressful because any problem that comes along is like a huge wave for a small boat. It can be so difficult to handle that it results in a breakup of the family, job loss, and/or severe financial problems.

People who are just trying to emotionally or financially keep their heads above water are not thinking about how to excel. They just want to live without being abandoned by their partner or their employer. Their fear motivates them to do only what is necessary to escape danger for another day. Without the pain or danger, the motivation for change is not there, even though they know they *should* change. People in this group are usually in severe pain or on the edge of some kind of social ruin (divorce, job loss, bankruptcy) when they enter counseling. They are in counseling because they "have

Motivations:

- Survival
- Comfort
- Advancement
- Excellence

The only way to advance is to go past your comfort zone. The only way to excel is to go way past it.

232

to" because things seem desperate (and may be). Unfortunately, once the danger has passed, they drop out of therapy and don't make any lasting improvement. They put out the emotional fires, but the embers are still hot and can reignite at any time. To be sure, though, they are much healthier than those who turn to escape or avoidance.

The Comfort Seekers

The majority of people (the third group) are not motivated solely by daily demands. They seek to create a life which is comfortable and stable. Some commit themselves to family, charitable organizations, church attendance, and/or civic responsibilities. While many of their activities may still be partially demand driven, they have also been able to find meaning in something other than mere survival and momentary pleasures. They are better able to delay gratification. They are likely to be better educated, in better physical condition, have fewer broken relationships, and have better jobs. If they use credit cards, they pay them off before interest is due. This group is better able to profit from counseling and are more likely to stay in counseling long enough to make some lasting changes. Most people in this group, however, also reach a point of "good enough" long before they reach their potential. They are usually unaware that they have the potential to be a whole lot more than they are. They use past achievement as a measuring stick for current success. The majority of people in counseling belong to this group.

The Growth Seekers

The fourth group is much smaller than the others; they seek to fulfill their potentials and to reach peak performance. They don't know what their potential is, but they are sure that they are not there yet. They will endure whatever short-term sacrifices are necessary in order to ensure long term success. They care about the big picture. They are the Rembrandts who painstakingly apply the brush day by day until they unveil a masterpiece that people will admire for centuries. These people could not care less what the Jones's are up to. They are gold

People are usually unaware that they have the potential to be a whole lot more than they are. We are all made in God's image.

233

medal winners and leaders. Although they have fears, they are neither motivated nor hindered by them. They risk what they have now in order to get something better for the future. Sometimes they fail, but they realize that the sum of their failures will never outdo the sum of their successes. They desire to make full use of their lives. Most therapists only meet a few such people in the course of a career. They often inspire their therapists.

Examples of Choice Points for Ending Counseling

(These are intentionally similar examples. Pay attention to the differences).

Crisis Management Choice Point #1

Rachel had no friends anymore, not since she lost her job and was unable to go out with them. Her relationship with her boyfriend was off again and on again, and recently there had been a lot of tension because he no longer wanted to help her financially with her bills. She was stressed and could only imagine the worst as she got further behind on her bills. She entered counseling because she "just couldn't take it anymore."

As her counselor, Rachel found me to be both supportive and practical. I helped her to establish priorities and to focus on getting at least a part time job. As soon as she managed to get some employment, she felt "100% better," and ended her counseling against my advice. With her head above water, she was no longer afraid of drowning.

Restoration of Good Functioning Choice Point #2

Ramona had no friends anymore, not since she lost her job and was unable to go out with them. Her relationship with her boyfriend was off again and on again, and recently there had

---

Choice Points for Ending Therapy:

- Survival—end therapy when the crisis is over.
- Comfort—end therapy when you are doing well again (back in the "comfort zone").
- Advancement—end therapy when you are doing better than in the past.
- Excellence—end therapy only after you move far ahead (a "breakthrough").

been a lot of tension because he no longer wanted to help her financially with her bills. She was stressed and could only imagine the worst as she got further behind on her bills. She entered counseling because she "just couldn't take it anymore."

As her counselor, Ramona found me to be both supportive and practical. I helped Ramona to establish priorities and to focus on getting at least a part time job. Encouraged by her success, she was willing to continue working in counseling on her relationship with her boyfriend. She learned how she had become increasingly dependent on her boyfriend and how that had changed the power structure of their relationship. As she became less dependent on him, she was also less desperate about the relationship. As she relaxed more about it, she was surprised to find that her boyfriend became more interested in her again. With her relationship and job going well, she was enjoying her life again and renewing her contacts with her friends. At this point, she was losing interest in counseling and could see no reason to continue.

Growth and Fulfillment Choice Point #3

Rebecca had no friends anymore, not since she lost her job and was unable to go out with them. Her relationship with her boyfriend was off again and on again, and recently there had been a lot of tension because he no longer wanted to help her financially with her bills. She was stressed and could only imagine the worst as she got further behind on her bills. She entered counseling because she "just couldn't take it anymore."

As her counselor, Rebecca found me to be both supportive and practical. I helped Rebecca to establish priorities and to focus on getting at least a part time job. Encouraged by her success, she was willing to continue working in counseling on her relationship with her boyfriend. She learned how she had become increasingly dependent on her boyfriend and how that had changed the power structure of their relationship. As she became less dependent on him, she was also less desperate about the relationship. As she relaxed more about it, she was surprised to find that her boyfriend became more interested in her again. With her relationship and job going well, she was enjoying her

Although the job she had was paying the bills, it was not personally fulfilling. It had always been Rebecca's dream to become a dental hygienist and to work in a dental office.

life again and renewing her contacts with her friends.

Although the job she had was paying the bills, it was not personally fulfilling. It had always been Rebecca's dream to become a dental hygienist and to work in a dental office. She had no idea how to go about it or if it were possible, but I told her that the only limits on her success came from her and that she could work on having what she really wanted in life. I didn't know for sure that she could become a dental hygienist, but if she didn't try, then I knew for sure she wouldn't.

I guided Rebecca into discovering that the first step for her would be to get some information. Rebecca decided she could do that by getting her teeth cleaned and asking her hygienist about it. Anyway, she had reasoned that it was time that she had her teeth cleaned again. Step by step, she followed a path to becoming a hygienist with occasional help from me when she got stuck.

There Is More to Life than Survival

These three types of people who use counseling—those motivated to end a crisis, those motivated to get their life back to the way it was, and those motivated to grow, all can benefit from counseling. Regardless of what motivates you, the reason you enter counseling is to improve upon something. Many of us have started out merely trying to survive and only later learned that there is more to life than survival. Although you will be the one who decides what to work on and when the work is done, you should carefully consider your therapist's opinion. While you have little experience with the therapeutic process, he will have seen hundreds or thousands of people. His goal will not only be to help you improve, but also to help you not to relapse.

We All Must Cope Before We Can Do More

While the therapist wishes to help clients to obtain the best results, clients who live on the edge quit as soon as their crisis is over. This is usually long before their newly acquired thinking

Your therapist's goal is not only to help you improve, but also to help you not to relapse.

236

and behavior has become a habit. Old behavior patterns then soon reemerge. They are likely to re-enter therapy the next time they have a crisis and are more likely than other groups to re-enter therapy, repeatedly, for the same reason. Without working until new habits replace old, they are very unlikely to actually change their way of life. Therapy for them is a short term way of coping with difficult situations. Their choice of therapy for coping, though, is a very healthy choice and is to be commended. It is likely one of their most healthy behaviors.

After Coping Comes Prevention of Future Problems

Those who see more of the big picture will work longer in therapy, will make some modest changes and reach a point where their problems are less likely to recur in the future. Not only do they learn to handle any crisis for the moment, they also learn new coping skills for the future. They manage future crises better and are less likely to need to return to therapy for the same kind of problem. This group of people comprise the majority of people in outpatient counseling. Since you are reading this book, you are likely to be either in this group or the next one.

After Prevention Comes Fulfillment

Those who are motivated by the desire to excel use therapists as consultants much like a wealthy person would use an investment broker. The therapist helps to provide a sense of clarity and direction. Those motivated to excellence realize that there is much they don't know and will gladly accept any wisdom they can get. Their commitment to excellence helps them to maintain new ways of thinking and behaving which are more in line with their long term goals. Another type of specialist, a life coach or relationship coach, can also fill the same needs (many coaches also are skilled therapists with years of experience).

Improvement Doesn't Happen by Accident

While you are still in counseling, you need to consider which group you *plan* to belong to. If you do not plan to belong to any of these, then by default, you will fall into group

Those who are motivated by the desire to excel use therapists as consultants much like a wealthy person would use an investment broker. The therapist helps to provide a sense of clarity and direction.

one—those who leave therapy as soon as their crisis is over. This group does not live according to plans, but according to feelings. For them, the avoidance of fears and problems outweighs the desire to risk and work for a higher level of success. This, however, is a perfectly valid way to live. Even the most determined and motivated people have no desire to live a life they can't enjoy. But, If you want to do more to prevent related problems in the future, you must resist the urge to drop out of therapy as soon as you are feeling better. Stay long enough to make sure the changes "stick."

Fear Motivates Us Not to Touch a Hot Stove, but It Doesn't Motivate Us to Make Beneficial Changes

While fear can motivate us to avoid an immediate danger, fear alone is not very effective if what is feared is perceived to be a long way off or unlikely. If people got fat the minute they ate junk food, they wouldn't eat it. If they got cancer the moment they smoked a cigarette, they wouldn't smoke. If relationships ended the moment they treated people badly, they wouldn't treat people badly. If children became demanding and belligerent the first time parents used poor boundaries with them, then parents wouldn't use poor boundaries with them. Lessons that have immediate, negative consequences are rapidly learned. Most social situations are not like that, however. There is too long of a delay between our choices and the results to learn from experience or to be motivated by fear.

Preventive Learning Requires Looking Ahead

You will never see a full length mirror in a fast food restaurant. Big, fancy mirrors seem to be a home decoration feature of a past, thinner generation. The easiest thing to do in the short term is always to *disregard* the impact of actions on the future ("I can always quit later"), *minimize* the importance of a single action ("Just one time won't hurt"), and *justify* our behavior based on the actions of others ("Everyone else is doing it"). Every healthy action you take will move you ahead one step. Every unhealthy action you take will move you back one step. To get anywhere different, to make changes, requires that you take many more healthy than unhealthy steps.

Why It's Harder to Move to New Ground Than to Just Stand on Our Feet

Bad habits are kind of like eating junk food. Knowing that eating junk food has such a bad effect on health, you would think that people would eat healthy food. Actually people would do just that if the next junk food they ate would immediately result in a 40 pound weight gain, diabetes, or a heart attack.

Imagine that you are in line at a fast food restaurant. The display behind the counter says "hamburger 40 pounds." Along with the burger they give you a toga to slip on since you will immediately gain 40 pounds and your clothes will not fit. Right after eating your burger, you will have a harder time going out to the car, you will get tired climbing the stairs to your apartment, you may need to start taking blood pressure medication, cholesterol medication, or insulin, and you will need to buy a completely new wardrobe of much bigger clothes.

Given that scenario, how many people do you think would buy the hamburger? But of course, we buy the hamburger, eat it and enjoy it, with no noticeable gain in weight. Over time, we may gain not just 40, but maybe even 60, 80, or more pounds. The short term consequences of eating a hamburger— delicious enjoyment. The long term consequences of living on junk—obesity and other diseases. The "junk food" of our lives may be TV, sarcasm, criticism, control or avoidance of others, or a disorganized lifestyle. A little bit at a time never seems so bad, but over time it can junk up our life.

The short term consequence of not showing up for work is being confronted by our boss. Even if this happens only a few times, we are likely to be fired. This would be a very unpleasant short term consequence. Compare this with the short term consequences for criticizing one's spouse or children and you start to see why people can hold their jobs more easily than they can their relationships. We learn to avoid short term

The "junk food" of our lives may be TV, computer games, sarcasm, control or avoidance of others, or a disorganized lifestyle.

consequences while ignoring long term consequences.

Staying in Therapy Takes More Guts than Starting Therapy

The desire to do what is easiest in the short term also prompts many people to drop out of therapy prematurely (therapy is not easy because it is work and costs time and money). Changing for the good is *always* difficult and the natural desire will be to do what is the easiest for the short term. Therapy is almost always easier to quit than to continue. Effectively used, however, the long term benefits of therapy include a happier and more successful life.

The importance of sticking to what we start can be said of many things that raise our quality of life—such as exercise, relationship building, becoming more spiritual, learning a second language, and becoming financially sound. None of these are easy, and none of them are helpful when done just a little, but all are worthwhile when practiced regularly.

Therapists help people to make lifestyle improvements so that they can enjoy their lives more fully. This takes both effort and time. You can't get into mental shape in one day any more than you can get into physical shape in one day. Your therapist expects you to make gradual and consistent changes to your life outside of therapy that match what is going on in therapy. The bulk of improvement from therapy happens between sessions and not within sessions. Without the sessions, however, it is easy to get off track, on the wrong track, and to backtrack.

A medical doctor can give you advice or a prescription and send you on your way. That is because medical doctors give something to you or do something to you. Therapists, on the other hand, do something *with* you. You work together first so that you can work on your own later. You are *expected* to run into difficulties, but your therapist will help you to trouble shoot those in your next session.

While some people are uncomfortable with this kind of gradual guidance and follow up, it can help you to make

Therapists have a saying, "Everyone wants things to be better, but no one wants to change." ...Well, you can't have one without the other.

progress like you never could on your own. It is important to remind yourself that the therapist is on your side and is not looking to do anything but help you. Don't let the discomfort of this way of working be a reason to quit. Consider the discomfort of therapy a sign of progress (getting out of your "comfort zone" is the only way you can make progress).

Therapy Is Like Mental Fitness Training

Those who are the most likely to succeed with therapy are those who have the most accurate expectations about it. One accurate expectation is that therapy means "short-term pain for long-term gain." If you repeatedly say this to yourself, it will help you to overcome the unrealistic cultural expectation that therapy makes you feel good the same as going to a spa. Another helpful belief is "the harder it is, the more progress I will make." Star athletes look forward to the "burn." It means they are getting stronger, faster, or better. Imagine doing weightlifting with a pencil in each hand rather than a dumbbell. It might be easy, but it would be a waste of time (and look silly). Think of therapy as "mental fitness training." How much emotional weight you lift will be up to you.

Keep Your Desired Outcome in Mind

Another way to encourage yourself to remain in therapy is to picture the final results. People go to college not because they envision the tests, but because they envision the career. Olympic athletes imagine crossing the finish line and getting the gold medal. They mentally see themselves succeeding long before they do. If instead, they focused on how much pain and difficulty they are going to have trying to be the world's best, they would soon quit.

Your life is as important to you as an Olympic athlete's life is to him or her. This is another reason for the importance of goals in therapy. They will give you a vision of how you will be when you succeed in making changes in therapy. We can endure a drive across country because we are looking forward to what we are going to do when we get there. The exercises on

Mental Fitness Training:

- **Use a correct posture (stop bad habits),**
- **Get a trainer (get help with your blind spots and with correct methods),**
- **Practice a little harder than you are used to (strength comes by successfully managing challenges),**
- **See pain as a sign of progress (every change is accompanied by temporary stress),**
- **Improve a little at a time (use many small goals instead of one big one),**
- **Don't expect others to compliment you (your doing well makes them feel bad),**
- **Amaze yourself with how much you've grown.**

Exercise: Keep Focused on What You Want to Achieve

When we are in the midst of a difficult situation, whether it is running a race or working on personal change, our minds tend to get focused on the pain involved in the process. We begin to have a stronger and stronger desire to quit. In order to counter this unproductive desire, we need to give our mind a positive outcome to focus on. Use this exercise to visualize a positive outcome to your diligence in attending and following through with counseling.

Complete the following sentences about ending therapy:

1. When I complete my therapy....

2. I will be able to....

3. I will feel....

4. I will no longer struggle with....

5. Other people will....

6. My future will be brighter because....

7. I will have more opportunities for....

Exercise: Visualizing a Successful Therapy Outcome

Everyone visualizes quite naturally, without thinking about it. If I cook lunch, I first have to visualize what I am going cook before I start cooking. If I ask you to draw a picture of something pretty, you will first need to visualize something pretty before you start to draw it. Visualization can be a mental "picture," but it could be simply a detailed thought.

For our success in therapy it is also important to visualize, as specifically as possible, what the results of going to therapy will be. The more detailed you can imagine something, the easier it will be to achieve. It is said that if we could imagine the result in 100% detail, we would already have it.

Instructions:

1. Find a quiet place where you won't be disturbed.

2. Spend a few minutes with your eyes closed, breathing slowly and deeply.

3. While continuing to breath slowly and deeply, use your responses to the previous exercise ("Focusing on the Benefits of Therapy") by thinking about what your life will be like for each of the responses.

4. Try to involve each of your senses as much as possible in your visualization.

　　Hear what people are saying to you.

　　Hear the way you are talking to others.

　　See the way others are treating you and responding to you.

　　See the way you are behaving and how much it is different from now.

　　Feel the confidence and contentment that you have.

　　If smell, touch, or taste come into play, imagine them too.

5. Make this your mental visit into the future.

6. Tell yourself, "This or something even better is waiting for me as I grow and change."

7. Return to these images often. Let them become your new daydream.

8. If you imagine any obstacles during this exercise, also imagine dealing positively and confidently with those obstacles.

9. If any of the things you imagine are unclear or confusing, they are good places to work with your therapist on getting more clarity

the next two pages are designed to help you picture your life as it will be when you finish therapy. Take time to fix that in your mind. The long-term gains are definitely worth the short-term pains.

Summary

Therapy can be used to resolve a crisis, to get back on track, or to achieve something altogether new. What will most determine what you get out of therapy is what you imagine you can become. To achieve big things, first dream big things. Then, work toward them while keeping your eyes fixed on the finish line.

17. DON'T QUIT JUST BECAUSE YOU FEEL BETTER

You've been in therapy for some time now and really feel much better than when you first started. You now look forward to seeing the therapist who you were at first unsure of. You feel so good about your therapy that you have been recommending it to your friends. Life has never felt so good. Surely, it must be time to finish therapy. You are expecting with some mixed feelings that your therapist is going to tell you it is time to leave the nest and fly on your own. Strangely though, your therapist doesn't say anything about stopping at all.

Ending Therapy Is Not a Common Sense Decision

Just how do therapists determine when it is time for you to end therapy? Of course some people must end therapy because of financial reasons, health problems, or geographic moves. But when there are no such limitations on therapy, when is the right time to graduate therapy? Some problems are never completely fixed, so does that mean that therapy should continue indefinitely? How do you know when you have made enough progress to continue working on your own?

If it was bad feelings that got you to enter therapy in the first place (and who doesn't feel bad, regardless of the type of problem he or she has?), then it makes common sense that when you are feeling better it is time to leave. However, this is another instance when common sense is a poor guide. Feelings can come and go like the wind and are a poor guide to action. If you were angry with the clerk in the store you wouldn't just haul off and hit him (hopefully). Although your angry feelings

Feelings are a good source of information, but they are a poor guide to action. Other important pieces of information:

- **Past results**
- **Advice from knowledgeable others**
- **Evaluation of the costs and benefits**
- **How effective you are in getting good results consistently**
- **The degree of alignment between your current thinking and behavior and your long term goals**

"If it feels good, do it," is poor advice for anyone with a history of psychological and/or relational problems.

might be relieved by hitting him, the consequences would not be good. If you find yourself attracted to strangers you wouldn't just grab them and press the issue. Following our feelings at times like these would be dangerous. Even with smaller matters, feelings often lead us astray. Although your feelings may have led you to get therapy in the first place, it is your rational mind that needs to make the decision about ending therapy—just as it does with many other important areas of your life.

Feelings give us important information, but feelings alone should never be used to make decisions. This is also true about leaving therapy. The decision to end therapy should be based on your *functioning* and *stability* in various areas of your life as well as your feelings.

Functioning: The First Factor to Consider Before Ending Therapy

Everyone has good days and bad days. Functioning has to do with what we usually do in our everyday lives and how well that is serving us. The major areas for which to consider your functioning are work or school, relationships, and self. All three of these areas are important to a satisfying life. Although you can limp along with good functioning in only two of these areas, you will never truly be happy until you get all three areas going well.

Functioning at Work or School

The most basic consideration about functioning at work or school is the ability to *continue*. Is your performance good enough for you to continue without threat of job loss or expulsion? The second aspect of functioning at work or school is *relational*. How well do you get along with your supervisors, supervisees, teachers, classmates, and/or coworkers? The third component of work or school functioning has to do with *satisfaction*. How satisfied are you? Do you like the way things are going? An ongoing problem in any of these three areas of continuing, relationships, or satisfaction would threaten to destabilize your life and create problems for your future.

School is not just about making grades, and work is not just about getting a paycheck. These are part of our identity and are an important source of social interaction. Whether you are seven years old or 37 years old, how you get along with others is vital to your success. A rich person without friends is a failure. Before leaving therapy, you should feel confident about your performance and satisfaction with work or school, and also have healthy relationships there.

Functioning in Social Relationships

Another area of functioning to consider before leaving therapy is that of relationships. Relationships with immediate family and friends are the most important relationships for our mental health. The significant people in our lives help us to be emotionally stable by providing for our emotional and physical needs on a regular basis. They help us to feel important and give us motivation for getting through the daily grind. It is impossible for us to meet all of our emotional needs outside of human relationships. Any threats to these relationships make us feel anxious for a good reason. Ongoing small problems can turn into big problems. The state of your relationships is an important factor when deciding whether to end therapy.

Functioning with Yourself

The third area of functioning, to consider before ending therapy, is that of self. How do you treat yourself? Even if you have a good job and good relationships, if you don't like yourself or mistreat yourself (self-sabotaging thoughts and behaviors), then you are headed for some kind of breakdown and it is only a matter of time. There are many possible ways to mistreat oneself. The top three are to not sleep enough, to eat an unhealthy diet, and to not exercise. Although we can survive for some time mistreating ourselves in these areas, they eventually lead to physical and mental deterioration and are among the most serious (although underemphasized by the media). It is only a matter of time.

Other common ways to self abuse include the use of drugs or alcohol to change the way we *feel* (this is different from

Wherever we are functioning poorly today will result in problems for the future:

- **Work**
- **School**
- **Relationships**
- **Self-care and self esteem**

The squeaky wheel either gets the grease or eventually falls off.

medication aimed at improving functioning), and making or thinking self disparaging thoughts or comments ("I'm so stupid, fat, ugly, weak, helpless, handicapped, etc."). Self-degrading comments are not a form of humility, but actually impact our physical and emotional well being, as well as our ability to function in all areas of our lives. Imagine if you had another person follow you around throughout your day making negative comments to you anytime you made the smallest mistake, got a negative reaction from others, or looked in the mirror. I think your relationship with the person following you around would be poor to say the least. You might even want to murder that person after a while. If that person is you, you will also be miserable and could even have thoughts of suicide (self-murder). If you are still putting yourself down, it is definitely not the time to leave therapy. You should be able to see yourself realistically and treat yourself well so that you can see others realistically and treat them well. If you have been in therapy for a while, your therapist is likely to be able to gauge how realistically you see yourself.

Stability: The Second Factor to Consider Before Ending Therapy

If you are functioning well in these three areas: work/school, relationships, and self, great! But, you are still not necessarily finished with therapy. If you are functioning well in all three areas, no doubt you feel very good and find it hard to imagine what could go wrong. But before deciding to end therapy, it is important to consider stability.

Stability refers to your having maintained good functioning in all three areas, school/work, relationships, and self, for a period of *at least* three months. Whenever we work to change ourselves, what we are really changing are our habits of thinking and behaving. This is true regardless of the style of therapy we are participating in. When we have only had a new behavior for a short period of time (or quit a behavior for a short period of time), we have a high probability of reverting back to our previous behaviors.

Stability Comes from Healthy Habits and Not from Recent Change:

- **What you have done over the past *three months* will tell you what your habits are.**
- **If someone with a history of anger, depression, anxiety, etc. told you that they are now a changed person, but they tell you they changed only last week, would you really believe they have changed?**
- **A person's sincerity does not relate to how much he or she has actually changed. It only relates to their *intention* to change at that moment.**

People are terrible predictors of whether they will relapse or not. Only time is a good predictor. This is because new behaviors don't instantly become new habits. And without support, new behaviors often give way to old ones. This is the New Year's resolution phenomenon. People set good goals with the new year, adopt a healthy behavior for a few weeks, then go right back to doing what they were doing before. It is always easier to revert to a long-held habit than to establish a new one—particularly if the new behavior is healthier. Sticking with therapy at this time is *critical* to make sure you don't lose important gains.

On the next page is an exercise you can do to assess your readiness to leave therapy. Whatever the outcome, my recommendation is to discuss the results of your self-assessment with your therapist before making your final decision.

Case Example: Cindy and Joseph

Cindy and Joseph came to me for marital counseling because they were having serious marital problems following some flirtatious behavior that Joseph was doing. Joseph had seen it as harmless when in fact it was undermining Cindy's trust and causing big problems in their relationship.

Although it was the flirtatious behavior which was the "identified problem" when therapy began, it soon became apparent that both were growing dissatisfied with their relationship even though they still loved each other. Given the growing shakiness of their relationship, Joseph's flirtatious behavior with other women made Cindy even more sensitive to this behavior.

As they started to work on restoring the kind of relationship that they had when things were going well, a new hopefulness entered the relationship. Cindy was naturally very watchful to see if Joseph was continuing the flirtatious behavior, as trust was not yet fully rebuilt. I helped Joseph to understand that Cindy's watchfulness was both normal and necessary. After some minor

Although it was the flirtatious behavior which was the "identified problem" when therapy began, it soon became apparent that both were growing dissatisfied with their relationship.

Exercise: Am I Ready to Leave Therapy?

Part A

Put a "Yes" or a "No" in each blank box in this table

	Just the way I want. Best described as "healthy."	Same or getting better over the past 3 months
My relationships are		
My work/school is		
I treat myself		
My feelings are		

If you have a "yes" in ALL eight of the boxes, you are ready to discuss termination with your therapist. After discussion with your therapist, you may find that you want to change some of your "yes" responses. It is hardest to see that which is under our nose, and often a therapist can help to point it out.

A "Yes" response in the first column will soon become a "No" response if it has not been stable or improving over the past three months. People who prematurely drop out of therapy most often do so because a situation has improved although it has not stabilized. They then drop back to pre-therapy levels and become demoralized. Ensure success by having three months of success before ending therapy.

Part B

Another way to consider progress is in terms of our projected future. Divide a piece of paper into two columns. In the first column, list any changes that you have made as a result of therapy. In the second column, write what affect those changes are likely to have on your future. When you are done, consider whether the changes you need to make for your future happiness have all been made. If not, you will want to continue to focus on such changes in your therapy. Your therapist can help you figure out *how* to get to where you want to go, as long as you know *where* you want to go.

setbacks and misunderstandings, they were able to make good progress on their relationship.

There came a point when their relationship was going well, with just an occasional hiccup. There was not much for them to work on in counseling except to say how well things were going and how they wanted to "bullet proof" their marriage so that such a thing could never happen again.

I admitted that I could not help them with the goal of "bullet proofing," since the risk of rejection is an inevitable part of every relationship. I suggested that we review how far they had come and if they had reached the goals they had set for therapy. They were in agreement that with trust rebuilt, and the marriage more enjoyable, their goals had been met.

They agreed to continue to occasionally meet in counseling until things had been going well for three months. At that time, they made maintenance a lifetime goal with a backup plan of reentering counseling if things started to slide back to where they had been. Both of them felt very comfortable with their plan and it made them feel even more secure knowing that they could reenter counseling if they needed to.

———

Stability Means a Minimum of Three Months of Change (Six for Addictions and Dependencies)

Most therapists use a three month guideline to determine stability. If you or someone else has maintained a behavior for three months or more, the likelihood is that you will stay with that behavior. If, during that three month period you slip up and do the old behavior—*even once*, the three-month count starts all over. You need to have three *uninterrupted* months of healthy behavior before you can be confident that it is going to stick. In the case of overcoming drug or alcohol addictions however, the period of required stability is six months. That means six months without using the drugs or alcohol at all.

They agreed to continue to occasionally meet in counseling until things had been going well for three months. At that time, they made maintenance a lifetime goal with a backup plan of reentering counseling if things started to slide back to where they had been.

One slip-up resets the count to day one.

Getting through those three months (or six months for addictions) would be very difficult to do on your own. The most important role the therapist plays during this time is that of accountability partner. Just knowing that your therapist is going to be checking on your progress will be a tremendous help in maintaining your healthy behavior. If you are doing very well and your temptations to revert to old behaviors are small, then it may be appropriate to decrease the frequency of counseling, but not to stop altogether. Many counselors see their clients one or two times a month for the final phase of therapy.

When it's Time to Go, It's Time to Go

When you are functioning well, and your behavior or way of thinking is stable, you are ready to "graduate." In fact, if you stayed in therapy at this point, you and your therapist would likely find yourselves watching the clock or making small talk for most of the session. You may even be healthier than your therapist at this point! I tell my clients that they have squeezed all the juice out of the grape (me) and there is nothing more that I can offer them at this time. Although therapists are used to saying goodbye, this parting (called termination) can be a difficult one for clients.

Parting Is Such a Sweet Sorrow

Depending on the style of therapy, the extent of your initial problems, and other factors, you may have been in therapy for months or even years (rare, but possible). You have probably shared things with your therapist that you never shared with anyone, all the while receiving help and support. Feelings of attachment can be very strong. And making it more difficult to say goodbye is the fact that you will not be able to continue the relationship when therapy ends. Counseling is a professional relationship that ends when treatment ends. There are strong legal, ethical, and moral prohibitions preventing the therapist from doing otherwise. It is time for you to stand on your own two feet and walk off into the sunset.

Indications That It Is Time to End Therapy:

- **There has been no change in the past three months,**
- **You and your therapist are primarily having small talk,**
- **Your goals have been met as much as possible in therapy,**
- **You are doing well at work/school, in relationships, and by yourself, and**
- **You are doing well seeing your therapist infrequently.**

252

If you have good functioning in the area of relationships, then termination will be easier (another good reason for making sure you have healthy relationships before termination). Several people in your life will do for you what your therapist previously did—give you encouragement and support, make you feel important and worthwhile, and be accountability partners. The reasons for those social goals in the treatment plan become even clearer when you end therapy. Healthy relationships will help you to maintain healthy functioning, and healthy functioning will help you maintain healthy relationships.

On Deciding to Leave Early

Although you are free to leave therapy at any time, it is always a good idea to discuss it with your therapist first. I know that it's difficult to bring up something if you think your therapist might disagree with you, but it's important to get the therapist's response. The danger is more on the side of leaving therapy too soon rather than too late. The easiest way to bring up the subject with your therapist is to ask when he or she thinks you will be ready to go it on your own.

If you don't bring up ending therapy however, there will eventually come a time when your therapist brings it up. It's important to keep in mind that this is not a personal rejection. Probably your past experience in relationships has taught you that when people talk about the end of a relationship they are rejecting you. This could not be further from the truth with psychotherapy. The therapist will be proud of you for staying in therapy until you are fit and able to go it on your own. The therapist will think fondly of you and remember you as one of his or her best clients. Successful treatment helps both the client and the therapist to feel good about themselves.

What to Do in the Last Sessions

Common issues to discuss in the last few sessions include a review of your progress, skills or changes to continue to work on (on your own), and when to make the decision to re-enter therapy should it become necessary.

Leaving Therapy Early:

- It's your right,
- Your therapist will not take it personally, and
- It does not prohibit you from going back.
- Be sure it's in your best interest.
- If you are making progress, leaving early will not allow you to see how much more you could have benefited.
- Unless your therapist is doing something seriously wrong, give therapy a month before deciding to leave.
- The main reason some people don't progress in therapy is that they leave before the work is done.
- Just like leaving the dentist's office in the middle of the procedure can make things worse, so can leaving psychotherapy too early.
- If your insurance benefits run out and you can't afford to continue, try negotiating a lower fee.

Remember that although a therapist can guide you, he cannot accomplish any goals for you. You have done that by yourself and the credit belongs to you.

Although you may have reviewed your progress several times during the course of therapy, a final review of progress compares your entry into therapy to your exit from therapy. Since change is accomplished slowly, we often don't consciously notice our progress. Doing a review can show us just how far we have come and can be very encouraging. One way to do such a review is to look at your first treatment plan with its problems, diagnosis, adjunct service recommendations, and goals. If you have a copy of the treatment plan, you can enjoy taking a red pen and crossing out the problems that you no longer have (perhaps all). You can check off the goals attained, and you can make a list of how you accomplished those goals. Remember that although a therapist can guide you, he cannot accomplish any goals for you. You have done that by yourself and the credit belongs to you.

Although you have completed your goals, and your problems are resolved, it is not the end to goals and goal making. Whether in therapy or on our own, we all need goals. A goal can be achieving something new or a goal can be maintaining what we have. It is typical to end therapy with such a "maintenance goal," with a backup plan of returning to therapy for a booster, if needed.

It may also be that you have made much progress in therapy but that you have not quite accomplished all of your goals. If you are able to continue to work toward your goal(s) without the help of your therapist and have demonstrated this over the last few months, then leaving may be the most appropriate thing. Some goals take years or even a lifetime to achieve. Other goals are never completely achieved, but are worth working on nevertheless. The therapist is mainly a help to people who get stuck on their way to a goal, or who are heading away from it rather than toward it. If you find that you are not stuck, and are going in the right direction, then you have become like the most successful people in the world who continuously set new goals and work to accomplish them. This is the work and the pleasure of life—to see our potential, and that of our loved ones, come to fruition.

Deciding on When to Re-enter Therapy

It is common for clients to feel like rushing back into therapy at the first sign of a returning problem. What you will find, however, is that you are not the same person that you were when you first entered therapy. You now are better prepared to fend off new problems rather than be overwhelmed by them. You know what to do. You will probably remember the things that your therapist told you. Although it may seem like the memory of your therapist is what is helping you, actually it is the part of you which has learned from therapy that is helping you. If a friend comes to you with the same problem, you will amaze yourself at what a fountain of wisdom you have become. Your successful venture through therapy may even turn you on to the idea of becoming a counselor yourself. Many a therapist has begun as a counseling client.

This said, however, there does come a point when it may be wise to re-enter therapy. Life *is* unpredictable. Indeed, that is what makes life an adventure. Perfect predictability is perfect monotony. When you find that circumstances are overwhelming your coping skills so that you cannot stop yourself from slipping into a hole, get help again before you slip all the way down to the bottom. There is no shame in re-entering counseling, and it is not that unusual. You may only need a few sessions as opposed to your initial set of therapy sessions. Your therapist will be happy to see you—really. This isn't because the therapist is happy you are having problems, but because you are staying healthy and know when to access help. Therapists are people, too. They know that sometimes life is harder than at other times. Therapists frequently see other therapists for their own counseling. We believe in what we do.

Saying "Goodbye"

The end of therapy comes with a "goodbye." "Goodbye" is a good word to end therapy with because it lends to a sense of closure. It is time for you to move on. Giving up the training wheels can be a little scary, but succeeding on your own will be

When you find that circumstances are overwhelming your coping skills so that you cannot stop yourself from slipping into a hole, get help again before you slip all the way down to the bottom.

exciting. Although unnecessary, a note after six months or so to your therapist to tell him or her how you are doing or just to say thanks will make your therapist's day. Your therapist won't respond, for various ethical reasons, so it is not a way to re-enter the relationship. But, when a therapist has spent such a length of time listening and helping and caring, a note or card means a lot. Therapists do not do their jobs just for the money. They really care.

Summary

Knowing when to end therapy is not a common sense decision. You will need to look objectively at the different areas of your life to determine how well you can function on your own. It is best not to quit therapy suddenly, regardless of how well you are doing. Instead, take the time to review with your therapist how you have progressed. Additionally, try to anticipate some potential future setbacks and how you can deal with them on your own. We can't anticipate all future events, and sometimes we may need to re-enter therapy. That is not a sign of failure, and is normal. Revisiting therapy is easier and more comfortable than the first time because you will know what to expect and will be able to more effectively identify what you need help with.

18. EVERYONE HAS MULTIPLE PERSONALITIES

Therapists do not apply a cookie cutter approach to the clients they treat. It simply is not possible. There are great variations in client's motivations, skills, background experiences, number of stressors and a host of other factors. In fact, even the same client is different on a day to day basis. Even psychiatrists and other medical doctors cannot apply a cookie cutter approach because biologically people react differently to medications and other medical treatments. And, their physical condition varies on a day to day basis.

The lack of a standard approach often frustrates clients because to some extent there is a trial and error period for psychological and psychiatric treatments. Therapists and medical doctors will start out with the types of treatment that work for most people, most of the time. After that, feedback from the client is very important to inform the doctor or counselor of whether the treatment is working or is causing other types of problems (biological, emotional, or social side effects). Then, adjustments have to be made.

Help Your Therapist to See the "Real" You

Sometimes the wrong treatment approach is chosen because clients leave out important information. In an ideal situation, therapists would interview not only you, but also your friends, family, and coworkers. The people in these three groups may have very different perspectives about you because they see you in three different contexts. For example, coworkers may see you as shy, friends as outgoing, and family as a trouble maker.

No Two People Are Exactly Alike. Implications:

- You can't just apply what works for others to yourself.
- You can't understand others without listening to their unique perspective.
- You can't convince others just by saying what would convince you.
- Conflicts and differences of opinion are a part of life.
- Therapists must adjust their treatment approach to every person they help.

Underreporting and over reporting symptoms are both common response sets. When a treatment provider doesn't know you well, he or she must guess about your response set in order to treat you appropriately.

The way you see yourself will be different still. Which one is the real you? Which one does the therapist see?

On the next two pages is a self analysis that will tell you more about who you really are than a personality test will. You may discover that you are not really the person you think you are, most of the time.

How Much Should You Tell Your Therapist?

Clients are often reluctant to reveal problem areas in their life not related to the presenting problem. They are also reluctant to reveal information that puts them in too good of a light, lest the therapist perceive them as not having a serious problem. The tendency for clients to respond in certain ways which don't accurately portray them is called a *response set*. When a practitioner doesn't know you well, he or she must guess about your response set.

An example of a doctor guessing my response set occurred one time when I had to visit a hospital emergency room. I had gone in with severe pain which had subsided hours later although I was still having some internal bleeding. The ER attending physician checked on me prior to admitting me to a room and asked me about pain. I told him truthfully that I no longer had any pain. He ordered an IV drip with a pain medication anyway. His belief was that I had a "faking good" response set and that I must surely have pain. Of course, he learned from nursing notes that I had no complaints of pain during the night and probably concluded that the pain medication that he ordered was the correct treatment. This was a case of a physician trying to be helpful by providing the usual treatment when the usual treatment was not warranted. Insistence on my part that I did not need pain medication only confirmed his belief that I was pretending to not have pain.

The disadvantage that the ER doctor had was that he did not know me. If he knew me, he would know that I hate pain and would always opt for pain medication if I were in pain. The doctor erred on the side of caution, which I can understand. For similar reasons, patients who complain of a lot of pain are

258

Exercise: Who Am I Really?

Completing the following chart will tell you more about your personality than a personality test will. If you don't know how a person sees you, try asking them. The more "bad" things you discover about yourself, the more opportunity you have for improving yourself. Try to help your therapist to see the "whole" you.

Person	How I see myself in regard to this person (5 adjectives)	How this person sees me (5 adjectives)	How I want to be seen (5 adjectives)
Spouse/significant other (**example**)	Caring Committed Loving Good sense of humor Good provider	Loving Stubborn Inactive Good provider Good sense of humor	Caring Loving Handsome Fun to be with Romantic
Spouse/significant other			
Child 1			
Child 2			
Mother			
Father			

(Continued on next page)

Brothers			
Sisters			
Boss/employer			
Employees/coworkers			
Best friends			
Casual friends			
Acquaintances/general population			

Any items which are identical for all three columns, for any person, represent a good sense of self and will make you more confident and likeable. Differences in the three columns will make you less likeable to others or to yourself. Thus, if you see yourself the way you want to be and others see you the way you want to be, you have an ideal situation. Note that these do not have to be the same qualities for each person (for example, you probably don't want both your boss and your spouse to see you as romantic!).

often viewed as over-reporting their pain (faking bad), while patients who complain little are often viewed as under-reporting their pain (faking good). The physician has the unenviable task of being a mind reader since she often cannot rely on the word of her patients. Of course the better the doctor knows you, the less mind reading is necessary.

Missing Information Can Delay Progress

When you have been in treatment for a while with a therapist and the therapist is continuing to provide treatment which is ineffective or is causing other problems, you need to ask yourself if the therapist has really received an accurate representation of you and your situation. The person who I see in therapy may be "on their best behavior" and not be the person that other people see. While this makes our interactions more pleasant, I often miss important social problems where the person needs help. One giveaway for this is listening to the person's answering machine message. Sometimes these messages are a real shock because they are so unlike the person that I have been treating. A seemingly shy person may have sung an Elvis song, a seemingly religious person may have a dirty joke on their machine, and so forth.

Sometimes it is not the answering machine, but the way the person answers the phone before they know it is me. Or it is the background conversation I hear when waiting for a client to come to the phone after their child has answered. Shouting and strings of expletives are not unusual. When I bring this up in therapy, the explanation that I get is that it was a particularly bad day and ordinarily they would never say things like that. The answering machine message? "Oh, I never realized that it was a dirty joke, I just thought it was funny," or some other incomprehensible thing. I'm not bringing this up to tell people how to talk at home or what to say on their answering machine. I am just saying that the less the therapist knows about the "real you," the less helpful will be the treatment goals and treatment methods.

The Cost of Withholding Important Information from Your Therapist:

- **The longer you withhold the information, the more reluctant you will be to share it,**
- **You won't get the feeling that your therapist really understands you,**
- **Treatment recommendations and goals may not fit your actual needs, and**
- **You may make little or no progress.**

If you want to get the best treatment possible, give your therapist as realistic an impression of yourself as possible. If your coworkers think you are stuck up, say in therapy, "My coworkers think I'm stuck up."

Misinformation Can Undermine Trust Important for the Therapeutic Relationship

There are also times when I will run into a person who is "feeling hopelessly depressed" very actively taking part in a public celebration, or run into them on the ski slope or at the tennis court. Once the truth is out, clients often drop out of treatment rather than confess to their therapist that they were not accurately portraying themselves. Ironically, though, it is the new information which will help the therapist to be able to better help them. Trying to appear either better off or worse off than you really are is ultimately not helpful to you because you will not receive the correct treatment.

Even Therapists Can't Read Your Mind

A similar kind of thing often happens with elderly medical patients. They will have aches and complaints of various sorts that they blame the "useless doctor" for to all their friends and family. However, when they enter the examination room and the doctor asks them how they are, they say that they are fine. If the doctor takes them at their word, they continue to suffer. If the doctor assumes that they have more problems than they report, he or she may give appropriate prescriptions based on a guess. Because so many elderly patients do this, when an elderly person actually tells it like it is, they may be assumed to still be understating things and receive more medication than they need. With therapists, often both young and elderly people understate their problems. Therapists can only be as helpful as your information.

If you want to get the best treatment possible, give your therapist as realistic an impression of yourself as possible. If your coworkers think you are stuck up, say in therapy, "My coworkers think I'm stuck up." The therapist may ask if that was also the case at previous jobs. If it was, then say, "Yes, I had the same problems at my previous jobs. People tended to not like me and to think that I was stuck up." Your therapist will not think badly of you for revealing this. In fact, your therapist will trust you even more, which will further promote the working alliance essential to progress. Because your therapist doesn't get to see you being "stuck up" (in this case), it gives him or her a more accurate picture of you than before.

Everyone Has Multiple "Personalities"

There was a time when psychologists held to the belief that "personality" is a stable construct. The idea of "personality types" became very popular and people still talk about their personality type. For example, some people say they are "extroverted" or outgoing, while other people say they are "introverted" or shy. While a few people are outgoing in all situations or shy in all situations, most people are shy in some situations and outgoing in others. They are introverted at a party, perhaps, and extroverted when they are among their friends. The same could be said of aggressive and passive, creative and realistic, organized and disorganized, as well as other dimensions of ourselves. Our personalities (our traits) shift according to the context (the states) that we are in. Instead of characterizing ourselves with single traits like "extroverted," it is more accurate to characterize ourselves and others by both trait and state—"I am extroverted with my friends, and introverted in new situations."

Therapy can help you to understand your personality state-trait characteristics. This is important because you will be most comfortable when your state-trait characteristics match the state-trait characteristics of others (a person who is outgoing at parties may do well with another person who is outgoing at parties, but not do well with someone who is outgoing at work). It also explains why we get along so well with people in one context (e.g., work), but cannot get along with the same person in another context (e.g., non-work, social situation).

State-trait analysis is also helpful for job selection. People who are being tested to see which job best suits them are tested for both their interests and state-trait characteristics in a job setting. If you have the right skills or interests, but are very different from your coworkers, you are likely to be unhappy and unsuccessful in your job.

Personalities Are Both Stable and Changeable:

- **We can predict that people will react similarly in the same circumstances.**
- **It is much harder to predict what someone will do in a completely different situation.**
- **To really know someone well, you need to know what she is like in many different circumstances.**
- **People who marry soon after meeting may have many "surprises," when they and their spouse have circumstances different from when they were dating.**
- **Some of your mild mannered coworkers may be tyrants at home.**
- **Some people behave very consistently from one setting to another.**
- **Some people are very different in different settings.**
- **The truly healthy person adjusts to the actual demands of each situation.**

The person your therapist sees in the office may not be the aspect of you that needs the most help.

The job that is the best choice for you is one where you have: 1) the appropriate skills; 2) an interest in that kind of work; and 3) similar personality characteristics as people who are already successful in that kind of job. For example, if successful wedding photographers tend to be *outgoing* (extroverted with strangers) and you have good photography skills, the motivation to be a good photographer, but are *shy* around strangers, then you would not be well suited to be a wedding photographer. A vocational aptitude test may suggest to you that you would do better as a wildlife photographer, where mixing with others was not so important.

Just as knowing how you are in different contexts can help you to find the right job, or the right partner, it can also help your therapist to help you do well in different contexts. The person your therapist sees in the office may not be the aspect of you that needs the most help.

Case example—Brent

Brent was a sophomore in college who was having difficulty deciding on his major. According to the rules of his school, he was supposed to have declared a major by the beginning of his sophomore year. His academic advisor recommended that he meet with a counselor at our counseling center to try to narrow his interests and to choose at least a temporary major.

Brent made an appointment at the counseling center. The first meeting was used to discuss Brent's concerns and why it was difficult for him to choose a major. It seemed that Brent felt some pressure to follow in his father's footsteps as a lawyer, but did not really have much interest in that. He also had little idea of what he would like to do instead. He had been using much of his emotional energy fighting the idea that he should become a lawyer.

I helped Brent to see the whole idea of choosing a major just as an experiment and that he could change later for any reason

264

he desired. I also explained to him how a vocational aptitude test could be an interesting way to consider some career directions that he may have never thought of. If the results didn't come out the way he liked, he was free to discard the whole thing.

With the idea of the aptitude test as potentially helpful and not committing him to any choices, Brent agreed to take the test. He was given a booklet with three sections containing various statements. All he had to do was to choose whether the statement was mostly true for him or mostly false for him. For example, one item was "I like to work with people more than things." I had told Brent that the more honest he could be in his answers, the more useful the results would be to him.

When he got the test results, Brent was both surprised and excited to find suggestions for several occupational areas that he had not considered. I encouraged Brent to take some classes in those areas and to choose a major related to the area that excited him the most. If, after taking the class, he found his interests had changed, he could then change his major. This plan was to Brent's liking and he was able to choose a major by the end of the month.

Your Success in Any Area Depends on Temperament as Much as Skills

Skills are only one aspect of a career or relationship. Temperamental suitability is another. Would you like to have an anxious pilot, an impatient surgeon, a disorganized teacher, an aggressive dentist, a passive commanding officer, or a perfectionist partner? State-trait characteristics are very important to your personal satisfaction with life and play an important role in the friends you make, the people you date (or marry), the jobs you hold, and the activities you do. Your therapist can help you to understand these things about yourself so that you can make better choices which, in turn, will make you a happier person.

Skills are only one aspect of a career or relationship. Temperamental suitability is another. Would you like to have an anxious pilot, an impatient surgeon, a disorganized teacher an aggressive dentist, a passive commanding officer, or a perfectionist partner?

Summary

Because your therapist only sees you in one context (therapy), it will be helpful for both you and your therapist if you help him or her to understand what you are like (how others see you) in other contexts. You don't want to become an expert at being a therapy client for example, if where you really need help is at work. Be open, be informative, and don't worry—your therapist will both accept you and help you.

Are you an "expert" therapy client:

- **Measure your progress in therapy not by how well you do in therapy but by how well you do in the other areas of your life.**

CHAPTER NINETEEN

19. POSITIVE WAYS TO WORK ON A MARRIAGE

Let's face it—relationships are tough. If we hadn't been stuck with our parents, we would have left home before the age of three. Fortunately though, we had to suffer the slings and arrows of childhood, bedtimes, school times and rules, rules, rules—never seeming to have control of our own lives. If we had healthy parents, we learned that someone can love us and still not give us everything we want. We learned self discipline that we initially didn't have. We learned that love, commitment, and getting our way all the time just do not go together. In our adult relationships we are better at give and take and because of that are more thoughtful about others needs. We also know that someone can be angry with us without rejecting us. Most of the important things we learned about relating to others, we learned before we even went to kindergarten.

What if we didn't have healthy parents? Although parents usually do what they believe is best for their children, sometimes their fears and insecurities get passed on to another generation—us. When that happens we can have fears and insecurities that we don't realize until the right (or wrong) situation brings them out. These hidden emotional bombs can set off behaviors which damage our relationships, endanger our careers, and lower our self esteem. Many trips to the therapist may be required to help us get these emotional bombs defused and to learn new ways of thinking and behaving to replace the old.

Self-Discipline Is:

- **Planned Behavior—As distinguished from people who react as crises occur.**
- **Internally Driven—As distinguished from people who do only because they have to comply with external demands.**

Self-Discipline in Relationships Is:

- **Planned Behavior—Actually doing what is in the best interest of the relationship, regardless of what your emotions are telling you.**
- **Internally driven—not because your partner will be upset if you don't.**

Battles over right and wrong may have a place in divorce, but not in marriage, and certainly not in marriage counseling.

People who have such hidden emotional problems most often marry other people who have hidden emotional problems. So, not only do we need to deal with our own issues, but we have to deal with our spouse's issues that come out in how he or she treats us. But, those issues just trigger more unhealthy reactions in us. Because of this interaction effect between our problems and our spouse's, and because problems can go unresolved, they start to stack up until they become overwhelming. It is at this point that most couples enter counseling or when individuals get help through marriage coaching.

The good news is that although we may be stuck with our genes, we are not stuck with fears, insecurities, or skills deficits. We can get the help we need to heal ourselves and our marriages before too much damage has been done. Although many couples fail to get help because they don't believe anything can be done, the truth is that for every difficult marriage problem, some people have been able to overcome it. Although you don't know how they did it, there is a good chance that your counselor does. If you are willing to try, at least experimentally, some new approaches, you and/or your spouse may be able to restore your marriage to health and happiness, too.

Is Marriage Counseling a Last Chance for a Marriage with Severe Problems?

People who enter therapy because of marital problems often feel like therapy is a "last chance" for their marriage. If therapy does not fix things, they think that things cannot be fixed. Often, by "fixing things," a client means "fixing" their spouse who is too stubborn, twisted, or dumb to make obvious changes so that the marriage can be wonderful.

If you have this mindset, that your spouse needs to be fixed, you will be in for a surprise when you get into marriage counseling. You will find that no matter how much "evidence" you present to prove how wrong your spouse is (or your spouse provides about you), that the therapist will refuse to take sides.

268

There are a couple of very good reasons why the therapist will not take sides: 1) taking the side of one spouse will alienate the other spouse and undermine the therapy, and 2) proving who is most in the wrong will not lead to problem resolution. Battles over right and wrong may have a place in divorce, but not in marriage, and certainly not in marriage counseling.

Being Right and Twenty-five Cents Won't Even Buy You a Pack of Gum

Let's suppose that you are having an argument (you can call it a discussion if it makes you feel better) with your spouse. You clearly demonstrate that your spouse is in the wrong. Then what? Are you closer or more distant after that? Does this sound likely—"Oh honey, you have shown me the evidence and the error of my ways. I appreciate you so much and my love for you is growing deeper"? Anybody who believes that has never had a relationship with a man or a woman.

You cannot fight, argue, or debate your way to a better relationship. A good example is the adversarial system on which our legal system and government is based. The slam of the judge's gavel and the written documentation signed by court officials does nothing to help a couple reconcile. Right and wrong do help (sometimes), in the division of monies and child custody. But, in trying to improve a relationship, determination of "rightness" or "wrongness" is not helpful.

Marriage Counseling Is About the Process of Relating

So, then, what is marriage counseling about if it's not about finding fault and correcting it? It is about the *process* of interacting. The results of your previous interactions are evident by the state of your current relationship. Poor process leads to poor outcomes, regardless of issues of right and wrong. Had the way you and your partner interacted gone a different way, your relationship would now be different. *How* you handled differences has determined how distant you have become.

Your therapist will take the time to talk about past issues

A Relationship is Not Something You *Have*, It Is Something You *Do*

- Once the interaction stops, the relationship stops.
- Changing what we do can make a relationship worse or better.
- The future of a relationship depends on the interactions of each person, *from here on out*.

that were resolved as well as past issues that were not resolved. Why were you able to work things out in one case, but not in another? Are there ways that you used to work things out a long time ago, but have since given up on? Are there strengths and skills that you have that you have simply stopped using?

Other therapists will be less interested in skills, but more interested in thoughts and behaviors. What did you think when your spouse was coming home late? What evidence did you consider? What did you do when your spouse got home? Was that helpful?

Still other therapists will be interested in patterns of thinking and behavior that you learned in your family of origin. Are you more suspicious of your spouse because you had a parent who was unfaithful?

Most therapists will use a combination of these ways of looking at how you and your spouse got to the point where you are now.

Marriage Problems Can't Be Solved in the Past

Although where you are *now* is a result of your past interactions, relationships are not the grand result of all previous interactions. Relationships are the very process of interacting. Relationships are ongoing. The way you interact *is* the relationship. Relationships change as the way you interact changes. What you have now can get instantly better or worse if you change the way you are interacting. Relationships only end when the interactions end.

The essence of good relationships then, are good interactions. Good interactions make people want to continue to interact. Bad interactions make people want to stop interacting, which leads to the death of a relationship. This is why therapists focus on the process of your interactions and not on who is right or wrong.

The Most Useful Questions for Couples in Trouble

I find that the most useful question to ask a couple in the

first session is "Why do you want to stay together?" It's much like asking a person who says he wants to kill himself why he hasn't done it already. It forces the couple to look at the positive motivations that hold them together even in the light of so much pain. Other useful questions are "What made you attracted to your spouse in the first place?" and "What would you miss about your spouse if you were divorced?" I have seen many couples who came in firing missiles at each other end up hugging in the parking lot after answering these questions. This is my early goal as a therapist—to change the process from an adversarial one to a collaborative one. Most of the time when I ask couples what they hope to accomplish as a result of the counseling, they both say the same thing. Then I say, "So you both want the same thing, but you just don't know how to get it, is that right?" This changes the focus from issues to process. Improve the process and you improve the relationship.

On the next page are some questions that you can use to help you find the value of your relationship and your partner, even if recently you haven't valued him or her at all.

When Blame Changes to Responsibility, Relationships Improve

The next surprise in marriage therapy is that the therapist will expect each spouse to work on his or her self. This is typically the opposite strategy to that of what clients do on their own. On their own, clients usually either try to change each other, or "patiently" wait for the other to change. Because each is focused on the other changing, there is no improvement and the relationship becomes more distant.

The Worse Your Partner, the More You Need to Change Yourself

Often, the partner most needing help with self change is the one who most feels like a victim. For example, do you think that a relationship is more likely to improve if a therapist works with an abusive person or with his/her abused partner? The common notion is that working with the abuse perpetrator brings the best results. But an abuser is rarely as motivated to change the situation as the victim. By working with the victim

Never refrain from entering counseling because you are not the one with the problem. The healthiest person in a family is the one most able to change the dynamics of the family.

271

Exercise: How Can I Discover the Value of My Relationship?

The more we value something, the better we take care of it. That goes for our relationships, too. Just like the air we breathe, it's easy to forget how valuable it is to us until we are deprived of it. By then, it may be too late. Becoming more aware of your relationship's value now, can motivate you to take corrective action before it is too late.

What initially attracted you to your partner?

What about your partner made him or her more special to you than others?

As a result of your relationship with your partner, what good things have come about in your life (e.g., children, nice home, etc.)?

What good qualities of your partner are hard to find in other people?

If you were to lose your partner through accident, illness, or breakup, what would you miss most about him or her?

If you were to suddenly lose your partner (such as through an accident), what would you regret not having done or said?

List all the reasons that you want to be with your partner, even if these things are not happening right now (e.g., companionship, sex, financial security, etc.).

The value of a person does not reside within that person, but within others who value that person. Even a person with no abilities and a severe illness could be highly valued by friends, family, or partner. Because of this, we can come to value our partners by working to change the way we think about them and treat them. We can't do this by trying to change them. Trying to change your partner can actually make you *devalue* your partner.

to help him/her no longer behave like a victim—to set healthy limits and no longer put up with or allow the abuse, the situation changes. The perpetrator then either stops or leaves. This is no less true for other, less serious behaviors.

Another good example of this is the treatment of children with behavior problems. Children are rarely as motivated to change as their parents are motivated to change them. By working with the parents—to change the way the parents respond to their children, the children in turn change their behavior. Who had the problem? The children? Or their parents? The answer is that they both did. Who had the most power to change the children's behavior? The parents. Parents may not be to blame for their children's behavior (therapists don't care about blame—it's not a helpful action), but they are the ones with the power to change it.

If Your Partner has a Problem, *You* Need Therapy

Healthier spouses are in a position to improve their relationships by changing the way they interact with their partners. Never refrain from entering counseling because you think you are not the one with the problem. The healthiest person in a group or family is the one most able to change, and therefore is in the best position to change the dynamics (the way people relate to each other) of the group or family.

On the next page is a brief assessment you can use to see how healthy your relationship behaviors are.

Regardless of the Type of Therapist You See, You Will Learn New Ways to Interact

Some therapists are skills-oriented no matter what type of client they see, while other therapists focus on insights as the basis of change. Most therapists are somewhere in between, especially when it comes to marriage counseling. Marriage therapy is ideal for learning skills because you have a real live partner to practice with.

Not every therapist uses the same techniques, but an example of my work may help you to understand the marriage

Marital Love:

- **Doing what is in the best interest of your partner.**
- **Doing what is in the best interest of the relationship.**
- **Refusing to participate in behavior which hurts your partner or the relationship.**
- **Is not always nice, submissive, or free of conflict.**

Exercise: How Healthy Are My Relationship Behaviors?

When we value something highly and are in danger of losing it, then we are motivated to work on making necessary changes. It is important to do what people with good relationships do. It is also important to stop doing what people with bad relationships do. Learning the difference between these two things is one benefit of relationship counseling.

I have dates with my spouse, outside of our home, without the children, at least once a week. (This is important for increasing intimacy).	☐ TRUE	☐ FALSE
I regularly spend time with friends without my spouse. (This is important to avoid neediness, dependency and resentment).	☐ TRUE	☐ FALSE
My partner and I know what each other most wants and we help each other to get it. (Measure of true partnership).	☐ TRUE	☐ FALSE
What I want and what my partner wants compliment, rather than conflict, with each other. (Necessary for minimizing conflict).	☐ TRUE	☐ FALSE
When my partner and I have conflicts, I respond in a constructive, not destructive, way. (Necessary skill to deal with inevitable conflicts).	☐ TRUE	☐ FALSE
I am committed to working on our relationship even at times when my partner is not. (Love and commitment should not depend only on what you can get from your partner).	☐ TRUE	☐ FALSE
I am willing to attend counseling to learn how to deal with issues I have with my partner, even if my partner is not willing to attend. (If there is a fire, someone must call the fire department).	☐ TRUE	☐ FALSE

A Note on Commitment: Your commitment to your relationship should never be based on the level of commitment your partner has to the relationship. If it is, then when one falls, you will both fall together. Commitment does not mean, however, that you patiently endure whatever your partner happens to do. Commitment means that you have made a decision, for better or for worse, that you will do what is necessary to preserve, protect, and nurture the relationship. At times, that may mean that you attend counseling by yourself. You can work on yourself and the way that you deal with your partner's actions. If your partner does not want *you* to go to counseling, you must weigh your partner's desires against the need for counseling. (If your partner was having a heart attack but did not want you to call for an ambulance, what would you do?). The right action is always in the best interest of both you and your partner.

counseling process better. For example, one beginning exercise I do with couples is to have them plan a date together during the session. Having to do that in front of me puts the couple on the spot and that alone changes the way they do the exercise. They talk nicely to each other because they don't want to argue in front of the doctor. Left on their own, couples may not be able to plan a date because they get sidetracked with other issues and an argument may make then just say "forget it!" With me watching, however, it normally takes less than five minutes for the couple to plan the date—which they then go on before the following session.

Knowing that I'm going to ask about how the date went helps to ensure that the date happens and that people are better behaved on their date. This is the familiar "accountability" role that the therapist plays. Because the therapist does not take sides, each partner is equally comfortable (or uncomfortable) and the couple returns to therapy. Because I work with couples who have severe problems, often this is the first date they have had in a long time.

The very interesting thing about this is that the couple had the skills to plan a date, cooperatively, and to follow through on it, but couldn't do that unless they were sitting in front of me. This is part of the reason that therapists have success getting clients to do what they *already know how to do*, but couldn't do, on their own.

Learning Alternatives to Complaining and Distancing

Do you believe that the best way to get someone to love you is to demand that they do? Or to complain until he or she loves you better? Or to stop interacting with your partner until he or she develops a desire to love you better? Although most people would answer "no" to these questions, this is another paradoxical situation that people get themselves into. They don't feel loved by their spouse and so either complain to their spouse ("you never want to do anything," "you never want to talk," "all you do is sit in front of that damned TV") or withdraw. Confrontation, followed by withdrawal, is a very

Without other sources of love and affirmation, we will become needy, desperate, and demanding whenever we are not receiving love from our partner.

275

natural thing to do. "Hit and run" is safer than hit and be hit back. It's true that if you close down or keep someone at a distance, they can't hurt you as much. But, we all need and want to be loved, and distance won't accomplish that. Neither will complaints or demands—even if our spouse has made promises such as wedding vows and we have it in writing. Rather than making demands, we must do three things that really promote love in marriage: 1) love our spouse; 2) not be a codependent; and 3) have other sources of love and affirmation in our lives.

Loving Someone Does Not Mean Being Submissive

Loving our partner does not mean doing whatever our partner wants or whatever makes him or her happy. (The same goes for a parent, child, or friend). Loving others means doing what is in their best interest, whether they like it or not. Generally, anything that will damage the relationship is not in their best interest. Sometimes saying "no" or temporarily walking away is in their best interest. It takes more guts to love than it does to be nice.

Not being a "codependent" means not helping our partner to do something which is harmful to him or her. Buying alcohol for an alcoholic, lying to protect your spouse, turning a blind eye to cheating, or allowing your spouse to abuse you are examples of codependency. In each case short-term conflict may be avoided but at the expense of long-term well-being for your partner, yourself, and the relationship. This behavior, when allowed to go on and on, leads to more and more problems, which can only end in crisis. Codependent people generally are acting out of a desire to avoid conflict rather than out of genuine love for their partners.

Dependency (Neediness), the Relationship Killer

In addition to loving your spouse by doing what is in the best interest of the relationship, and avoiding codependency, it is essential to have other sources of love and affirmation. Without other sources of love and affirmation, we will become needy, desperate, and demanding whenever we are not

Which of These Behaviors Shows More Love?

- Buying alcohol for your alcoholic husband as you watch his health and your relationship deteriorate? Or
- Requiring that your partner go to rehab if he wants to continue the relationship?
- Giving in to your partner's jealousy and control, gradually becoming more resentful? Or
- Refusing to be controlled by your partner, even though it may cause conflict at first?
- Genuine love does what is in the long term interest of others and our relationships with them.

receiving love from our partner. We also will hesitate to take a firm stance when we need to, for fear of losing the only person in our life who makes us feel loved. Needy people have no power in the relationship and their partners feel like they have to be careful not to upset the needy person. Intimacy is lost. Partnership is lost. And, eventually, the relationship is lost. The more sources of love and validation you have in your life, the less emotionally dependent (needy) you will be on your partner. That will help you to maintain intimacy and partnership. Your therapist will therefore encourage you both to have your own interests, friends, and activities. Protecting the future of your relationship is as important as fixing it now.

If Your Partner Is Your Only Friend, You Are Headed for Trouble

Friends help us to meet our emotional needs. It is not all up to our partners to do that. The less emotionally needy we are, the more emotionally available we will be to love our spouses instead of demand our spouses love us. Not having friends creates neediness, and neediness takes away from our ability to love others and instead motivates us to focus on seeking love for ourselves. When we are not needy, then we have an abundant supply of love to give to others. The controlling person, who is jealous when his or her partner has friends, is attempting to get all the love for himself or herself. But, the fact is, he will get less and less love because he is depriving and depleting his partner's love. Withholding love from someone is not a way to get more of it from them.

Feeling Love Attaches You to Your Partner, But Only the Genuine Expression of Love Builds the Relationship

Your therapist plays a vital role in keeping a careful watch on the way you express your love for each other—not just whether or not you have it. Many times people are not aware that the way they are attempting to show love is not really experienced as love by their partner and is not, in fact, in their partner's best interest. For example, codependent people are notorious for not realizing that they are helping to maintain

The controlling person, who is jealous when his or her partner has friends, is attempting to get all the love for himself or herself. But, the fact is, he will get less and less love because he is depriving and depleting his partner's love.

their partner's problems (if they were, they would probably stop being codependent). An example of this is that many spouses have given up having friends of their own, to satisfy their partner, although the end result is bitterness and resentment. Showing love has a lot to do with when to say "Yes," and when to say "No."

The Therapeutic Use of Separation Can Save a Relationship

Sometimes, the therapist will recommend that a couple separate. This may come as a big surprise to a couple who is working to stay together. A *therapeutic separation* is very different from the common idea of marital separation. The common act of separation is to distance the couple in preparation for divorce. A therapeutic separation, on the other hand, is for the purpose of putting an end to destructive behavior in order to save the marriage. Therapeutic separation is recommended when staying together will lead to damaging the relationship further. After the damage has been stopped and a couple are relating in a way that builds the relationship, the separation ends. During a therapeutic separation, therefore, it is important that the couple be participating in marital counseling.

Therapeutic Separation:

- **Is necessary when continued damage would otherwise result.**
- **Is always for the purpose of improving the relationship.**
- **Takes place while a couple is in counseling.**
- **Is at least three months in duration, to ensure stability of progress.**

Case Example—Raymond and Yuko

Raymond and Yuko were at the end of their wits. They had been married for only three years. They described their relationship as "sheer hell." By the time they entered counseling with me, they were ready to call the marriage quits.

As their therapist, I told Raymond and Yuko that I could certainly understand their desire to divorce. No person in their right mind would want to live in "sheer hell." I certainly wouldn't. What I then asked them was, "Why haven't you already filed for divorce?"

Neither Raymond nor Yuko wanted to answer the question. They had so much anger toward each other and were so walled off to protect themselves that it was hard to say anything positive. Raymond did admit that their relationship "used to be fun," although he was sure to add that it wasn't anymore. Yuko could agree that they used to have good times together, "a long time ago."

I focused on their agreement and got them talking about how it used to be. As each talked about how they had enjoyed the relationship, the atmosphere lightened and the mood was less tense.

I summarized for them their situation and put in words what they were having difficulty saying. "Now you want to recover what you once had, but you don't know how to do that and a lot of damage has been done." I then asked each of them what they believed would happen if they continued as they are, without taking drastic steps to save their marriage. They both agreed the marriage would end in divorce and very soon.

Because this first session was critical and because this couple might not have returned to therapy, I laid out the best choice that I saw for them to save their marriage. They could either continue as they are, which they knew would result in divorce, or separate. The separation would give them some breathing space and a chance to calm down. They would continue to see each other in therapy and work on restoring what they once had.

Raymond and Yuko saw a separation as impractical and difficult, but as necessary, if they were to save their relationship. I framed their agreement to separate as their desire to save their marriage, while deciding to continue as they were would just be a desire to kill their relationship once and for all. Then, they would end up separated anyhow, but with little hope of reconciling.

When they returned to therapy the following week, Yuko was living with one of her friends and was less angry. So was Raymond. They then started the work of being a couple rather than adversaries.

———

The separation would give them some breathing space and a chance to calm down. They would continue to see each other in therapy and work on restoring what they once had.

Therapists will generally recommend separation if: 1) one of the spouses is in physical danger; or 2) staying together is breaking down the marriage faster than it can be built up. Therapeutic separation is an intervention designed to prevent extreme damage to the relationship. During the separation, counseling, dating, and other skills practice continues. The idea is to use the time of separation for the couple to have positive interactions together, learn how to more constructively handle their differences, and prepare to again live together. The therapist is an important guide as to when to separate, the things to do during the separation, and in determining when to end the separation. Used in this way, therapeutic separations can save marriages that would otherwise be difficult or impossible to rescue. When couples separate on their own, without the guidance of a therapist, their interactions typically do not improve and they grow further and further apart.

Summary

In order to become closer to a person emotionally, our positive interactions have to greatly outnumber our negative interactions. Whether separated or together, learning to change the way you interact with your partner can make that happen. In the process, trust will be built. Remaining in therapy with or without your spouse until you have had at least three good months together is essential to the long term success of your relationship.

SPECIAL TOPICS

CHAPTER TWENTY

20. HELPING YOUR KIDS WITH COUNSELING

Being a parent is one of the most difficult jobs in the world. Anyone who thinks it is a hobby and not a job has not yet been a parent. It is a 24 hour a day, 7 days a week, high responsibility job. Job duties are constantly changing and the unexpected can happen at any moment. At the same time you are parenting, you have other responsibilities such as earning money, and taking care of other people. Even if someone (like a babysitter) takes over for you temporarily, you remain on call. If you are a parent, then you know that there are even more demands on you than this. If we were to list them all, it would be a wonder why people have children in the first place. Fortunately, when all goes well, the demands of parenting are equaled by the rewards.

Are Kids Worth It?

If all goes well, we are happy with the time and effort that we have spent in raising a child. Although there are always some problems along the way, we will never regret having had our children and will desire to remain involved in their lives for the rest of ours. That "if all goes well" is a very scary part, though, because so much can go wrong. Scary as it is, we must do our best without fearing the results. Otherwise, we will lose the joy. Doing our best means "our educated best" so that we can get things mostly right (no one gets them all right).

Children are more vulnerable and impressionable than adults. They live in a world full of dangers to their body, mind, and soul. No matter how good care a parent takes of a child,

Parenting is a Full Time Job

- **Anybody who is capable of devoting as much time and effort to a career as people do to raising children can rise to the top of the corporate ladder and spend their retirement lying on the beaches of Hawaii.**

there is plenty of room for things to go wrong. When they do, fortunately, there are professionals available to help. There may come a time when you call on a therapist to help you with your child, or your relationship with your child.

Meeting Children's Needs Develops Trust

When children are just babies, they need almost constant monitoring, but their needs are simple. They need food and drink, protection from the elements, to be kept clean, and love and affection. Parents know to give their babies milk and not soft drinks, baby food and not french fries. They cuddle their babies rather than just setting them in front of the television. They know that because their baby is helpless and not capable of much, not to put demands on them to dress themselves or to use the toilet instead of diapers. In short, parents match their care with their baby's needs and abilities. That fosters healthy development in their child as well as trust. Trust and bonding go hand in hand.

As children grow bigger, they grow in ability and need less constant supervision. Although most parents take care of babies in the same way, there is a lot of variation in the way they take care of older children. And, because children differ more (individuate more) as they get older, it makes sense that parents differ somewhat in how they care for their children.

Determining the Needs of an Older Child

The first step in taking care of *anyone* properly is determining his or her needs. This is also true in taking care of things. Caring for a piece of furniture requires cleaning and polishing. Taking care of a plant entails providing the right amount of sunlight, the correct nutrients, and the correct amount of water. Caring for a pet takes the right kind and amount of food, exercise, play, etc. "Each according to his or her needs," is a wise rule of thumb.

To figure out what a child needs, it is helpful to think in categories. First, there is the body category. Essential to the body's health is getting enough sleep, exercise, and nutrition. These are "needs" of the body because without them, health

No matter how good care a parent takes of a child, there is plenty of room for things to go wrong. When they do, fortunately, there are professionals available to help.

284

will deteriorate. Children, like all people, have built-in indicators to signal when a need is not being met. When they are babies, they will cry and you need to figure it out (are they wet? hungry? sleepy?). When they are able to speak they will tell you their need directly ("Mom, I'm hungry") or you will be able to tell from their behavior (e.g., fussing and rubbing their eyes when they are tired, for example). Fortunately, the body is somewhat flexible and children can adapt to different eating and sleeping schedules and be deprived for short periods of time without harm.

Problems with the body arise when the body's needs are not met. Children who sleep too little will be moodier, sick more often, and have worse performance in school and otherwise. Children who receive improper nutrition may be obese and overfed though lacking in essential nutrients necessary for healthy development. Children who don't exercise will have inferior coordination skills, as well as delayed physical and social development. Of course, bodies can also be injured by accident, genetic predisposition and illness. Sometimes no matter how well a parent cares for a child's physical needs, there will be problems.

The Emotional Needs of Children

Children also have emotional needs. The most basic emotional need is to feel safe. When children live in predictable environments without receiving verbal, sexual, or physical abuse or neglect, they develop a sense of security. *Neglect* is the deprivation of needs—not the deprivation of desires. Children also need to have secure and loving attachments to their families. Children have a need for socialization—enjoyable interaction with other children. Children need to feel important and valued regardless of their ability to achieve or succeed. Again, even with the best of care by parents, things can go wrong.

When Your Child Needs Counseling

When a child is brought to the attention of a mental health professional such as a therapist, the therapist will gather a lot of

Physical Needs Include:

- **Food**
- **Water**
- **Sleep**
- **Activity**
- **Shelter**
- **Safe Environment**
- **Clean Environment**

Psychological Needs Include:

- **Nurturing/guidance**
- **Bonding/attachment**
- **Trust**
- **Security**
- **Feeling Important**
- **Feeling Competent**
- **Socialization**
- **Intellectual stimulation**

information about earlier development. Sometimes parents of teenagers are surprised to find the therapist asking about things such as when the teen first learned to talk or walk or other "milestones of development." Just as adults get asked about their childhood, therapists want to know about children's early childhood development. If you can't remember at what age your child sat up, don't worry about it. In asking such things, therapists are most concerned when children are early or late in their development. When children are sufficiently different from the norm, parents generally remember. You will also get asked about school problems at each grade, early friendships, activities, and interests. Again, the things that are most relevant you will be able to remember. The therapist is just helping you to mentally check each of these areas. Knowing a child developed and achieved milestones normally is just as important as knowing he or she didn't. Usually, problems don't just come out of nowhere, but when they do, it's very important to know.

Case Example—Jeremy

Jeremy was a 10 year old boy who was brought into counseling by his parents for "depression." At the first session, I met with Jeremy for half the session while his parents completed several checklists and questionnaires about him. During the second half of the session, I met with Jeremy's parents while Jeremy waited in the waiting room.

I praised Jeremy's parents for their concern and desire to help him. I assured them that Jeremy was not destined to be depressed, but that we had to figure out what was causing the depression so that we could plan a truly effective treatment. A thorough evaluation would be the most important way to start to help him.

I explained that there are several different kinds of problems that can result in the symptoms of depression. They could be something internal to Jeremy, like a physical problem or some difficult thoughts that he is struggling with. On the other hand, they could be a reaction to something that is difficult for Jeremy to deal with in his environment, such as bullying or poor grades. Because of this, it would be necessary to gather information from Jeremy's parents, teachers, activity leaders (such as Boy Scout leader, soccer coach, etc.), and Jeremy. It was also necessary for Jeremy to have a complete physical examination by a medical doctor.

I explained to Jeremy's parents that we could spend months of time treating the wrong problem without such thorough information. We needed to be sure we were on the right track and also whether counseling or medical treatment would be the best place to start. If they would sign the release forms and arrange for the medical exam, I would contact the school and activity leaders.

I continued to meet weekly with Jeremy and his parents while the information was being gathered. Jeremy's parents liked my team approach and the way I supported them. I never suggested that they were at fault for Jeremy's depression. Jeremy also completed some simple tests with me. At no time did Jeremy ever dislike coming to therapy. His parents also felt assured— knowing that they were doing something effective to help their son. Later it would be just a small part of his growing up, but at that time, it was something important that he really needed.

———

Therapists try to meet with both parents and sometimes siblings. Therapists also want to get information from school teachers even though a child may not have any problems at school. Knowing about the environments where your child both succeeds and has difficulty are important for comparison purposes. It also helps to reveal when the problem is more likely to be biological, as biological problems impact most contexts the same.

I explained to Jeremy's parents that we could spend months of time treating the wrong problem without such thorough information. We needed to be sure we were on the right track and also whether counseling or medical treatment would be the best place to start.

When Needs are Deprived, Problems Eventually Result

Most of the time when children or adults enter therapy it is because their physical and/or emotional needs are not being met. The deprivation may have had to go on for some time for the symptoms to become noticeable. But, they are likely to become even worse if the need is not identified and met in an appropriate way.

Teenagers who come for counseling are notorious for being sleep deprived. Often, the parent has no idea how much the teen is sleeping. A common problem is teenager's desires for socialization or stimulation (such as from talking on the phone, text messaging, using the internet, playing games, or watching television) combined with their poor judgment (about how much sleep they need), and desire for immediate gratification, which results in physical deprivation. *Physical deprivation always has mental consequences.* This can occur with younger children as well.

Don't Take It Personally

The therapist will help you to determine if your child's needs are being met. Although parents tend to take this personally, that's unnecessary. The fact that you brought your child to counseling shows your concern for the welfare of your child. Therapists know that raising a child involves all kinds of variables and is not as straightforward as looking up the answer in a book. After all, therapists realize the same thing with all other problems—you can't just look up the answers in a book, do them, and have a wonderful life. Even therapists can't do that (therapists go to other therapists).

Get the Need Met as Soon as Possible

If one or more of your child's needs are not being met (whether physical or emotional), the therapist will either refer you to another kind of specialist who can help you with meeting that need (an education specialist, pediatrician, psychiatrist, etc.) or will directly work with you and your child.

All Psychological Problems Relate to Needs:

- **Needs that are unmet, or**
- **Needs which are being insufficiently met, or**
- **Needs that are being met in unhealthy ways.**

Therapists Don't Blame Parents:

- **Placing blame does not help a child.**
- **You are responsible for helping your child to overcome problems.**
- **Even if you were at fault somehow, focus on what you can do—not on what you have done.**

288

Unless a problem obviously has an environmental cause, going to a *psychologist* is a good first step because of the careful evaluation that the psychologist will do (and because psychologists are qualified to do psychological testing). The psychologist will also guide you in selecting the best treatment approach and help you and your child to deal with any stresses that come with that. Even a seemingly simple solution can create stress. Early intervention is always more effective and easier on you and your child than the "wait and see" approach.

Why Children Don't Get to Vote About Their Physical or Emotional Health

When parents discover such deprivation is occurring, they must choose between meeting their child's *needs* (e.g., getting enough sleep), and meeting their child's *desires* (e.g., staying up all night on school nights). Some parents choose to meet their child's desires in order to avoid conflict with their child. They would rather allow their child to use the computer all night, for example, than argue with them about it. For a child who is already having problems, in the long run, this will both harm the child as well as the parents' relationship with the child. Just as with adults, long term needs must take priority over short term desires.

Of course, if the child was not having problems, intervention would not be needed. This too, illustrates the importance of seeing what your child's actual needs are. Too many parents pick a battle that is totally unnecessary because a child is doing well.

If we take the example where your teen is staying up late, and using the internet rather than getting needed sleep, the solution is simple *on the surface*—disallow the use of the internet after a certain time at night. This solution only seems simple to people who have yet to have teenage children. Once a teenager has acquired a habit, it is difficult to get them to give it up. This underscores the importance of working with children from a young age to acquire healthy habits. If you have always had a house rule that there is to be no use of electronic devices after a set bedtime, it will be easier for the teen to tolerate

Just as with adults, long term needs must take priority over short term desires. Of course, if the child was not having problems, intervention would not be needed.

although they won't necessarily like it. What do you think will happen when you introduce this rule when it hasn't been in place before? Your teen will predictably become angry and try to talk you out of it, coerce you out of it, and then work around you. Experienced parents can see this coming.

See Your Own Difficulties Realistically to Be Able to Empathize More with Your Child

When your child's behavior is interfering with her needs being met, you have two choices: 1) attempt to change your child's behavior in order to help her to get her needs met; or 2) allow your child to get what she desires rather than what she needs. This decision of whether to give a child what she needs or what she desires is one that is revisited throughout childhood.

As adults, we have this struggle in our own lives and may often choose what we desire—to our own detriment. Our choices may not be much better than those of our children. To expect our children to have the ability to make good choices without our help is unreasonable. Adults must make decisions for children, and help them to follow through with those decisions. Especially when not to do so would have long-lasting consequences.

If you choose to give your child what she desires rather than what she needs, she will be pleased in the short-run. She will consider you to be the good parent who is loving and caring. Unfortunately, because your child is being deprived of a need, she will accumulate problems which will eventually lead to failure for her and to greater conflict with you. Giving in to your child's desires, *when they prevent an important need from being met*, brings short-term peace at the cost of long-term failure (just as you saw with marriage in the chapter on marriage counseling). It is the strategy of giving a drunk a drink. He will be happy for the moment, but you will have done nothing to help him to improve his prospects for the future. With children, this comes in many forms—play as a substitute for sleep, TV as a substitute for social interaction, money as a substitute for quality time with family, fast food as a

Rules are Not Just for Kids:

- The rules in our workplaces, in public, and in our relationships are designed to keep us safe, functioning well, and benefiting from our efforts.
- When adults break these rules, they end up jobless, in traffic accidents, divorced, with big debt, or in prison.
- Helping your child with the appropriate use of rules is responsible parenting and may save your child and you from a lot of heartache later.
- Children don't grow up to hate their parents for rules which were appropriate, no matter how much they complain at the time.

substitute for proper nutrition, handouts as a substitute for chores, etc. These strategies don't work for adults—why would they work for children?

The More Serious the Consequences, the Stronger Your Intervention May Need to Be

When the consequences are critical, rather than choose to give children what they desire, you can choose to give children what they need. You can also establish conditions under which your child's needs can be met. In removing all electronic devices after a certain time of night, you do not ensure that your child will sleep. You do make it more likely that your child will sleep. Requiring that your child participate in activities and get extra academic help also won't ensure that your child will make friends or do well in school, but it does create the possibility for that. A child that has no participation with others outside of school does not have the possibility for making friends. A child who is doing poorly in school without receiving extra help does not have the possibility for improvement. As much as they can, parents need to establish the conditions which make it *possible* for their children to be healthy and to experience success. Experiencing success is more important to long term happiness than instant gratification. Whether a child has a genius IQ or is developmentally delayed, he or she needs to feel successful at something.

Explanation Helps, But Don't Expect Agreement

When you choose to meet your children's needs before their desires, there will be short-term conflict. Although it is good to tell your reasons to your child, no amount of reasoning will prevent the conflict. Such conflict is not caused by a lack of understanding. It is caused by the opposition of your desire and your child's desire. After an initial adjustment period, your child will perform better (due to more sleep, more friends, academic success, etc.) and conflict will be reduced. In fact, your relationship with your child will improve in the long term. Your child will learn self-control and responsibility, and as a result, be better prepared for adulthood.

Experiencing success is more important to long term happiness than instant gratification. Whether a child has a genius IQ or is developmentally delayed, he or she needs to feel successful at something.

Conflict:

- Is inevitable.
- Can help us to grow.
- Is an opportunity to teach win-win problem solving to our children.

Happiness:

- Is not something we can feel all of the time.
- If your child is more often unhappy then happy, it signals an unmet need.

Some parents have told me that they would never take their child to therapy against their will:

- I ask them if they feel the same way about the dentist or the medical doctor.

When Children are Unhappy

When a child (or an adult) is unhappy, it is because one or more of their needs are not being met. This can result from personal choice, as a result of crime or poverty, social oppression, or an underlying biological disorder. Figuring out what those needs are and how to get them met are only two of the tasks of the therapist. The third is to work with you, your child, and other family members to get the need or needs met, while preserving relationships. When that's hard to do on your own, it is entirely appropriate to enlist the help of a therapist.

When the problem is caused by a conflict between what your child needs and what he desires, he will not be motivated to enter counseling. He will have an instinctive sense that the therapist will not work to get him what he wants, but will work with his parents to get him what he needs. Asking a child if he wants to go to counseling is like asking him if he wants to get his tooth pulled. He will say yes only if he's in extreme pain.

Talking to Your Child About Going to Therapy

There are ways that will soften the blow for bringing unwilling adults and children into therapy. The best way is to share the problem. Rather than telling the other person that she has a problem and needs counseling, you can say truthfully that you both have a problem. For example, let's say that the problem is that your daughter appears depressed and withdrawn. You say, "Rachel, we have a family problem. You seem to be unhappy and because of that *we* are unhappy too. *We* are going to go to counseling together to get help so that *we* can *all* be happy." Another example, "Tom, I know that you would like to get better grades in school, and we would like you to get better grades, too. The things that *we've* tried don't seem to be helping so *we* are going to counseling so that *we* can *all* get help with this issue."

Emotional Problems vs. Behavioral Problems

Besides determining which of your child's needs is not being met, the therapist will determine if your child's problem is

292

mainly emotional, mainly behavioral, or both. When the problem is mainly emotional, the therapist will spend most of the therapy time with your child. When the problem is mainly behavioral, the therapist will spend most of the time with you. Adults have more control over a child's behavior than the child does. If the problem is both emotional and behavioral, the time will be more evenly divided between child and adult.

Family therapists will often meet with the child and adults (and possibly other family members) at the same time, combining behavior management and emotional help. The skill of the therapist rather than the type of therapy is the most important. A skilled family therapist can accomplish a lot. So can a skilled clinical therapist. Therapists who work with children must have knowledge of both child and adult dynamics and a number of other skills not required for working with adults. Skills are a result of training plus experience. Be sure to ask your therapist about both and to get a referral to a counselor rather than selecting one at random.

Why Therapists Play Games with Children

When a therapist works with a young child, therapy will be in the form of play. For the older child, therapy is in the form of talk. Actually, even with the younger child there is a good deal of talk but in the context of play which is easier for the child. They often will remember only the play although the therapist will have been talking with them about very serious subjects. Young children usually find it more important to remember the outcome of a game rather than what they talked about during the session.

Children Need Confidentiality, Too

Older children often quickly come to see that therapy is enjoyable although they are not likely to say so to their parents. In therapy they receive one on one attention, unconditional positive regard, and what they say and think is valued without judgment. Because the counseling is confidential, they can talk about things with the therapist that they may not be able to talk about with another adult. The most important thing you can

When the problem is mainly emotional, the therapist will spend most of the therapy time with your child. When the problem is mainly behavioral, the therapist will spend most of the time with you.

Older children often quickly come to see that therapy is enjoyable although they are not likely to say so to their parents. In therapy they receive one on one attention, unconditional positive regard, and what they say and think is valued without judgment.

do as a parent is to trust the therapist and not insist on breaking your child's confidentiality. That would only undermine the therapist-child relationship. With younger children, the therapist will share more with you but you must not reveal this to your child or your child will become guarded in the session. You have to choose between helping your child and knowing everything your child says in the session. You cannot have both.

Be Careful Not to End Therapy as Soon as Things Seem Better

As with therapy for adults, therapy can be used with children to handle: 1) crisis issues; 2) a return to normal functioning; and 3) working to do better than before. The same dangers also apply to removing your child from counseling too soon. If you see improvement in your child's emotions or behaviors, but it has been less than three months, there is a high risk of falling back to previous moods and behavior. Just like adults, children need time to firmly establish new habits and to adjust to them.

Summary

Parents cannot be expected to know how to help their child with every conceivable problem over an 18 year period. A counselor can be just as important of a resource as a pediatrician. Regardless of the style of therapy, the therapist will always work to help your child as well as to improve your relationship with your child. Determining needs, not where to lay blame, is the key for successful change.

Exercise

On the next page is a checklist of concerns for children. This checklist can help you to identify concerns to raise with the therapist and/or areas where your child has an underlying need. The more concerns that you have for your child, or the more severe the problems, the greater the need for therapy for you and your child.

Exercise: Checklist of Concerns for Children

Check the lines that describe your child's characteristics in the <u>past three months</u>:

☐ Aggressive or violent, starts fights
☐ Always complains of feeling sick
☐ Anxiety, nervousness
☐ Argumentative and/or defiant
☐ Bad peer group
☐ Clinging, dependent, immature
☐ Complains often
☐ Conflicts with parents over rules, chores, schoolwork
☐ Cruelty toward animals
☐ Delayed development of skills or abilities
☐ Difficulty adjusting to loss of a family member
☐ Difficulty adjusting to new family member
☐ Difficulty adjusting to parental separation or divorce
☐ Difficulty displaying affection
☐ Difficulty learning in some areas
☐ Difficulty making friends
☐ Difficulty separating fantasy from reality
☐ Disobedient, uncooperative
☐ Disorganized
☐ Disruptive, attention seeking
☐ Drug or alcohol use or attempts
☐ Easily distracted, inattentive, poor concentration
☐ Easily frustrated, gives up quickly, irritable
☐ Eats too much or too little, always hungry
☐ Fire setting
☐ Foul language, inappropriate language
☐ Frequent nightmares
☐ Immature, has only younger friends
☐ Irresponsible, cannot be trusted, doesn't follow through with commitments
☐ Isolates, prefers to be alone, withdraws
☐ Lack of concern for others
☐ Lack of exercise
☐ Lacks respect for adults, provokes adults
☐ Law breaking
☐ Lying
☐ Overly talkative, overly loud
☐ Mental retardation
☐ Moody, sullen
☐ Nail biting
☐ Needs high degree of supervision
☐ Negativism
☐ No participation in social activities of peers
☐ Obese
☐ Overactive, hyper, fidgety, wound up

☐Overly compliant, seeks to please too much
☐Picks on or bullies other children
☐Poor grades, failures
☐Poor peer or sibling relationships
☐Prejudiced, intolerant of differences (race, gender, etc.)
☐Preoccupation with sex or self-stimulation
☐Procrastinates, delays, wastes time
☐Recent move to new school or away from friends
☐Refuses help even when needed
☐Rocking, hand flapping, or other repetitive movements
☐Refuses to speak
☐Rule breaking, cheating
☐Runs away
☐Sad most of the time
☐Self-injures or threatens to self-injure
☐Sensitive, Cries easily, feelings are easily hurt
☐Shy
☐Speech difficulties, speech delays
☐Stubborn
☐Sudden and uncontrollable rapid movements, noises, or words
☐Suicide threats or attempts
☐Sulks, pouts
☐Teased or picked on by others
☐Temper tantrums, fits, rages
☐Thumb sucking, hair chewing
☐Timid, fearful
☐Truancy, skipping classes, dropping out of school
☐Underactive, low energy, lethargy
☐Uncoordinated, accident-prone, clumsy
☐Victim of physical, sexual, and/or emotional abuse
☐Wetting or soiling clothes
☐Wetting or soiling bed

For each item that is checked, consider: 1) the length of time your child has had this problem; 2) what you are doing to help; and 3) how effective your help is, so far.

The need for a therapist increases with: 1) the number or severity of problems your child has; 2) the length of time your child has had these problems; 3) your difficulty in knowing how to help your child with this problem; and 4) the ineffectiveness of your interventions.

CHAPTER TWENTY-ONE

21. HELPING YOUR CHILD TO SUCCEED

When you think about success for your child, what comes to mind? Do you think about her grades in school, her social relationships, her health, her happiness, her ability to contribute to your family and her preparation for contributing to the world, her values and how she sees herself in the world? The fact is, that most parents don't think about all of these things. As long as their children are doing reasonably well (no complaints from school and good behavior at home), they assume that all is well. Then, if a problem does occur, it is seen as something that just happened—seemingly springing out of nowhere. Although there often are "trigger events" that precede the need for psychological help, most problems started much earlier. This is true for adults, and it is true for children as well.

Developmental psychologists talk about the various stages of growth that children need to successfully complete before they will be ready for the next stage of development. In other words, success today depends on success yesterday; and success tomorrow depends on success today. When something goes wrong today, what has (or hasn't) gone on before may be largely responsible.

Here are some examples of modern day problems that kids have which actually have been building for quite some time: Obesity related diseases are the result of years of being overweight. Poor self esteem is the result of years of getting negative messages about the self. Lack of friends and conflicts

Measures of Success:
- **Physical Health**
- **Mental Health**
- **Financial Health**
- **Social Health**
- **Personal/Spiritual Meaning**

When people (which includes children) feel that what they do is important, but that they themselves are not personally important, they lose motivation. We all need to feel personally important to someone, even if we really mess up.

with peers are the result of years of inadequate social skills and socialization. Selfishness and disregard for others is the result of years of living with values that promote the self over others. And psychological problems are often the result of years of inconsistency, stressful environments, and poor coping. Many other problems of childhood (and adulthood) could be added to this list.

Psychologists necessarily must look both backwards (to how problems developed) and forwards (to how to prepare children for more success), because they see children only after problems have developed. As a parent, you have the luxury of focusing forward—preparing your child to have success in areas important for adults in this world. When you do that, you not only help your child to not have problems later, you help your child to have success later.

If we "let children be children," with few rules and little guidance, then they would have to become adults before they learned to "grow up." They wouldn't know how to get along with people who are not their friends, how to deal with the inevitable problems and stresses of life, how to work through conflict with a loved one, how to use their strengths to help others, how to manage money, or many other very practical skills necessary to live and be successful as a person. Most of us as adults can look back and see how learning a particular skill as a child would have gotten us off to a much better start in our relationships or careers.

Friends as a Measure of Success

Schools use grades to measure performance, but as a parent you need to take more than grades into consideration. Sometimes in an effort to get their children to have good grades, parents actually neglect other factors important for success. There are several.

Considering some examples from the adult world can help us to put things into perspective. Would you consider an adult who has a nice, high-paying career, to be successful? What if he or she had no friends and has been unable to have any long term relationships? Would you rather be well-paid with no friends or a poor person with many friends? If you are like most people, you wouldn't want to be either. You would rather be well-paid with a lot of friends. You don't have to be well-paid to be successful, but it is easier than being poor. You don't need friends in order to be well-paid, but life is not very enjoyable without them. Similarly, children must be able to make and keep friends. Schools do little to promote friendships and you won't be able to see "friendship ability" on your child's report card. That is, unless there is a serious problem which affects the teachers.

Feeling Important as a Measure of Success

Besides friends, and job or school performance, another vital factor to anyone's success is a feeling of importance. When people (which includes children) feel that what they do is important, but that they themselves are not personally important, they lose motivation. We all need to feel personally important to someone, even if we really mess up. This means that children need to feel important to their parents even if their grades aren't so good, or their sports ability isn't so good, or even if they have any kind of physical, emotional, or academic handicap. In short, children's emotional needs are the same as adult's needs. The single most important factor in children's success is their relationship with their parents, and secondly, with their peers. Academics, while important, don't come close to the powerful positive impact of each of these things. Parents must be careful not to sacrifice a good relationship with their children in the effort to improve their child's academic performance.

Punishment Doesn't Improve Grades

Sometimes well meaning parents use punishment to try to improve their children's grades. While punishment can be used to stop a behavior, it is not good for starting a behavior. If a child is punished for getting 3 out of 10 words wrong on a spelling test, grades on the next test are likely to be worse rather than better. Rather than learning to improve, what children would learn from the punishment is that their performance is

There is one thing worse than ignoring mistakes— focusing on them.

What motivates both children and adults to succeed is a positive perspective, even when they have a poor performance.

inadequate. Feelings of inadequacy are inhibiting rather than motivating. Can you imagine if you were criticized whenever you made a negative comment to your partner while any positive comments you made were ignored? How long do you think it would be before you would not want to talk to your partner at all? How about if your negative comments were ignored while your positive comments were praised? How would that change your behavior? Wouldn't you want to talk more and more to your partner?

Ignore Mistakes

Rather than seeing children's mistakes as performance failures, their mistakes are better *ignored*. For most of us, this is a radical idea that doesn't match our own upbringing. But can you ever remember being motivated by getting errors marked on your paper or getting bad grades? These things discourage, not motivate.

Once, when I was trying to improve my fluency in the Japanese language, I hired a Japanese tutor. I told her that I wanted to become comfortable talking, and that fluency, rather than having perfect grammar, was my goal. Unfortunately, she stopped me from talking whenever I made the smallest mistake. It was hard for me to be able to finish a single sentence without getting a grammar lecture. My motivation to study Japanese dropped to about zero, until I fired my tutor. If she had focused on what I said well, instead of my mistakes, I'm sure that I would have both liked it and improved. Focusing on my mistakes had the opposite effect.

What motivates both children and adults to succeed is a positive perspective, even when they have a poor performance. Positive facts encourage us while negative facts shut us down. People would rather have a glass which is half full than one which is half empty. How can we make this kind of positive presentation to children?

Let's consider an example using a spelling test. Getting 5 out of 10 words wrong on a spelling test could be either a glass half-full or glass half empty situation. Scoring 5 out of 10 is not

Which Would Motivate You to Improve?

- **Someone pointing out your mistakes? or**
- **Someone pointing out where you were doing well?**
- **Why would that be any different for children?**

really bad behavior—it is half of an excellent performance. If we tell a child that she did excellent on those five words that she spelled correctly, we are telling the truth. We are also encouraging her to want to have more words right. If instead we punish her for the five words that she got wrong (even if the punishment is just in the form of mild disapproval), she will discount the words she got right, and her desire for learning will decrease. She will try not to make mistakes because she doesn't want the punishment, but she will wish that she didn't have spelling tests at all so that she didn't have to worry about it. Spelling will become a source of stress.

Stress not only interferes with performance, but it takes away our desire to continue. If you were doing something that made you feel stressed, would you rather continue doing it or quit? Would it be more motivating for you to have someone praise your successes or criticize you for your mistakes? If you could choose a magical message to appear either whenever you did something wrong, telling you how lousy you are; or, whenever you do something right, telling you how wonderful you are, which would you choose? Which would frustrate you and which would encourage you?

Use Your Child's Natural Motivation

Children are naturally motivated to get adult attention, so wherever you focus your attention will get you more and more of what you are focusing your attention on. If you tell a girl that she has a pretty smile, she will feel better about herself, smile more, and be more interested in taking care of her teeth. If you tell her that she should take better care of her jack-o-lantern teeth, she will smile less, feel worse about her teeth, and take worse care of them. People seem to instinctively know this when they are on dates. They look for what is good in the other person and point it out. In return, they get a favorable response and more of whatever they complimented. People who point out faults in their dates do not wind up with much improved dates—they wind up with no dates at all! Spouses also can be lured out of a marriage if the only place they hear compliments is from strangers.

The child who is motivated to learn will not need to have constant supervision and will feel good about herself when she does well. She will see intelligence as an important quality in herself. The child who gets good grades only under threat will feel relieved when she doesn't have to learn things.

Take Every Opportunity to Turn Your Child On To:

- Learning
- Living
- Loving

Many teenagers hear more compliments from their friends than from their parents. A very common complaint among teens is that their parents don't say anything nice to them. Some believe that their parents are disappointed in them and don't love them. When is the last time you complimented your child? What was the compliment about? Was it sarcastic? Did it have a "but" attached to it ("You are really talented in basketball, *but* I wish you would help out more around the house)?

On the following page is a "quiz" for parents who want their children to be more successful. This quiz is to encourage you that there is a lot that you can do to help your child. If you really want to get good at these skills, take the quiz again for each significant person in your life—your partner, your family members, your coworkers, etc. Helping other people to be successful is one of the best ways of creating success for yourself.

Grades vs. Love of Learning

Which do you think is more important—for a child to get good grades even if she hates school, or to have mediocre grades but develop a love for learning? Which one will lead to continued success? The child who is motivated to learn will not need to have constant supervision and will feel good about herself when she does well. She will see intelligence as an important quality in herself.

Train Your Child for Success:

Celebrate your child's achievements, no matter how they compare to others, and help your child to see the good in others.

The child who gets good grades only under threat will feel relieved when she doesn't *have to* learn things. If she goes to college, she is likely to avoid studying as much as possible. Without constant supervision, she realizes that no one can make her study anymore. She is likely to study only when she has to in order to pass her courses, afraid of the consequences of failing. Without a love of learning, however, she is not likely to get a graduate degree.

It is very difficult for people who don't have a love of learning to spend the number of years required to get master

302

Exercise: Quiz for Parents Who Want Their Child to Be Successful

I use praise, touch, and occasional, unexpected rewards (not promised payment) for what my child does well.
☐ True ☐ False

Rather than telling my child what is unacceptable, I tell him/her what is acceptable.
☐ True ☐ False

My child feels competent socially, academically, and physically.
☐ True ☐ False

I encourage my child's natural talents, even when they are different from the talents I wish he/she had.
☐ True ☐ False

I examine each of my child's efforts for things that he/she does well and focus on them.
☐ True ☐ False

I do not criticize my child.
☐ True ☐ False

I provide my child with extra help, where needed, without making my child feel inadequate.
☐ True ☐ False

I enforce rules to help my child to develop rather than punish or retaliate for my child's behavior.
☐ True ☐ False

I listen to my child with my full attention and don't interrupt.
☐ True ☐ False

I point out positive things about other people to my child so that he/she can learn to look for the positive in others.
☐ True ☐ False

Whenever possible, I promote my child's skills by using questions to teach rather than just giving answers.
☐ True ☐ False

When it is necessary to punish/discipline my child, I quickly get us back on track without letting bad feelings linger.
☐ True ☐ False

This is not an all-inclusive list, but includes core parenting competencies. The more "True" responses you have, the greater the likelihood for your child's long term success. The more "True" responses you have, the greater the likelihood that you will have a long term good relationship with your child. You can choose to work on any items that you answered "False," if you believe that would be helpful for you and your child.

and doctoral level degrees. Even if your child doesn't decide to go to college, her love of learning and self-confidence will help her in whatever endeavor she undertakes. So, focus more on helping your child to love learning than on making the grades.

Don't Weed Your Kids (or Anyone Else)

There's an old story about a vegetable gardener that spent all of his time pulling weeds. He wanted to grow beautiful vegetables and tried to keep his garden weed free. But every day, when he went to look at his garden, he would find more weeds to pull. It got so that instead of enjoying seeing his nice vegetables, his eyes would quickly shift to looking for weeds. In his efforts to get rid of the weeds, he would buy more and more powerful weed killers. If someone complimented him on his garden, he would thank them politely and tell them how much of a chore it is continuously getting rid of the weeds.

One day, the gardener had an insight—his hobby wasn't growing vegetables—it was killing weeds. And more than that, he realized he didn't like his hobby of killing weeds. He used his new insight to make a change in his life. Rather than pulling and spraying weeds, he started to focus on the vegetables themselves. He made sure that they had the water, sun, and nutrients that they required. He pruned them to make them strong. He avoided watering the weeds or giving them any attention.

Meanwhile, the weeds multiplied in his garden but without water, they didn't get very big and the vegetable plants grew big and strong and overshadowed the weeds. Each day the farmer would enjoy going to his garden to see how the plants were blossoming and producing fruit. His vegetable garden thrived and he enjoyed gardening once again.

Some parents spend the bulk of their time weeding their kids. Others focus on raising them.

Be Careful Not to Train Your Kids to be Self-Weeders

Many kids have been turned off to gardening because it was

Learn from Your Past:

- **Can you think of one thing you wish your parent(s) had said to you more?**
- **Do you say that to your child?**
- **How do you wish your parents had handled your mistakes?**
- **Do you handle your children's mistakes that way?**

their chore to pull the weeds when it should have been their chore to harvest the crops instead. Many kids have been turned off to school because it was their chore to fix their mistakes ("John, you made some rather bad mistakes. Correct them before you do anything more.") rather than to make more successes ("That's good John, you wrote a very nice paragraph. Now write another one just like it").

When your child brings home a report card with some good grades and some bad grades, praise your child for the good grades. Don't even mention the bad grades. Your child may point out his bad grades but you should pay little attention to them. If you are standing in a garden with a woman and her prize vegetables, don't point out the weeds around her. Tell her how impressed you are with her vegetables and how delicious they look. You can be sure that next season she will have some to share with you. Take your child out and celebrate the good grades, brag about the good grades to other people (without mentioning those other grades). The more you do this, the better your child's grades will become and the happier you will be parenting your child.

Examples of Comments that Tear Down

I know you can do better than that.

Why can't you be more like your brother?

When I was your age, I did 5 hours of homework per night.

You need to be more careful, you need to think.

You used to do better, what happened?

Do you want to have to be put in a special class?

If you tried harder, you'd do better.

Do get your child any extra help that she needs to do well and do require that homework be done and that tests be studied for. And then, sincerely praise her for all the answers she gets right.

Therapy Can Help You to:

- Determine the cause of the difficulty,
- Make sure that you get the correct help for your child, and
- Preserve your relationship with your child in the process.

Examples of Comments that Build Up

I really like the way you _____.

I believe in you.

Together we can do anything!

You have a good eye for details.

With a little extra help, you can get better and better.

I love you just the way you are.

I am proud of you.

I'm glad you're my son/daughter.

_____

Hopefully, no matter what wrinkles or blemishes your significant other has, you tell him he is handsome, or her that she is beautiful. In so doing, you create a more handsome, beautiful, and happy person.

On the next page is an exercise for identifying more positives in your child or others. Identifying and praising these positives will build up your child and your relationship with your child. Of course, the same goes for your relationship with anyone. Sincere appreciation builds where criticism and flattery fail.

Substitute Assistance for Criticism

Do get your child any extra help that she needs to do well and do require that homework be done and that tests be studied for. And then, sincerely praise her for all the answers she gets right. Continue this pattern: extra help as needed, study rules, and praise for whatever your child gets right (even if it's just a little). You will have a winning formula for success. You can apply the same formula to yourself while you are at it. You may need to overcome a "self-weeding" habit that you

Exercise: Why My Child Deserves Praise

Too often people fail to praise performance unless it is completely, or almost completely good. As a result, people who are already very competent get much praise, while people who are not very competent feel more and more discouraged. Children are the least competent of people because of their lack of experience. Even naturally talented children are not naturally talented in every area. But, they too, need to feel encouraged to grow in other areas.

Instructions: For each of the following areas, list examples (no matter how small) of what your child does well. Challenge yourself to write at least 10 items for each area. If you have a hard time coming up with positives, try to look for smaller things to praise. No one is *completely* incompetent in any area.

Social Skills:

Examples: my child returns my greeting, my child answers the phone politely, my child makes eye contact when listening

Academic Performance:

Examples: my child is good as spelling words up to 5 letters long, my child is good at adding numbers, my child does most of his homework independently

Physical Attributes and Skills

Examples: my child has shiny hair and a pretty smile, my child can run fast, my child can ride a bicycle safely

Emotional Expression

Examples: my child stays in control when he is disappointed, my child uses feeling words to express her emotions ("I'm mad," "I'm scared," etc.), my child comes to me when she is confused learned from your parents.

Apply this Principle Everywhere

While the focus has been on grades in this chapter, the same principles apply to all that children do, and adults as well. Take the time to ask yourself if the way you manage your children would be motivating to you if you were your child. If you are a teacher, consider whether your teaching style would be motivating to you. Whether parent or teacher, ask yourself what would be likely to happen if you praised more for success while ignoring mistakes.

Therapy Can Help Your Child Do Better Academically

Therapy is often a very good place to get help when your child is doing poorly academically. It is necessary to break the patterns—both within your child and within your family—that continue to create the poor performance. When you bring your child to therapy, it shows how much you care and how motivated you are to help your child to succeed. It shows your love toward your child. Your therapist or your child's therapist will not criticize you for the problems, but rather help the both of you to have success and a stronger relationship. Don't let your fear of being a bad parent get in the way of helping your child to be successful.

CHAPTER TWENTY-TWO

22. OVERCOMING WORK STRESS

For most people, work is a major portion of their lives. They are likely to spend more time on the job than in any other activity except sleeping. Some people spend more time working than sleeping, even including their days off. While it is not always possible to change jobs, it is almost always possible to reduce the amount of stress you have at work. That's because stress isn't simply a matter of what you have to do. Stress is also related to the way you *do* what you have to do. Because stress is connected to our physical health, making just a few changes in your thinking or the way you communicate with others can literally make a life or death difference.

Work Isn't Just for Money

Work gives people both a sense of purpose and of identity—two key psychological needs. If I were to ask you to tell me about yourself, no doubt you would include your occupation in your description. "My name is Jack Ito, I'm a psychologist and relationship coach, I live in…." Even people without a paid job usually identify themselves with a job title such as homemaker or hospital volunteer. Since work is a part of our identity, people who enjoy their jobs feel better about themselves, and are more satisfied with their lives. People who believe that their jobs are unimportant, or beneath them in some way, feel worse about themselves. They may try to psychologically distance themselves from their jobs by saying or thinking things such as, "This is only temporary until I find something better."

Work

- **Provides income**
- **Provides emotional stability**
- **Provides a sense of importance**
- **Provides a sense of identity**
- **Is a social environment**
- **Consumes the bulk of our waking hours**
- **Can be a source of physical stress**
- **Can be a source of emotional stress**
- **Can contribute to a longer life or a premature death**
- **Needs to go well for us to be well**

If you are already in a job for which your personality is not well suited, the best way for you to reduce stress will be to look for a job you are more suited for, even if the job is less prestigious.

Since work is an important part of our identity and life satisfaction, one of the best ways to avoid job stress is by choosing a job or career that we like. There are many reasons why that is often not possible, but to some extent it usually is.

Your dream job might be a teaching job. But, because of lack of training, funding, time, etc. you may not be able to become a teacher. Knowing you would like to be a teacher, however, provides clues as to what other kinds of jobs would be a good match for you. Looking at the reasons you want to be a teacher can help with finding equally satisfying jobs. For example, you may want to be a teacher because you enjoy working with children. You also may like the aspect of being part of a school system, working with colleagues and so on. Applying to work at a day care would then be a better choice for you than trying to get a job in an industrial mill.

On the other hand, if your dream job involves working with things (machines for example) rather than with people, then you will have less stress working at an industrial job than as a day care worker. In a day care you would not only need to care for a diversity of children, but would also need to deal with their parents on a daily basis.

Reduce Stress by Doing Work that Suits You, Even if It Is Less Prestigious than What You Are Doing Now

If you are already in a job for which your personality is not well suited, the best way for you to reduce stress will be to look for a job you are more suited for, even if the job is less prestigious. Many people start out in jobs which they think they will like, but which really don't suit them. The opposite is also true—people sometimes become attached to jobs that they never thought they would like.

Psychologists, who are the ones with the training to do psychological testing, have tools to help you match your personality, skills, and interests to an occupation. These tools are called vocational aptitude tests. They are easy to complete and can give you many ideas for jobs that you have never considered—jobs that would excite you rather than stress you.

Other Ways to Reduce Job Stress

Although having a job that you are well-suited for is important, it is not the only way to reduce job stress. Sometimes stress is not caused by the job itself, but by the way that we handle the job. A good way to check this out is to see if other people with the same position that you have are also stressed. If everyone with your particular job is stressed, then it may be the nature of the job. On the other hand, if other people in your position are able to do their job without stress, there is a much greater likelihood that some personal changes will make your job less stressful.

You can use the exercise on the next page to see if some of your beliefs are making your job much worse than it has to be.

Counseling for Job Stress

People entering counseling for job stress usually are stressed beyond what is normal for people in their position. Sometimes they seek out counseling by themselves, and other times they are referred to counseling by their employer.

Your therapist will want detailed information about the nature of your job and your interactions with other people on the job. You should feel free to express this information as is natural to you. You don't need to fear that any of it will get back to your employer. Of course, if you threaten to kill your boss or some such, then the therapist will need to notify your intended victim and the authorities in order to protect others as well as you. Any other exceptions to confidentiality will be spelled out for you at the beginning of therapy.

The Cause of Stress

Stress is caused by loading a system beyond its design capacity. Both objects and people have load capacities. If you have a small car and tow a trailer with it, it puts stress on the engine and although it may do fine for a while, it will start making strange sounds and shortly afterward need repair—

Ways of Reducing Job Stress:

- **Find a more satisfying job**
- **Ask for help from your employer**
- **Get help on your own**
- **Improve your relationships with your coworkers**
- **Become more knowledgeable about your job/industry**
- **Work at a pace that you can maintain**
- **Take breaks**
- **Be well rested before you go to work**
- **Eat healthy lunches and drink water rather than coffee**
- **Personalize your work space**
- **Have a back-up plan and savings in case of a lay-off**

Exercise: Self Assessment of Healthy and Unhealthy Workplace Beliefs

Instructions: Check off whether you believe each statement is mostly true or false.

Even if my boss tells me to do something that would hurt myself and/or my family, I should do it: ☐ True ☐ False

The workload that I am given is hurting me and/or my family: ☐ True ☐ False

I am responsible to do everything my boss tells me to, regardless of its impact on me: ☐ True ☐ False

If I don't work at the same pace as my coworkers, then something must be wrong with me: ☐ True ☐ False

Complaining is the best way to handle work overload: ☐ True ☐ False

It's ok to neglect my family or mistreat them because of my work stress or work overload. ☐ True ☐ False

Burnout only happens when one is overloaded with work. Being under challenged is ok. ☐ True ☐ False

Feeling stressed is a normal part of having a job. ☐ True ☐ False

I need to work as fast as I can. ☐ True ☐ False

I work for the company, but I'm not part of the company. ☐ True ☐ False

All of my work is equally important. ☐ True ☐ False

I see work evaluations as a threat rather than an opportunity. ☐ True ☐ False

My pace and productivity should be the same as others. ☐ True ☐ False

I am easily replaceable. ☐ True ☐ False

Each "True" response indicates that you have problems in your beliefs about work which can have long-term harmful effects. No matter how strongly you believe these things, it is not helpful and contributes to work stress. Talk with your therapist about improving your work conditions, your beliefs, or seeking an alternative position.

To work on this on your own, try to write an alternative, helpful belief for each statement that you marked as "true."

possibly costing several thousand dollars. Small cars are not designed to tow trailers. To avoid costly repairs, you need to either get a more powerful vehicle to tow the trailer or carry only light loads with your small car.

In the same token, we generally don't ask children or elderly people to carry heavy loads for us. They would likely be injured. Many people are inaccurate about how much of a physical or psychological load they can safely carry at work without doing physical or psychological damage to themselves. Sometimes, something has to "break down" before they realize their limits are less than what they thought.

Physical Symptoms of Job Stress

Just as a car often makes strange sounds or emits strong smells prior to a serious problem, people also have indications that they are exceeding their load capacities. On the physical side, there are aches and pains, headaches, fatigue, nausea, and dizziness. To have aches and pains in a *new* job is part of the job adjustment—using muscles that you are not used to using.

When aches and pains continue past the initial stages or when they begin on a job that previously did not give you aches and pains, it is a sign that you are physically stressed. If you continue working in the same manner, something will break down. There are many possibilities for physical breakdown such as carpal tunnel syndrome, bones getting out of alignment (especially in the spine), hernias, accidents, and illnesses caused by a weakening of the immune system. Disability or death would not be an unusual result from prolonged work stress, occurring either directly, as the result of an accident, or from a weakening of the immune system. Even auto accidents can be caused by job stress as people's ability to pay attention and to stay awake or aware on their way to or from work may be seriously impaired.

If you are having physical symptoms of job stress, the most important thing to do is to remedy the cause of the stress. Sometimes this is as simple as getting an extra hour of sleep, making sure you drink enough water (not coffee), and taking

Disability or death would not be an unusual result from prolonged work stress, occurring either directly, as the result of an accident, or from a weakening of the immune system.

By the time you experience symptoms of work stress, some damage has already been done.

The number one cause of psychological stress is the same as for physical stress— overloading your design capacity.

regular breaks during which you relax. Other measures might be changing the way that you lift or move things, using wrist or back supports, getting help with difficult tasks, and slowing your pace. What may have been a natural pace at age 20 may be too fast a pace at age 30. You may need new glasses, different lighting, or you may need to improve your posture.

Besides remedying whatever is putting a strain on your system, you will also need to get a full physical exam. By the time you recognize symptoms from your body, you may already have a serious condition (such as high blood pressure or diabetes).

Psychological Stress and Physical Symptoms

Physical symptoms can also be the result of psychological stress. When we are under stress, our minds and bodies attempt to compensate by releasing natural hormones into our blood stream. These hormones are not meant to help with long-term stressors. They are there primarily to give you energy for fighting or fleeing in an emergency. In the absence of such an emergency, they can upset your stomach (causing ulcers, and other such problems), make your muscles tense (pulling bones out of alignment, restricting blood flow, and causing headaches and cramps), and take away energy from other body functions that regulate such critical systems as oxygen absorption, digestion, blood pressure, blood sugar level, and on and on.[11] As capable as human beings are, we are much more fragile than a car and require continuous care and adjustment. Our "load" must be matched to our ability in order to stay healthy.

The Number One Cause of Psychological Stress

The number one cause of psychological stress is the same as for physical stress—overloading our design capacity. An easy way to overload ourselves psychologically is to work faster than our normal speed. Everyone has a natural pace, not just for walking, but for everything they do.

You can try this exercise right now: stand up, go outside, and do one lap around your building at a fast walking speed.

Not running—but a fast walking speed. You will find an increase in your heart rate and breathing. That's your body adjusting to stress. Now, go out and walk around your building a second time at a very slow speed—baby steps. Don't step more than 12 inches at a time. Physically, it's easier than fast walking, but psychologically it's much harder.

You will find that with either the fast walking or baby step pace you feel relieved when you finally make it around the building. You feel relieved when you stop because you stop stressing your mind and body. It was physically difficult to maintain the fast pace; it was mentally difficult to maintain the slow pace. The least stressful way to walk around your building would be at your *normal* walking pace. At that pace, both your body and mind are relaxed. At your normal walking pace you could circle your building many more times than you could if you went faster or slower.

We will always be able to walk further than we can run—no matter how good our condition is. If you get lost in the desert or forest, don't try to run your way out of it. This exemplifies our need to walk or work at a pace which fits us both physically and mentally. By working at a normal pace, you can actually get more done with little stress on yourself. Backpackers hike more slowly than hikers because they are carrying a heavy load on their back. But, they walk many more miles than hikers, even under a heavy load. If a backpacker walked like a hiker (faster pace), she would soon fatigue and would be more likely to twist an ankle, overheat, or to have other problems. Also, she couldn't cover nearly as much ground. Likewise, the most productive worker works at a normal and steady pace. Notice that I didn't say "slow and steady." *Normal* and steady wins the race.

Coping with a Heavy Work Load

Some people say that they cannot change their pace because of the demands that are put on them by their bosses. They believe that no matter how much work their boss gives them, that they have to do it and to push themselves while they do. For people who get "extra" work routinely, this is a major

Pace:

- The rate of speed you perform some action.
- Can be accelerated for short periods with positive benefit, such as when we exercise.
- When pace is accelerated or decelerated for prolonged periods it leads to physical and psychological damage.
- You have a normal pace for everything you do.
- Working at a normal pace for long periods of time will result in greater productivity with no damage to ourselves.

A rabbit should work at a rabbit's pace; a snail should work at a snail's pace. It just won't work any other way.

problem. They believe their stress is coming from their boss. They reason that if the boss gave them less work, they wouldn't be stressed. But not everyone is stressed by bosses, even when they get a lot of work.

You might guess that the difference is a positive attitude, but you would be wrong. People with a positive attitude still have to work at their normal pace in order to not be stressed. The answer is using the skill of cooperation. Don't confuse cooperating with your boss to submitting to your boss. Submitting means giving in without resistance. Cooperation means working together. Cooperation builds strong marriages and strong work forces. Learn the following cooperation skill to become a more valuable employee (or even spouse!) without becoming overloaded again.

Dealing with the Boss

Bosses are authority figures and it is hard for many people to deal with them in an effective way that still maintains a good working relationship (someone in your family may also be playing the role of your boss). This is one reason that therapists are so helpful to people in this kind of situation. Typically people who blame their boss for their stress also blame other people in their lives for other stresses. They tend to see themselves as a victim—a fall guy for others. This is a role your therapist can help you stop playing.

The essential skill in this situation is to work at your normal pace and when the boss approaches you with more work, *don't argue*. Arguing increases stress without improving the situation, because the work still needs to be done. Rather than arguing, tell your boss that you would be happy to do the new work, but that you won't be able to do all of your regular work *and* get this new work done (if that is actually true).

This will create a small problem for your boss that is not your job to solve. It is important that you do not try to solve the problem for your boss. If your boss asks why you can't, just say that it is more than you can do in the allotted time (which is honest; e.g., although you could theoretically drive to the store

Not everyone is stressed by bosses, even when they get a lot of work. You can learn to be that way, too.

at over 100 mph, you would not tell someone that you could because it would be dangerous).

Invariably, the boss will solve the problem for you. She may tell you what to put aside so that you can work on the new stuff, may change her mind about giving you the new stuff, or may delegate some of your work to other people. If your boss insists that you do it all anyhow, accept the work without arguing. Then work only at your natural pace (not too fast or too slow). Take your scheduled breaks and don't work overtime. Don't take work home with you.

Since you were overloaded with work, you will not be able to get it all done. At first, your boss may be upset but will soon adjust to your capacities. A fair day's work for a fair day's wage truly is fair. But doing two days work for one day's pay is not fair. Just as with all changes that a person makes, it takes time for others to adjust to those changes, but when they do, you feel less stressed, they will feel less stressed, and your health and relationship with them *improve.*

To do anything else jeopardizes your wellbeing and also creates increased risk for your employer (due to quitting, workplace injury, etc.) without creating a better relationship with your boss. When you learn this skill, you will find that your stress never actually came from your boss—it came from your belief that you had to do whatever the boss told you to do, no matter how harmful that was to you. You, in effect, victimized yourself with your belief.

Case Example: Margery

Margery generally was a passive and friendly person, but she had found herself becoming more and more irritable. Although her irritation was not apparent to others and she wore a pleasant face, she could feel it inside. She described it to me as her face getting hot and as her being "ready to boil over like a tea kettle."

Margery could easily identify the source of her irritation. She had been at her job as a clerical worker in a small business for the past seven years. She had enjoyed the job and her

Many people are surprised that by having good boundaries and being agreeable, they can get along better with their employer, while having less stress and a reasonable amount of work. Most employers want to get along with their employees and get the job done.

relationship with her boss. Recently though, her boss (who was the owner), retired and the boss's daughter took over the business.

Margery knew the job better than her new boss and resented the amount of direction and oversight her new boss was giving her. She was also given an additional responsibility for contacting advertising companies that was previously handled by her former boss. She did not believe that she should have to do this work. She also said that she could not go home on time because of the new work. Not going home on time meant difficulty preparing dinner for her family, which caused more resentment.

At the time Margery entered counseling, she considered her only alternative to be quitting a job that she had enjoyed for the past seven years. Her family and her sanity had to come first. I quite agreed with her—her family and her sanity certainly were more important than the work she did for her employer, but I suggested that there may be a way for her to keep her sanity and her job, too.

I told Margery that making her situation better would involve temporarily increasing the tension between her and her employer, but was likely to result in both of them being satisfied after this initial period. And, she was likely to have tension with her employer anyhow, if she quit or lost her temper at work. Her choices really were to try my approach, quit, or hate her job. It was her choice to make. I could not choose her priorities for her.

Margery agreed to try my way, although she didn't see how she was going to change her boss, who she believed was the source of her stress. I told Margery that it would be completely unnecessary to change her boss and that trying to change her boss would just cause more tension. Margery could certainly agree with that.

I encouraged Margery to work at the same pace as she had for the past seven years and to accept any work that her boss gave her. But, she was to be honest with her boss about the amount of work that she would be able to do, and also say that she could

At the time Margery entered counseling, she considered her only alternative to be quitting a job that she had enjoyed for the past seven years.

not work overtime because of her family responsibilities. I role played this with Margery, with both of us taking turns in the roles of Margery and her new boss. She learned how to refuse overtime assertively, without being aggressive.

Margery reported back to me that when she told her boss what she would honestly be able to do, she felt good about it because it was the truth and she was calm. Her boss had been upset and her boss's face had flushed red. Margery had expected that and knew from her counseling that was a normal response on her boss's part that would be temporary. Margery did not have to be upset just because her boss was upset. She knew both her job and her ability.

After a while, Margery's boss actually asked her how the advertising had been handled in the past. Margery told her and also told her that she would make whatever changes her boss wanted as long as she could leave on time. That helped them to work together. Margery was able to go home on time, and it seemed that her relationship with her boss was likely to improve. The work stress faded away.

Therapy Can Help a Lot, Even if You Think Your Job Situation Is Unchangeable

It is important to be in therapy when you are working on job stress because of the tremendous pressure that you will feel, both internal and external, to return to a submissive or hostile posture at work. You will continue to feel trapped unless you find a way out of your stress. If it takes you two hours to recover from an eight hour job, then you actually have a 10 hour job. A therapist will provide the emotional support and practical guidance to help you make positive changes. These changes will improve conditions for you and for others. Your workplace will benefit from your improved mood and productivity. Your family will also benefit from your improved mood and energy. You can begin in your next session to make your work more pleasant by discussing your work stresses with your therapist.

Margery did not have to be upset just because her boss was upset. She knew both her job and her ability.

If it takes you two hours to recover from an eight hour job, then you actually have a 10 hour job.

Summary

Work is much more than a way to make money and is where we will spend a major portion of our lives. It is normal to experience stress in a new job, but when stress is ongoing it creates problems. Both psychological and physical problems can result from job stress. That stress, in turn, will affect our life satisfaction and other areas of our lives. Rather than take a fatalistic view of job stress, we can learn to manage aspects of ourselves that make the job stress worse. In cases where job stress is beyond our ability to manage, we will need to seek another job. Therapy can be helpful for learning how to deal with job stress. Therapy can also be helpful in identifying other careers you may be better suited for.

CHAPTER TWENTY-THREE

23. MAKEOVER YOUR LIFE

Except for people who are court ordered or coerced into coming to therapy, people who come into therapy want to create some kind of change in their life. Clients who are experiencing difficulties in their lives naturally believe that if only their situation were different, then their life would be better.

These "if only" beliefs are often stated in terms of significant others—"If only my husband/wife would come to his/her senses," "If only my son/daughter/boss would just listen," and so on. Often clients want their therapist to commiserate with them in focusing on this other person who is not sitting in front of the therapist. Often the client has expended a great deal of effort to try to change this other person before entering therapy.

You will learn in this chapter why trying to change others is the wrong approach—even if other people are the cause of your problems. In 20 years of marriage counseling and coaching, I have never seen a marriage improved by focusing on changing one's spouse. Neither have I seen work stress alleviated by focusing on changing one's employer. I have never seen anxiety cured by making the world a safer place. I have never seen a depressed person recover by waiting for the world to become a happier place. And, I have never seen someone become successful by waiting for things to become easier.

What I have seen is people improve their marriages by

Fault Finding vs. Taking Responsibility:

- **When we find fault with others and try to get them to change, they resist.**
- **When we take responsibility for change, no matter whose "fault" something was, our life improves.**
- **Becoming a person who we respect results in getting more respect from others as well.**

making changes in the way they interact with their spouses. I have seen work stress alleviated by changing the way one thinks about work, and gets along with others at work. I have seen Anxiety cured by learning to think realistically, planning to overcome obstacles and learning to relax. I have also seen people overcome depression in much the same way. I have also seen people become successful by taking on challenges and becoming more and more capable.

Improving Our Lives Means Changing Ourselves, Even When Other People Have Done the Damage

No matter how much someone else may be at fault, therapists will not support the goal of changing someone else in order to improve one's own life. Not only does the therapist not have access to this other person, but the therapist would have no more luck in changing an unwilling person than the client did. Changing one's life for the better involves changing oneself.

Occasionally, the idea of working on oneself is met with a great deal of resistance from the beginning of therapy. The client reasons, "Why should I change if it is someone else who is causing the problem?" This is an example of some clients' desire to continue to use the same strategy in therapy that hasn't worked at home (changing the other person).

Trying harder, using the same methods, will only result in more frustration. No matter how much sense a strategy seems to make, *if it doesn't work, it doesn't work.* A bad strategy is a bad strategy—no matter who is using it and no amount of "trying harder" will make it work. "It would be easier to climb the mountain if it weren't so high," is a correct belief but working on making the mountain smaller is a bad strategy. Learning how you can climb the mountain, despite the fact that it is high, is helpful.

The Person Who Will Come to Our Rescue Needs to Be a Healthier Part of Ourselves

In order to make positive change in our lives, we must be willing to give up our current ways of thinking and behaving.

No matter how much sense a strategy seems to make, if it doesn't work, it doesn't work. A bad strategy is a bad strategy—no matter who is using it and no amount of "trying harder" will make it work.

To do otherwise results in more of the same old stuff. Therapy is about the process of change. It is about using the best parts of ourselves to do better than we have done before. The part that blames others and holds onto hurts is not the better part of ourselves. That part needs to grow up.

Often people honestly believe that other people need to make changes before they can change. This belief provides a convenient excuse for not changing and it also keeps the person stuck. It's a belief without a basis in reality. Changing another person is *never* a good goal for therapy and waiting for others to change is damage that we do to ourselves—on top of whatever someone else has done.

When we try to push others to change, they push back. The net effect is no change. On the other hand, changing ourselves can draw people closer, help them to see us differently, and often get them to treat us better. If you really want someone else to change, the most effective way to make that happen is to change the way that you interact with them—without trying to directly get them to change.

Picture trying to push a donkey who does not wish to move. The donkey is stronger than you and you can wear yourself out trying to push it. Rather than trying to move it, you can hold a carrot in front of the donkey and lead it in the direction you want it to go. Did you move the donkey? No. The donkey chose to move *after* you chose to hold out the carrot. Although people aren't donkeys, the principle remains the same. Changes that you make motivate others to move either toward or away from you. By controlling what you do, you influence (not control) what others do. It is not control because the other person still has free will. A donkey, or a person, may choose to ignore whatever carrot you hold out.

A prime example of this is with a job interview. In a job interview you dress to fit the job you are applying for, and ask and answer questions in a way that influences the interviewer to hire you. You can't control the interviewer, but you do have influence. If you don't make a nice appearance (which is under your control), you are not likely to get hired. The same

Creating Change in Ourselves and in Others is Like Moving a Stubborn Donkey:

- **Pushing really hard won't work.**
- **Pulling really hard won't work.**
- **A little reward can get things moving.**

Everybody wants something. When we connect what they want to what we want, we get a win-win solution.

- **Employers want a good employee, we want a good job.**
- **Children want good parents, we want good children.**
- **Partners want good relationships, and so do we.**

We are constantly in a state of change. The reason we usually don't notice this is that we usually bounce forward and backward inside the bubble of our comfort zone. We need to take conscious and willful control of our actions to head off in another direction.

principle applies in meeting people, and in improving relationships with friends and family members. The people who are best at influencing other people to do things know what changes to make in themselves that create the desire to change in others.

Whether you want change for yourself or for someone else, the best and only *effective* way to start is by looking at different choices that you can make. Seeing that we have choices is often enough to get us "unstuck," and working on productive changes. On the next page is a formula you can use to look at as many choices as you like. I suggest trying to see every difficult situation in your life as involving choices.

Change Is Nothing New

We have, of course, been making changes all of our lives. If not, we would still be wearing diapers and crawling around on the floor. Most of the people who are reading this book are no longer doing that.

Whenever you learn something, your mind is no longer the same as before. Every experience we have changes what we think and also changes our ability to think. Doing something the second time is never the same as doing it the first time because of your prior experience. The more you do something, the easier it becomes to continue doing it. This is one of the key principles of change.

Change Happens All the Time

Getting dressed each day is a change from being undressed. Eating is a change from being hungry. Getting angry is a change from not being angry. Standing up is a change from sitting down. Thinking about what to cook for dinner is a change from thinking about your job at the moment. Every single moment that we are alive, we are changing. To cease to change is to cease to live. Change is not hard, it is inevitable.

When we take *conscious* control of the changes that we are making, we move forward. Things happen and our life gets better. When we just let random forces and thoughts guide us,

Exercise: What Drives Me?

Becoming empowered to improve your life is about seeing that you have choices. Unhealthy choices often have a positive short term benefit, but a large long term cost. Use this formula with any of your unhealthy thoughts or behaviors to see what small benefit you are getting for a large cost.

Formula for Discovering Our Bad Choices

I am choosing _____(a bad thing) in order to get _____(a short term benefit), although it means I am sacrificing my _____ (a long term cost).

Example 1: I am choosing <u>to sleep less</u> (a bad thing) in order to <u>get more done</u> (a short term benefit) although it means I am sacrificing my <u>future health</u> (a long term cost).

Example 2: I am choosing to <u>avoid making friends</u> (a bad thing) in order to <u>feel more comfortable</u> (a short term benefit) although it means I am sacrificing my <u>long-term relationships</u> (a long term cost).

Example 3: I am choosing to <u>not work on my relationship</u> in order to have a <u>peaceful relationship</u> (a short term benefit), although it means I am sacrificing my <u>relationship satisfaction</u> (a long term cost).

After you have done that, you can flip your bad choices around so that they become good ones. Healthy choices often have a short term negative outcome, but long term positive benefits. Use the following formula to see the large benefit you can receive for only a small cost.

Formula for Making Healthier Choices

I can choose to _____(a good thing) which will cause _____(short term cost), although it will lead to _____ (long term benefit).

Example 1: I can choose to <u>sleep more</u> (a good thing) which will cause me to <u>lose an hour of free time</u> (short term cost) although it will lead to <u>better health, mood, and energy level</u> (long term benefit).

Example 2: I can choose to <u>make friends</u> (a good thing) which will cause me <u>to be more anxious at first</u> (short term cost), although it will lead to <u>feeling less lonely</u> (long term benefit).

Example 3: I can choose to <u>work on my relationship</u> which will cause <u>stress at first</u> (short term cost), although it will lead to <u>a more satisfying relationship</u> (long term benefit).

we become like a small piece of wood floating back and forth on a wave. Although each day we are constantly changing, the changes are not productive, and we end up where we started.

Change Follows Maturation and Preparation

One reason that people have difficulty making changes is because they don't have the physical or mental capacity to make the desired voluntary change. An infant cannot be potty trained. It first has to grow both mentally and physically. Most people will not be able to be Olympic athletes or Nobel Prize winners due to their physical and mental limitations.

Many of the things that you have the potential to do, you will also not be able to do until after you have made progress with lesser achievements. You may have the potential to climb a mountain, but if you don't get in shape first, that potential won't be realized. Inside of you is the potential to do and be a countless number of things if you first do the "basic training" that opens up those opportunities for you.

Another reason that someone can have difficulty changing is because of a lack of knowledge. An animal trainer can't just decide to be a surgeon. A couple can't just stop arguing and resolve their problems peacefully if all they know how to do is argue. A person who is not initially relaxed may not know how to relax, no matter how much she wants to. Provided that people have the mental and physical ability, they can acquire the knowledge needed to make changes.

Many people would like to be rich, but believe that they are not able to for lack of opportunity. Yet, if you take everything away from a rich man, he will soon become rich again. Because of his knowledge, he can see his opportunities and take advantage of them. If you have a cage full of monkeys and put a banana just out of reach, on the outside of the cage, many of the monkeys will try unsuccessfully to reach for the banana. But, if you put another monkey in the cage who knows how to reach the banana using a stick, all of the other monkeys will learn how to reach that banana by observing the first monkey reach it with a stick. They won't do it as quickly, but they will do it eventually. The same principle applies to humans.

To be successful, you need to learn what successful people do and do it. You must do it over and over again until you become as good at it as the successful person. Insisting on trying to "reach for the banana" your old way will just get you frustration without getting you any rewards.

Change Often Requires Un-Learning

Sometimes people are both physically and mentally able to make a change and know how to make a change, but still have difficulty making changes. For example, when people learn to communicate in assertive rather than aggressive ways, they still can have a very hard time changing from being aggressive to being assertive. Teaching children to be nice doesn't assure that they will be nice. What we already know and what we already do interferes with us doing and being something different from what we are. For this reason, many employers would rather hire an employee with no experience than an employee with experience. An employee with no experience will be easier to train to do things the way they are done in the new company. An employee with experience may have to unlearn previous training (e.g., "This is how we did it on my other job"—"This is not your other job, this is how we do it here"). In a similar manner, people can have the same pattern of interactions from one relationship to the next. Rather than learn from mistakes, each mistake we make further cements a bad habit and makes it more likely that we will make the same mistake again.

If experience teaches us anything, it is that experience alone is not enough to create change. If it were, then we would get better and better with every mistake we made—learning from our experiences what not to do. The truth is, we learn more from our successes than we do from our mistakes. The memory of our mistakes actually makes learning harder.

The imagined image of future success is more helpful to future success than any memory of failure that you have. For people who have had a lot of failures, it can be really hard to be

If we learned from our mistakes, then people who make a lot of them would make rapid progress. This is not the case. Mistakes teach us what not to do, not what to do. Only our own and other people's successes can teach us what to do.

motivated to change. To start that ball rolling, it is helpful to create as many small successes as possible. These small successes will help to provide the momentum and positive attitude necessary for learning and doing things in a better way.

Four Principles for Un-Learning Bad Habits

In overcoming the pull of a habit, there are four principles that we can use to our advantage to promote change: 1) the principle that things tend to remain the same (homeostasis), 2) the principle that we can't intentionally forget something, 3) the principle of substitution, and 4) the principle that big goals are most easily reached with small steps.

The Principle of Homeostasis

The tendency for things to remain the same teaches us the importance of doing things right the first time. And the second time. And the third time. And so on, until the behavior becomes automatic. If you are well trained to drive a car and to follow the rules of the road and you practice driving that way every time you drive, you will have safe driving habits that will last you a lifetime. An experienced driver does not think about driving. Because it is done so often, driving becomes an automatic behavior that is done without much conscious thought. Our subconscious mind drives according to earlier, consciously acquired habits.

We begin to learn habits from the first time that we perform an action and we continue our habits, without thinking, when they become unconscious. Most of what we do, say, and think is a result of these over-learned, unconscious habits that are totally beyond our level of conscious awareness. You can tell a behavior is a habit if you can think of something else while you do it.

If you want your children to grow up to be responsible adults, then you must teach them to be responsible *as soon as they are able to learn*. This usually means that they start helping to pick up their toys and to do other small tasks from the time they are two. As children grow, you give them more and more responsibility. When they are adults, it will be second nature to be responsible. The idea that children should just be given freedom to play and be themselves, without cares or concerns, does not help a child. Firstborn children have higher success rates as adults, in part because they had more responsibilities when they were children.[12]

Although you are already an adult, this is the first day of the rest of your life. Today is the infancy for all that you can become in the future. You can "raise" yourself in the way you want your life to go from here on out. If you are acquiring a new skill, get the best training and supervision from the start. Learn one step well before proceeding to the next step. And always keep your attention on your successes and not your mistakes. Good habits, learned pleasantly, stimulate the desire to learn and progress. Use this principle for yourself and your children.

"Intentional Forgetting" Can Aid Memory Retention

The idea that you cannot intentionally forget something is very useful for making changes to a behavior that you already have (changing an established habit). Here is a way to demonstrate this concept to yourself. I have a "magic number" for you and it is 42. Now, close your eyes and forget what the magic number is. Walk away, get a drink, whatever you like. But, before you come back to reading this book, ask yourself what the magic number is just to make sure that you have forgotten it. The effort that you made to rid the number 42 from your mind will actually have cemented it in your mind. Most likely, you will still remember the number 42 tomorrow if I were to ask you what the magic number is. If you want to make sure your spouse or child remembers something, tell them emphatically to "forget it and never remember it again."

When we *try not to* remember something, we remember it all the more. And, just like remembering, when we intentionally try *not* to do something, we are more likely to do it. A person who has to give a speech and tries to not mispronounce words is much more likely to mispronounce words. Tell a child not to do something, and you guarantee that he will think about it and be more likely to do it. Tell a

This tendency to tell others what not to do is one of the most frequent habits of unsuccessful communicators and people with relationship problems.

329

toddler not to touch something and leave the room and spy on the toddler. The toddler will approach the object and look at it and probably touch it. The toddler may have never touched it if you didn't plant the idea in her mind. Telling someone not to yell at you makes it much more likely that they will— particularly if they already have a habit of yelling. Even if they don't, tell them not to enough times and they are much more likely to start. This tendency to tell others what not to do is one of the most frequent habits of unsuccessful communicators and people with relationship problems. They create in others the negative reactions that they fear. Be sure you are not creating negative changes by telling others (or yourself) what *not* to do!

Rather than try to get negative thoughts out of your mind or out of others' minds, try putting positive thoughts into your mind and that of others. Tell others what you *want* them to do rather than what you don't want them to do. Tell your children what behavior you expect of them and don't mention the other behavior. For example say, "Alex, I expect you to stay in the cart and listen to what I say while we are shopping." Do not say, "Alex, I expect you to stay in the cart instead of climbing out and trying to run around the store. You need to listen to me instead of ignoring me." The first sentence plants the good idea. The second sentence plants the bad ideas. Which one do you want your child to have? Successful gardeners don't plant weeds along with their healthy plants.

The Principle of Substitution

The point is to work on developing a *competing behavior* rather than trying to work on reducing a bad habit behavior (remember, trying not to do something increases its strength in our mind). Although eating junk food is unhealthy, trying not to eat junk food is counterproductive. You cannot just "intend" to put junk food out of your mind. It will make junk food be on your mind all the more. Instead, try doing a competing behavior. Try eating healthy food. Think about what is healthy food. When you shop, search for healthy food. Let healthy food be on your mind. Have salad fantasies.

Trying not to spend money on foolish things is another

Practice Competing Behaviors to Remove Old Habits:

- Listen for things you can agree with when others are talking, instead of what you disagree with.
- Drink a tall glass of water before taking another cup of coffee.
- Leave the house everyday during the times you normally watch television.
- Pay off your bills and put money into savings before buying any luxury items.
- Go study with better students instead of hanging around with worse ones.
- Every behavior you want to stop has an opposite—focus on doing that.

counterproductive behavior. Instead, try to spend money on important things. Focus on saving and paying off your debts. Have debt free fantasies of financial freedom. Let your future goals fill your mind. Think about your priorities. Write down what are really the most important things for you. Spend your money there first.

The exercise on the next page will give you practice in the principle of substitution.

As you can see, the first step to changing an established behavior is to learn the most appropriate competing behavior or thinking that will help you to have success. The second step is to start to do the competing behavior and to think as well as you can—focusing on success rather than mistakes. Thirdly, you need to maintain the competing behavior long enough for it to become an over learned, unconscious habit. It needs to become as second nature to you as being able to touch your nose with your eyes closed.

Change Happens in 21 Consecutive Days

It takes 21 days to create a new habit—if the new habit is done for 21 days *in a row*. If you miss even one day, then start the count over again. For example, let's say that you want to learn to praise your children for their good behavior rather than criticize them for their bad behavior. After all, you know that criticizing them will only make it more likely that they will misbehave because it keeps the misbehavior firmly planted in their minds.

Let's further suppose that whenever you get the urge to criticize them, you instead find something to compliment them about and have done that for the past 10 days. You know that it's 10 days because you have been marking your daily successes on a calendar. Now, if on the 11th day you criticize rather than compliment, then your number of successful days will revert to zero. You will need to start from day one to work toward having 21 consecutive days of your new, desired, behavior. People can rarely acquire a new habit without sliding back into old behaviors several times. For this reason, it may take 6

It takes 21 days to create a new habit—if the new habit is done for 21 days in a row. If you miss even one day, then start the count over again.

Exercise: Becoming More Positive

Improvement is about *thinking* and *doing* positively. Remove your negatives by substituting positive thoughts and actions. Using this method can improve <u>every</u> aspect of your life. Practice making positive goals by completing this chart. The last three are for converting your problems to goals.

Negative Goal (contain the word "not" or "don't")	Positive Goal (contain only things you want to do or should do)
Not eating junk food	Eat only foods without refined sugars and processed oils.
Not yelling at people	Use a calm, friendly tone whenever I talk to people, including my family.
Not making a mess	Clean up before changing tasks. Leave my workspace cleaner than it was when I started.
Not wasting time	Make a to-do list each day and do important things first
Not thinking of things to complain about	
Not using credit cards	
Not staying home all the time	
Not arguing	
Not panicking	
Not going off my medication	
Not being shy	
Not worrying about the future	
Not putting myself down	
Not watching television	
Not missing therapy appointments	
(from you)	
(from you)	
(from you)	

months to achieve 21 consecutive days of a new behavior. If you are not used to making changes, make small ones at first; maintain them for 21 consecutive days, and then choose a new one. You can become an expert at change and makeover your life and relationships as much as you desire.

A Method for Tracking Goals

Tracking goals are easy when you use an ordinary calendar. Make a smiley face on the calendar for each day that you do the new behavior. Count the number of consecutive smiley faces to determine when you have reached 21 consecutive days. Then work on the next step toward your desired changes. It will do you little good to work on the second step before completing the first (you can't climb the top half of a mountain before you climb the bottom half).

The Principle of Small Steps

The fourth condition for successfully changing a behavior is working on one very small step at a time. It is much easier to maintain a small change for 21 consecutive days than to maintain a large change for 21 consecutive days. For this reason alone, we can usually make changes to our lives faster by taking small steps than by taking big ones. Additionally, the longer it takes someone to make a change, the more likely they are to give up on changing. Making small changes feels good, is rewarding, is encouraging, and results in more overall change than working on big steps.

In my work with people with failing marriages, I help them to rebuild even the most severely damaged marriages by taking small steps. Even people on the brink of divorce can improve their marriages by taking small steps.

Almost everyone who works at the top started at the bottom. They got to the top by continuously taking small steps without wasting their time looking for shortcuts. Good therapists help their client to break their problems into small pieces and deal with them one at a time. This process is a sure way to get more of what you want out of life.

The advantages of taking small steps:

- It's easier to get started.
- It's easier to maintain.
- It creates many more successes.
- It feels good.
- You can more easily achieve 21 consecutive days.
- You can make more progress than by taking big steps.

Summary

Making positive change is very possible and very rewarding with the correct selection of goals and methods: The method that absolutely does not work is trying to get other people to change so that our life can be better. Changing ourselves, though, influences others to change. When you follow the four basic principles of change, you can change as much as your potential allows and enjoy a richer life.

Therapists are experts at helping people decide on the changes they need to make, as well as providing support until the desired changes have become established. Many people who have been unable to change on their own have been able to make very significant changes in a relatively short period of time through counseling. Being in counseling may be the single most productive and positive time of your life. Enjoy it!

ENDNOTES

CHAPTER ONE

1. Office of the Assistant Secretary for Health, U.S. Department of Health and Human Services (1999). *Mental Health: a Report of the Surgeon General.*

2. National Institute of Mental Health. *Statistics.* Retrieved from the NIMH website: http://www.nimh.nih.gov/statistics/index.shtml on May 12th, 2013.

3. Focus on the Family. http://www.focusonthefamily.com

CHAPTER TWO

4. US Department of Health and Human Services, National Institutes of Health. *Depression.* Booklet. NIH Publication No. 11-3561. Available at http://www.nimh.nih.gov/health/publications/depression/depression-booklet-pdf.pdf.

5. Meichenbaum, D. (1995). *A Clinical Handbook/Practical Therapist Manual for Assessing and Treating Adults with Post-Traumatic Stress Disorder (PTSD).* Pub: Don Meichenbaum.

CHAPTER FOUR

6. Norcross, J. C. (2012). *Changeology: 5 Steps to Realizing Your Goals and Resolutions.* New York: Simon & Schuster.

CHAPTER SEVEN

7. Røysamb, E., Tambs, K., Reichborn-Kjennerud, T., Neale, M. C. and Harris, J. R. (2003). *Happiness and Health: Environmental and Genetic Contributions to the Relationship Between Subjective Well-Being, Perceived Health, and Somatic Illness.* Journal of Personality and Social Psychology, Vol 85(6), Dec 2003, 1136-1146.

8. Metcalf, E. MPH (2013). Pain Medication: Are You Addicted? Retrieved from WebMD website: http://www.webmd.com/pain-management/features/pain-medication-addiction on May 15, 2013.

CHAPTER EIGHT

9. Norcross, J. C. & Lambert, M. J. (2010). *Evidence-Based Therapy Relationships, Chapter One.* Retrieved from NREPP SAMHSA's National Registry of Evidence Based Programs and Practices website: http://www.nrepp.samhsa.gov/Norcross.aspx on May 16, 2013.

CHAPTER ELEVEN

10. Knapen, J., Vancampfort, D., Schoubs, B., Probst, M., Sienaert, P., Haake, P., Peuskens, J., & Pieters, G. (2009). *Exercise for the Treatment of Depression*. The Open Complimentary Medicine Journal, 2009, 1, 78-83.

CHAPTER TWENTY-TWO

11. Schneiderman, N., Ironson, G., & Siegel, S.D. *Stress and Health: Psychological, Behavioral, and Biological Determinants*. Annual Review of Clinical Psychology, 2005; 1: 607-628.

CHAPTER TWENTY-THREE

12. Jones, D. *First-born kids become CEO material*. USA Today, Sep 3, 2007.

BONUS

Has this book helped you? I hope it has. If you would be willing to leave a brief review telling others how this book helped you, I will give you, as my special thank you, a relationship assessment of your choice.

This assessment will help you get closer to your significant other. You can use it on your own or together as a couple's exercise. If you are in counseling, you can also use this assessment to identify specific issues to work on with your therapist.

Which assessment would you like?

❖ <u>Knowledge and Acceptance</u>: How well do you and your partner know each other?

❖ <u>Financial</u>: Can you talk about and solve financial issues with your partner?

❖ <u>Physical Togetherness</u>: Do you both like the way that you touch and are sexual?

❖ <u>Spiritual Beliefs</u>: Are different spiritual beliefs stressing your relationship?

❖ <u>Relating to Friends</u>: Shared friends? Separate friends? No friends?

❖ <u>Intimacy and Sharing</u>: How open and honest can you enjoy being with your partner?

❖ <u>Family Relationships</u>: Can you work as a team for managing other family members?

❖ <u>Learning and Growth</u>: Are you achieving your dreams or forgetting about them?

❖ <u>Home Environment</u>: Is your home really a "home" for the both of you?

❖ <u>Fun</u>: How much do you enjoy each other outside your home?

To get your free bonus assessment, leave your review on the online website where you bought your book (e.g., Amazon, Barnes & Noble, etc.). Then go this link to get your free assessment:

http://coachjackito.com/review-bonus/

ABOUT THE AUTHOR

Jack Ito, Ph.D., is a licensed clinical psychologist, marriage and relationship coach. He has been on both sides of the therapist's couch and is well qualified to speak to the experiences of both client and therapist. He is a graduate of Fuller Theological Seminary's Graduate School of Psychology and formerly was a psychology professor at Geneva College. "Coach Jack" has 20 years of experience in marriage and family counseling and coaching. His coaching specialty is reconciling broken or strained marriages in which one spouse refuses to work on the marriage. Coach Jack's deep desire to save and improve marriages comes out of his own experience as a child in a highly dysfunctional home.

Coach Jack was both witness and victim to physical and emotional abuse inflicted on his mother and himself throughout his early childhood. Through his own personal therapy, Coach Jack came to realize something that he could not as a child—although his parents did not get along, they desperately needed each other. Unfortunately, they did not have the skills to manage the stresses of their relationship or to create a healthy home environment. He is thankful that God used his tragic experiences for good in preparing him to rescue failing marriages. Although Coach Jack believes that *skills* are essential to be able to improve our lives, it is our *love* for God and for each other which gives life meaning. With these two traits, we can be secure and make the most of our lives, without feeling like something is missing.

Coach Jack made the change from counseling to coaching because of coaching's positive emphasis on skills and success, but he remains a believer in the importance of therapy. "Therapy is essential for dealing with the symptoms of a psychological disorder and returning people to a healthy level of functioning; coaching is essential for doing better, once our symptoms have been removed. Counseling helps people to walk; coaching helps people to run. We learn both of those things, *in order.*"

Coach Jack has brought some of his skills as coach into this volume for people in therapy. It is his goal to encourage people to take a more active role in therapy. By doing that, therapy becomes a more powerful agent for change. Research has demonstrated that clients benefit significantly more from therapy when they play an active role in their treatment. Therapists are experts in intervention, but clients are experts on themselves. Working together, and combining their abilities, they can create something new, vital, and exciting that would be difficult for a client to do on his or her own. This is the same view that Coach Jack has about marriage. "We marry because we can be so much more together than we could be on our own."

Coach Jack's practice includes people from many countries, cultures, and religions. He gets email from all over the world and tries to respond personally to everyone. You are welcome to write to Coach Jack or to visit his website for free downloads and helpful information on a variety of marriage and relationship problems.

Website:

coachjackito.com

Contact Information:

email: coachjack@coachjackito.com

Abbreviated Biography

Birthplace: Vermont, USA

1985 Bachelor of Arts in Psychology, St. Michael's College, Colchester, Vermont

1988 Master of Arts in Psychology, East Tennessee State University, Johnson City, Tennessee

1993 Master of Arts in Theology, Fuller Theological Seminary, Graduate School of Theology, Pasadena, California

1994 Doctor of Philosophy in Clinical Psychology, Fuller Theological Seminary, Graduate School of Psychology, Pasadena, California

Undergraduate and Graduate Professor of Psychology at Geneva College, Beaver Falls, Pennsylvania

Director Olive Branch Counseling Services, Chippewa, Pennsylvania

Post Traumatic Stress Specialist, United States Navy, Bremerton, Washington, and 29 Palms, California

Graduate MentorCoach Certified Coaching Program

Books: What to Do When He Won't Change (2011), Connecting Through "Yes!" (2013)

Coaching Specialties: Fostering Intimacy in Severely Damaged Marriages and Committed Relationships

Coaching Venues: Individuals and Couples

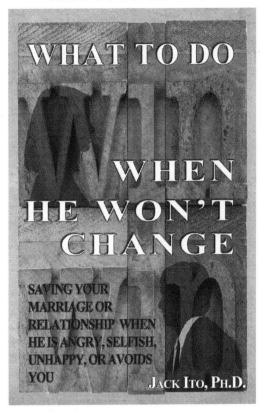

What to Do When He Won't Change

Saving Your Marriage or Relationship When He Is Angry, Selfish, Unhappy, or Avoids You

(2011) 249 pages

Has your spouse become an angry, selfish, unhappy, or avoidant person? Does he refuse to go to counseling or work on your relationship? Would you like a way to make things better without having to end your relationship or threaten to?

In *What To Do When He Won't Change*, you will learn the four major motivations that drive men's behavior in relationships. You can then use the down to earth examples and win-win interventions to work with your partner's motivations rather than against them. The result? Faster change with less conflict.

Available at online bookstores in paperback or as a downloadable Kindle eBook from Amazon.com

Connecting Through "Yes!"

How to Agree When You Don't Agree to Get Cooperation and Closeness in Your Marriage

(2013) 292 pages

Do you know how to use agreement to transform your biggest areas of marital conflict into closeness, cooperation, and the changes that YOU want in your relationship?

In Connecting Through "Yes!" Marriage and Relationship Coach Jack Ito shows you with clear, easy to follow examples, how to positively communicate about the biggest problems that couples face. These are the same techniques his coaching clients use to reconcile marriages, end affairs, deal with addicted spouses, solve problems, end blaming, improve dating, handle money issues, and much more.

Available at online bookstores in paperback or as a downloadable Kindle eBook from Amazon.com

INDEX

Made in the USA
Middletown, DE
02 August 2018